LANGUAGE
IN ACTION

LANGUAGE IN ACTION

S. I. HAYAKAWA

ASSISTANT PROFESSOR OF ENGLISH
ILLINOIS INSTITUTE OF TECHNOLOGY

NEW YORK

HARCOURT, BRACE AND COMPANY

PRINTED AND BOUND IN THE UNITED STATES OF AMERICA
BY THE HADDON CRAFTSMEN, INC., CAMDEN, N. J.

CONTENTS

INTRODUCTION

FROM the moment Mr. Smith switches on an early morning news broadcast to the time he falls asleep at night over a novel or a magazine, he is, like all other people living under modern civilized conditions, swimming in words. Newspaper editors, politicians, salesmen, radio comedians, columnists, luncheon club speakers, and clergymen; colleagues at work, friends, relatives, wife and children; market reports, direct mail advertising, books, and billboards—all are assailing him with words all day long. And Mr. Smith himself is constantly contributing to that verbal Niagara every time he puts on an advertising campaign, delivers a speech, writes a letter, or even chats with his friends.

When things go wrong in Mr. Smith's life—when he is worried, perplexed, or nervous, when family, business, or national affairs are not going as he thinks they should, when he finds himself making blunder after blunder in personal or financial matters—he blames a number of things as responsible for his difficulties. Sometimes he blames the weather, sometimes his health or the state of his "nerves," sometimes his glands, or, if the problem is a larger one, he may blame his environment, the economic system he lives under, a foreign nation, or the cultural pattern of society. When he is pondering over the difficulties of other people, he may attribute their troubles too to causes such as these, and he may add still another, namely, "human nature." It rarely, if ever, occurs to him to investigate, among other things, the nature and constituents of that daily verbal Niagara as a possible cause of trouble.

Indeed, there are few occasions on which Mr. Smith thinks about words as such. He wonders from time to time about a grammatical point. Sometimes he feels an uneasiness about his own verbal accomplishments, so that he begins to wonder if he shouldn't take steps to "improve his vocabulary." Once in a while he is struck by the fact that some people (although he never includes himself among these) "twist the meanings of words," especially during the course of arguments, so that words are often "very tricky." Occasionally, too, he notices, usually with irritation, that words sometimes "mean different things to different people." This condition, he feels, would be cured if people would only consult their dictionaries oftener and learn the "true meanings" of words. He knows, however, that they will not—at least, not any oftener than he does, which is not very often—so that he puts this down as another instance of the weakness of human nature.

This, unfortunately, is about the limit of Mr. Smith's linguistic speculations. But in this respect Mr. Smith is representative not only of the general public, but also of many scientific workers, publicists, and writers. Mr. Smith, like most people, takes words as much for granted as the air he breathes, and gives them about as much thought. Mr. Smith's body automatically adjusts itself, within certain limits, to changes in climate or atmosphere, from cold to warm, from dry to moist, from fresh to foul; no conscious effort on his part is required to make these adjustments. Nevertheless, he is ready to acknowledge the effect that climate and air have upon his physical well being, and he takes measures to protect himself from unhealthy air, either by traveling to get away from it, or by installing air-conditioning systems to purify it. But Mr. Smith, like the rest of us, also adjusts himself automatically to changes in the verbal climate, from one type of discourse to another, from one set of terms to another, without conscious effort. He has yet, however, to acknowledge the effect of his verbal climate upon his mental health and well being.

Nevertheless, in the words he absorbs daily and in the words he uses daily, Mr. Smith is profoundly involved. Words in the newspaper make him pound his fist on the breakfast table. Words his superiors speak to him puff him out with pride, or send him scurrying to work harder. Words about himself, which he has overheard being spoken behind his back, worry him sick. Words which he spoke before a clergyman some years ago have tied him to one woman for life. Words written down on pieces of paper tie him down on his job, or bring bills in his mail every month, which keep him paying and paying. Words written down by other people, on the other hand, keep them paying him month after month. With words woven into almost every detail of his life, it seems amazing that Mr. Smith's thinking on the subject of words should be so limited.

Mr. Smith has also noticed, if he keeps himself informed about the world, that when large masses of people, for example in totalitarian countries, are permitted by their governments to hear and read only carefully selected words, their conduct becomes so strange that he can only regard it as mad. Yet he has observed that some individuals who have the same educational attainments and the same access to varied sources of information that he has, are nevertheless just as mad, and, as the present crisis deepens, getting progressively madder, whether in the direction of escapist fantasy, mouth-foaming hysteria, or catatonic apathy. Does such madness, he asks, illustrate again the "inevitable frailty of human nature"? Mr. Smith, especially if he is an American accustomed to regarding all things as possible, does not like this conclusion, but often he can hardly see how he can escape it.

The reason for this impasse is that Mr. Smith believes, as most people do, that words are not really important;

what is important is the "ideas" they stand for. But what is an "idea" if it is not the *verbalization* of a cerebral itch? This, however, is something that has rarely, if ever, occurred to Mr. Smith. The fact that the implications of one set of terms may lead inevitably into blind alleys while the implications of another set of terms may not; the fact that the historical or sentimental associations that some words have make calm discussion impossible so long as those words are employed; the fact that language has a multitude of different kinds of uses, and that great confusion arises from mistaking one kind of use for another; the fact that a person speaking a language of structure entirely different from that of English, such as Japanese, Chinese, or Turkish, does not even think the same thoughts as an English-speaking person—these are unfamiliar notions to Mr. Smith, who has always assumed that the important thing is always to get one's "ideas" straight first, after which words would automatically take care of themselves.

Whether he realizes it or not, however, Mr. Smith is affected every hour of his life not only by the words he hears and uses, *but also by his unconscious assumptions about language.* These unconscious assumptions determine the way he takes words—which in turn determines the way he acts, whether wisely or foolishly. Words and the way he takes them determine his beliefs, his prejudices, his ideals, his aspirations—they constitute the moral and intellectual atmosphere in which he lives, in short, his semantic environment. If he is constantly absorbing false and lying words, or if his unconscious assumptions about language happen to be, as most of our notions are that have not been exposed to scientific influence, naïve, superstitious, or primitive, he may be constantly breathing a poisoned air without knowing it.

What this book hopes to do is to present certain principles of interpretation, or semantic principles, which are intended to act as a kind of intellectual air-purifying and air-conditioning system to prevent the poisons of verbal superstition, primitive linguistic assumptions, and the more pernicious forms of propaganda from entering our systems. These poisons, if unchecked, wastefully consume our energies in the fighting of verbal bogey-men, reduce our intellectual efficiency, and may ultimately destroy our mental health and well being. Nature to some extent provides her own safeguards against these poisons, as she does against germs and dust in the atmosphere; that is, we all intuitively learn, and at least part of the time unconsciously practice, sane semantic principles. But we live in an environment shaped and partially created by hitherto unparalleled semantic influences: commercialized newspapers, commercialized radio programs, "public relation counsels," and the propaganda technique of nationalistic madmen. Citizens of a modern society need, therefore, more than ordinary "horse sense"; they need to be scientifically aware of the mechanisms of interpretation if they are to guard themselves against being driven mad by the welter of words with which they are now faced.

I should be distressed, however, if my readers found in this book only negative injunctions. If the emphasis seems mainly to be on what not to do, it is only because a book on how to stay healthy cannot as a rule even begin to tell us what to do with our health when we have it. I have tried to indicate nevertheless, even if briefly, some of the positive values, the far-reaching cultural and democratic implications, of semantic health widely established. Semantics is not, as some have accused it of being, a purely destructive discipline, an "anatomy of disbelief." I hope I have not made it appear in that light.

S. I. H.

Illinois Institute of Technology
Chicago

LANGUAGE
IN ACTION

A STORY WITH A MORAL

O NCE upon a time (said the Professor), there were
two small communities, spiritually as well as geo-
graphically situated at a considerable distance from each
other. They had, however, these problems in common:
both were hard hit by the depression, so that in each of
the towns there were about one hundred heads of families unemployed. There was, to be sure, enough food for
them available, enough clothing, enough materials for
housing, but these families simply did not have money
to procure these necessities.

The city fathers of A-town, the first community, were
substantial businessmen, moderately well educated, good
to their families, kindhearted, and "sound-thinking."
The unemployed tried hard, as unemployed people usually do, to find jobs; but the situation did not improve.
The city fathers, as well as the unemployed themselves,
had been brought up to believe that there is always
enough work for everyone, if you only look for it hard
enough. Comforting themselves with this doctrine, the
city fathers could have shrugged their shoulders and
turned their backs on the problem, except for the fact
that they were genuinely kindhearted men. They could
not bear to see the unemployed men and their wives and
children starving. In order to prevent starvation, they felt

that they had to provide these people with some means of sustenance. Their principles told them, nevertheless, that if people were "given something for nothing," it would "demoralize their character." Naturally, this made the city fathers even more unhappy, because they were faced with the horrible choice of (1) letting the unemployed starve, or (2) destroying their moral character.

The solution they finally hit upon, after much debate and soul-searching, was this. They decided to give the unemployed families "relief" of fifty dollars a month, but to insure against the "pauperization" of the recipients, they decided that this fifty dollars was to be accompanied by a moral lesson, to wit: the obtaining of the assistance would be made so difficult, humiliating, and disagreeable that there would be no temptation for anyone to go through the process unless it was absolutely necessary; the moral disapproval of the community would be turned upon the recipients of the money at all times in such a way that they would try hard to get "off relief" and regain their "self-respect." Some even proposed that people "on relief" be denied the vote, so that the moral lesson would be more deeply impressed upon them. Others suggested that their names be published at regular intervals in the newspapers, so that there would be a strong incentive to get "off relief." The city fathers had enough faith in the goodness of human nature to expect that the recipients would be "grateful," since they were "getting something for nothing," something which they "hadn't worked for."

When the plan was put into operation, however, the recipients of the "relief" checks proved to be an ungrateful, ugly bunch. They seemed to resent the cross-examinations and inspections at the hands of the "relief investigators," who, they said, "took advantage of a man's misery to snoop into every detail of his private life." In spite of uplifting editorials in A-town *Tribune* telling them how grateful they ought to be, the recipients of the "relief" stubbornly refused to learn any moral lessons, declaring that they were "just as good as anybody else." When, for example, they permitted themselves the rare luxury of a movie or an evening of bingo, their neighbors looked at them sourly as if to say, "I work hard and pay my taxes just in order to support bums like you in idleness and pleasure." This attitude, which was fairly characteristic of those members of the community who still had jobs, further embittered the "relief" recipients, so that they showed even less gratitude as time went on and were constantly on the lookout for insults, real or imaginary, from people who might think that they weren't "as good as anybody else." A number of them took to moping all day long, to thinking that their lives had been "failures," and finally to committing suicide. Others found that it was "hard to look their wives and

kiddies in the face," because they had "failed to provide." They all found it difficult to maintain their club
and fraternal relationships, since they could not help feeling that their fellow citizens despised them for having
"sunk so low." Their wives, too, were unhappy for the
same reasons and gave up their social activities. Children
whose parents were "on relief" felt inferior to classmates
whose parents were not "public charges." Some of these
children developed inferiority complexes which affected
not only their grades at school, but their careers after
graduation. A couple of other relief recipients, finally, felt
they could stand their "loss of self-respect" no longer
and decided, after many efforts to gain honest jobs, to
earn money "by their own efforts," even if they had to go
in for robbery. They did so and were caught and sent to
the state penitentiary.

The depression, therefore, hit A-town very hard. The
relief policy had averted starvation, no doubt, but suicide,
personal quarrels, unhappy homes, the weakening of social organizations, the maladjustment of children, and,
finally, crime, had resulted during the hard times. The
town was divided in two, the "haves" and the "have-nots,"
so that there was "class hatred." People shook their heads
sadly and declared that it all went to prove over again
what they had known from the beginning, that "giving
people something for nothing" inevitably "demoralizes
their character." The citizens of A-town gloomily waited

for "prosperity" to return, with less and less hope as time went on.

The story of the other community, B-ville, was entirely different. B-ville was a relatively isolated town, too far out of the way to be reached by Rotary Club speakers and university extension services. One of the aldermen, however, who was something of an economist, explained to his fellow aldermen that unemployment, like sickness, accident, fire, tornado, or death, hits unexpectedly in modern society, irrespective of the victim's merits or deserts. He went on to say that B-ville's homes, parks, streets, industries, and everything else B-ville was proud of had been built in part by the work of these same people who were now unemployed. He then proposed to apply a principle of insurance: that if the work these unemployed people had previously done for the community could be regarded as a form of "premium" paid to the community against a time of misfortune, payments now made to them to prevent their starvation could be regarded as "insurance claims." He therefore proposed that all men of good repute who had worked in the community in whatever line of useful endeavor, whether as machinists, clerks, or bank managers, be regarded as "citizen policyholders," having "claims" against the city in the case of unemployment for fifty dollars a month until such time as they might again be employed. Naturally, he had to talk very slowly and patiently, since the idea was entirely new to his fellow aldermen. But he described his plan as a "straight business proposition," and finally they were persuaded. They worked out the details as to the conditions under which citizens should be regarded as "policyholders" in the city's "social insurance plan" to everybody's satisfaction and decided to give checks for fifty dollars a month to the heads of each of B-ville's indigent families.

B-ville's "claim adjusters," whose duty it was to investigate the "claims" of the "citizen policyholders," had a much better time than A-town's "relief investigators." While the latter had been resentfully regarded as "snoopers," the former, having no moral lesson to teach but simply a business transaction to carry out, treated their "policyholders" with businesslike courtesy and got the same amount of information as the "relief investigators" with considerably less difficulty. There were no hard feelings. It further happened, fortunately, that news of B-ville's plans reached a liberal newspaper editor in the big city at the other end of the state. This writer described the plan in a leading feature story headed "B-VILLE LOOKS AHEAD. Great Adventure in Social Pioneering Launched by Upper Valley Community." As a result of this publicity, inquiries about the plan began to come to the city hall even before the first checks were mailed out. This led, naturally, to a considerable feeling of pride on the part of the aldermen, who, being "boosters," felt that this was a wonderful opportunity to "put B-ville on the map."

Accordingly, the aldermen decided that instead of simply mailing out the checks as they had originally intended, they would publicly present the first checks at a monster civic ceremony. They invited the governor of the state, who was glad to come to bolster his none-too-enthusiastic support in that locality, the president of the state university, the senator from their district, and other functionaries. They decorated the National Guard armory with flags and got out the American Legion Fife and Drum Corps, the Boy Scouts, and other civic organizations. At the big celebration, each family to receive a "social insurance check" was marched up to the platform to receive it, and the governor and the mayor shook hands with each of them as they came trooping up in their best clothes. Fine speeches were made; there was much cheering and shouting; pictures of the event showing the recipients of the checks shaking hands with the mayor, and the governor patting the heads of the children, were published not only in the local papers but also in several metropolitan rotogravure sections.

Every recipient of these "insurance checks" had a feeling, therefore, that he had been personally honored, that he lived in a "wonderful little town," and that he could face his unemployment with greater courage and assurance, since his community was "back of him." The men and women found themselves being kidded in a friendly way by their acquaintances for having been "up there with the big shots," shaking hands with the governor, etc. The children at school found themselves envied for having had their pictures in the papers. Altogether, B-ville's unemployed did not commit suicide, were not haunted by a sense of failure, did not turn to crime, did not get personal maladjustments, did not develop "class hatred," as the result of their fifty dollars a month. . . .

At the conclusion of the Professor's story, the discussion began:

"That just goes to show," said the Advertising Man, who was known among his friends as a "realistic" thinker, "what good promotional work can do. B-ville's city council had real advertising sense, and that civic ceremony was a masterpiece . . . made everyone happy . . . put over the scheme in a big way. Reminds me of the way we do things in our business: as soon as we called horse-mackerel tuna-fish, we developed a big market for it. I suppose if you called relief 'insurance,' you could actually get people to like it, couldn't you?"

"What do you mean, 'calling' it insurance?" asked the

Social Worker. "B-ville's scheme wasn't relief at all. It *was* insurance. That's what all such payments should be. What gets me is the stupidity of A-town's city council and all people like them in not realizing that what they call 'relief' is simply the payment of just claims which those unemployed have on a community."

"Good grief, man! Do you realize what you're saying?" cried the Advertising Man in surprise. "Are you implying that those people had any *right* to that money? All I said was that it's a good idea to *disguise* relief as insurance if it's going to make people any happier. But it's still relief, no matter what you *call* it. It's all right to kid the public along to reduce discontent, but we don't need to kid ourselves as well as the public!"

"But they *do* have a right to that money! They're not getting something for nothing. It's insurance. They did something for the community, and that's their prem—"

"Say, are you crazy?"

"Who's crazy?"

"You're crazy. Relief is relief, isn't it? If you'd only call things by their right names . . ."

"But, confound it, insurance is insurance, isn't it?"

(Since the gentlemen are obviously losing their tempers, it will be best to leave them. The Professor has already sneaked out. When last heard of, not only had the quarrelers stopped speaking to each other, but so had their

wives—and the Advertising Man was threatening to dis-
inherit his son if he didn't break off his engagement with
the Social Worker's daughter.)

This story has been told not to advance arguments in
favor of "social insurance" or "relief" or for any other
political and economic system, but simply to show a fairly
characteristic sample of language in action. Do the words
we use make as much difference in our lives as the story
of A-town and B-ville seems to indicate? We often talk
about "choosing the right words to express our thoughts,"
as if thinking were a process entirely independent of the
words we think in. But is thinking such an independent
process? Do the words we utter arise as a result of the
thoughts we have, or are the thoughts we have determined by the linguistic systems we happen to have been
taught?

The Advertising Man and the Social Worker seem to be
agreed that the results of B-ville's program were good, so
that we can assume that their notions of what is socially
desirable are similar. Nevertheless, they *cannot agree*. Is
it because of ignorance on the part of one or the other or
both that they quarrel? This cannot be so, because, as the
reader may verify for himself by reading controversies in
newspapers, magazines, or even learned journals, well
educated people are often the cleverest in proving that
insurance is *really* insurance or that relief is *really* relief.

Quarrels of this kind, therefore, are especially bitter among social philosophers, lawyers, and publicists.

It will be the thesis of this book that disagreements of this kind—fundamental, doctrinal disagreements which seem to admit of no solution—are due not to stupidity or stubbornness, not even to an unscientific attitude towards the problems involved, but to an unscientific attitude towards language itself. In fact, a number of apparently insoluble problems which face us in our personal lives, in our society, and in our politics—and it must be remembered that these problems are formulated in *words*—may prove to be not insoluble at all when viewed through a clearer knowledge of the workings of language. It will be the purpose of this book, therefore, not only to acquaint the reader with some elementary facts about language such as are revealed by modern linguistics, anthropology, psychology, philosophy, literary criticism, and other branches of learning, *but also to change his very attitude towards language.*

Such a change of attitude, it is believed, will, first of all, make him a more understanding reader and listener than he was before. Secondly, it should increase the fruitfulness of whatever conversation and discussion he enters into, because, depending on our unconscious attitudes towards the words we hear and utter, we may use them either as weapons with which to start arguments and verbal free-for-alls or as instruments with which to increase our wisdom, our sense of fellowship with other human beings, and our enjoyment of life.

P.S. Those who have concluded that the point of the story is that the Social Worker and the Advertising Man were "only arguing about different names for the same thing," are asked to reread the story and explain what they mean by (1) "only," and (2) "the same thing."

1. THE IMPORTANCE OF LANGUAGE

> *One cannot but wonder at this constantly recurring phrase "getting something for nothing," as if it were the peculiar and perverse ambition of disturbers of society. Except for our animal outfit, practically all we have is handed to us gratis. Can the most complacent reactionary flatter himself that he invented the art of writing or the printing press, or discovered his religious, economic, and moral convictions, or any of the devices which supply him with meat and raiment or any of the sources of such pleasure as he may derive from literature or the fine arts? In short, civilization is little else than getting something for nothing.* JAMES HARVEY ROBINSON

Co-operation

WHEN someone shouts at you, "Look out!" and you duck just in time to avoid being hit by a thrown ball, you owe your escape from injury to the fundamental co-operative act by which most of the higher animals survive: namely, communication by means of noises. You did not see the ball coming; nevertheless, someone did see it, and he made certain *noises* to *communicate* his alarm to you. In other words, although your nervous system did not record the danger, you were unharmed because another nervous system did record it. You had, for the time being, the advantage of an extra nervous system in addition to your own.

Indeed, most of the time when we are listening to the noises people make or looking at the black marks on paper that stand for such noises, we are drawing upon the experiences of the nervous systems of others in order to make up what our own nervous systems have missed. Now obviously the more an individual can make use of the nervous systems of others to supplement his own, the easier it is for him to survive. And, of course, the more individuals there are in a group accustomed to co-operating by making helpful noises at each other, the better it is for all—within the limits, naturally, of the group's talents for organization. Birds and animals congregate with their own kind and make noises when they find food or become alarmed. In fact, gregariousness as an aid to self-defense and survival is forced upon animals as well as upon men by the necessity of uniting nervous systems even more than by the necessity of uniting physical strength. Societies, both animal and human, might almost be regarded as huge co-operative nervous systems.

While animals use only a few limited cries, however, human beings use extremely complicated systems of sputtering, hissing, gurgling, clucking, and cooing noises called *language,* with which they express and report what goes on in their nervous systems. Language is, in addition to being more complicated, immeasurably more flexible than the animal cries from which it was developed—so flexible indeed that it can be used not only to report the tremendous variety of things that go on in the human nervous system, but to report those reports. That is, when an animal yelps, he may cause a second animal to yelp in imitation or in alarm, but the second yelp is not *about* the first yelp. But when a man says, "I see a river," a second man can say, "He says he sees a river"—which is a statement about a statement. About this statement-about-a-statement further statements can be made—and about those, still more. *Language, in short, can be about language.* This is a fundamental way in which human noise-making systems differ from the cries of animals.

The Pooling of Knowledge

In addition to having developed language, man has also developed means of making, on clay tablets, bits of wood or stone, skins of animals, and paper, more or less permanent marks and scratches which *stand for* language. These marks enable him to communicate with people who are beyond the reach of his voice, both in space and in time. There is a long course of evolution from the marked trees that indicated Indian trails to the metropolitan daily newspaper, but they have this in common: they pass on what one individual has known to other individuals, for their convenience or, in the broadest sense, instruction. The Indians are dead, but many of their trails are still marked and can be followed to this day. Archimedes is dead, but we still have his reports about what he observed in his experiments in physics. Keats is dead, but he can still tell us how he felt on first reading Chapman's Homer. From our newspapers we learn with great rapidity, as the result of steamship, railway, telegraph, and radio, facts about the world we live in. From books and magazines we learn how hundreds of people whom we shall never be able to see have felt and thought. All this information is useful to us at one time or another in the solution of our own problems.

A human being, then, is never dependent on his own experience alone for his information. Even in a primitive culture he can make use of the experience of his neighbors, friends, and relatives, which they communicate to him by means of language. Therefore, instead of remaining helpless because of the limitations of his own experience and knowledge, instead of having to rediscover what others have already discovered, instead of exploring the false trails they explored and repeating their errors, he can *go on from where they left off*. Language, that is to say, makes progress possible.

Indeed, most of what we call the human characteristics

of our species are expressed and developed through our ability to co-operate by means of our systems of making meaningful noises and meaningful scratches on paper. Even people who belong to backward cultures in which writing has not been invented are able to exchange information and to hand down from generation to generation considerable stores of traditional knowledge. There seems, however, to be a limit both to the trustworthiness and to the amount of knowledge that can be transmitted orally. But when writing is invented, a tremendous step forward is taken. The accuracy of reports can be checked and rechecked by successive generations of observers. The amount of knowledge accumulated ceases to be limited by people's ability to remember what has been told them. The result is that in any literate culture of a few centuries' standing, human beings accumulate vast stores of knowledge—far more than any individual in that culture can read in his lifetime, let alone remember. These stores of knowledge, which are being added to constantly, are made widely available to all who want them through such mechanical processes as printing and through such distributive agencies as the book trade, the newspaper and magazine trade, and library systems. The result is that all of us who can read any of the major European or Asiatic languages are potentially in touch with the intellectual resources of centuries of human endeavor in all parts of the civilized world.

A physician, for example, who does not know how to treat a patient suffering from a rare disease can look up the disease in a medical index, which may send him in turn to medical journals. There he may find records of similar cases as reported and described by a physician in Rotterdam, Holland, in 1873, by another physician in Bangkok, Siam, in 1909, and by still other physicians in Kansas City in 1924. With such records before him, he can better handle his own case. Again, if a person is worried about ethics, he is not dependent merely upon the pastor of the Elm Street Baptist Church, but he may go to Confucius, Aristotle, Jesus, Spinoza, and many others whose reflections on ethical problems are on record. If one is worried about love, he can get advice not only from his mother or best friend, but from Sappho, Ovid, Propertius, Shakespeare, Havelock Ellis, or any of a thousand others who knew something about it and wrote down what they knew.

Language, that is to say, is the indispensable mechanism of human life—of life such as ours that is molded, guided, enriched, and made possible by the accumulation of the *past* experience of members of our species. Dogs and cats and chimpanzees do not, so far as we can tell, increase their wisdom, their information, or their control over their environment from one generation to the next. But human beings do. The cultural accomplishments of the ages, the invention of cooking, of weapons, of writing,

of printing, of methods of building, of games and amuse-
ments, of means of transportation, and the discoveries of
all the arts and sciences come to us as *free gifts from the
dead*. These gifts, which none of us has done anything
to earn, offer us not only the opportunity for a richer life
than any of our forebears enjoyed, but also the opportunity to add to the sum total of human achievement by
our own contributions, however small.

To be able to read and write, therefore, is to learn to
profit by and to take part in the greatest of human
achievements—that which makes all other human achievements possible—namely, the pooling of our experience in
great co-operative stores of knowledge, available (except
where special privilege, censorship, or suppression stand
in the way) to all. From the warning cry of the savage
to the latest scientific monograph or radio news flash,
language is social. Cultural and intellectual co-operation
is, or should be, the great principle of human life.

The Worlds We Live In: Map and Territory

There is a sense in which we all live in two worlds.
First, we live in the world of the happenings about us
which we know at first hand. But this is an extremely
small world, consisting only of that continuum of the
things that we have actually seen, felt, or heard—the flow
of events constantly passing before our senses. As far as

this world of personal experience is concerned, Africa, South America, Asia, Washington, New York, or Los Angeles do not exist if we have never been to these places. President Roosevelt is only a name if we have never seen him. When we ask ourselves how much we know at first hand, we discover that we know very little indeed.

Most of our knowledge, acquired from parents, friends, schools, newspapers, books, conversation, speeches, and radio, is received *verbally*. All of our knowledge of history, for example, comes to us only in words. The only proof we have that the Battle of Waterloo ever took place is that we have had reports to that effect. These reports are not given us by people who saw it happen, but are based on other reports: reports of reports of reports, and so on, that go back ultimately to the first-hand reports given by the people who did see it happening. It is through reports, then, and through reports of reports, that we receive most of our knowledge: about government, about what is happening in China, about what picture is showing at the downtown theater—in fact, about anything which we do not know through direct experience.

Let us call this world that comes to us through words the *verbal world,* as opposed to the world we know or are capable of knowing through our own experience, which we shall call the *extensional world*. The reason for the choice of the word "extensional" will become clear

later. The human being, like any other creature, begins
to make his acquaintance with the extensional world from
infancy. Unlike other creatures, however, he begins to
receive, as soon as he can learn to understand, reports,
reports of reports, reports of reports of reports, and so
on. In addition, he receives inferences made from reports,
inferences made from other inferences, and so on. By the
time a child is a few years old, has gone to school and
to Sunday school, and has made a few friends, he has
accumulated a considerable amount of second- and third-
hand information about morals, geography, history, nature, people, games—all of which information together
constitutes his verbal world.

Now this verbal world ought to stand in relation to the
extensional world as a *map* does to the *territory* it is supposed to represent. If the child grows to adulthood with
a verbal world in his head which corresponds fairly closely
to the extensional world that he finds around him in his
widening experience, he is in relatively small danger of
being shocked or hurt by what he finds, because his verbal
world has told him what, more or less, to expect. He is
prepared for life. If, however, he grows up with a false
map in his head—that is, with a head crammed with
false knowledge and superstition—he will constantly be
running into trouble, wasting his efforts, and acting like
a fool. He will not be adjusted to the world as it is; he

may, if the lack of adjustment is serious, end up in an insane asylum.

Some of the follies we commit because of false maps in our heads are so commonplace that we do not even think of them as remarkable. There are those who protect themselves from accidents by carrying a rabbit's foot in the pocket. Some refuse to sleep on the thirteenth floor of hotels—this is so common that most big hotels, even in the capitals of our scientific culture, skip "13" in numbering their floors. Some plan their lives on the basis of astrological predictions. Some play fifty-to-one shots on the basis of dream books. Some hope to make their teeth whiter by changing their brand of tooth paste. All such people are living in verbal worlds that bear little, if any, resemblance to the extensional world.

Now, no matter how beautiful a map may be, it is useless to a traveler unless it accurately shows the relationship of places to each other, the structure of the territory. If we draw, for example, a big dent in the outline of a lake for, let us say, artistic reasons, the map is worthless. But if we are just drawing maps for fun without paying any attention to the structure of the region, there is nothing in the world to prevent us from putting in all the extra curlicues and twists we want in the lakes, rivers, and roads. No harm will be done unless someone tries to plan a trip by such a map. Similarly, by means of imaginary or false reports, or by false inferences from good reports, or by mere rhetorical exercises, we can manufacture at will, with language, "maps" which have no reference to the extensional world. Here again no harm will be done unless someone makes the mistake of regarding such "maps" as representing real "territories."

We all inherit a great deal of useless knowledge, and a great deal of misinformation and error, so that there is always a portion of what we have been told that must be discarded. But the cultural heritage of our civilization that is transmitted to us—our socially pooled knowledge, both scientific and humane—has been valued principally because we have believed that it gives us accurate maps of experience. The analogy of verbal worlds to maps is an important one and will be referred to frequently throughout this book. It should be noticed at this point, however, that there are two ways of getting false maps of the world into our heads: first, by having them given to us; second, by making them up for ourselves by misreading the true maps given to us.

2. SYMBOLS

I find it difficult to believe that words have no meaning in themselves, hard as I try. Habits of a lifetime are not lightly thrown aside.

STUART CHASE

Signal and Symbol Reaction

ANIMALS struggle with each other for food or for leadership, but they do not, like human beings, struggle with each other for things that *stand for* food or leadership: such things as our paper symbols of wealth (money, bonds, titles), badges of rank to wear on our clothes, or low-number license-plates, supposed by some people to stand for social precedence. For animals the relationship in which one thing *stands for* something else does not appear to exist except in very rudimentary form. For example, a chimpanzee can be taught to drive a car, but there is one thing wrong with its driving: its reactions are such that if a red light shows when it is halfway across a street, it will stop in the middle of the crossing, while if a green light shows while another car is stalled in its path, it will go ahead regardless of consequences. In other words, so far as a chimpanzee is concerned, the red light can hardly be said to *stand for* stop; it *is* stop.

Let us then introduce two terms to represent this dis-

26

tinction between the "red light *is* stop" relationship, which the chimpanzee understands, and the "red light *stands for* stop" relationship, which the human being understands. To the chimpanzee, the red light is, we shall say, a *signal,* and we shall term its reaction a *signal reaction; that is, a complete and invariable reaction which occurs whether or not the conditions warrant such a reaction.* To the human being, on the other hand, the red light is, in our terminology, a *symbol,* and we shall term his reaction a *symbol reaction; that is, a delayed reaction, conditional upon the circumstances.* In other words, the nervous system capable only of signal reactions *identifies the signal with the thing for which the signal stands;* the human nervous system, however, working under normal conditions, understands *no necessary connection* between the symbol and the thing for which the symbol stands. Human beings do not automatically jump up in the expectation of being fed whenever they hear an ice-box door slam.

The Symbolic Process

Human beings, because they can understand certain things to *stand for* other things, have been able to develop what we shall term the *symbolic process.* Whenever two or more human beings can communicate with each other, they can, by agreement, make anything stand for anything. Feathers worn on the head can be made to stand for tribal chieftainship; cowrie shells or rings of brass or pieces of paper can stand for wealth; crossed sticks can stand for a set of religious beliefs; buttons, elks' teeth, ribbons, special styles of ornamental haircutting or tattooing, can stand for social affiliations. The symbolic process permeates human life at the most savage as well as at the most civilized levels. Warriors, medicine men, policemen, doormen, telegraph boys, cardinals, and kings wear costumes that symbolize their occupations. Savages collect scalps, college students collect dance programs and membership keys in honorary societies, to symbolize victories in their respective fields. There are very few things that men do or want to do, possess or want to possess, that have not, in addition to their mechanical or biological value, a symbolic value.

All fashionable clothes, as Thorstein Veblen has pointed out in his *Theory of the Leisure Class,* are highly symbolic: materials, cut, and ornament are dictated only to a slight degree by considerations of warmth, comfort, or practicability. The more we dress up in fine clothes, the more do we restrict our freedom of action. But by means of delicate embroideries, easily soiled fabrics, starched shirts, high heels, long and pointed fingernails, and other such sacrifices of comfort, the wealthy classes manage to symbolize the fact that they don't have to work for a living. The not so wealthy, on the other hand, by imitating these symbols of wealth, symbolize their conviction that, even if they do work for a living, they are just as good as anybody else. Again, we select our furniture to serve as visible symbols of our taste, wealth, and social position; we trade in perfectly good cars for later models, not always to get better transportation, but to give evidence to the community that we can afford such luxuries; we often choose our residential localities on the basis of a feeling that it "looks well" to have a "good address"; we like to put expensive food on our tables, not always because it tastes better than cheap food, but because it tells our guests that we like them, or, just as often, because it tells them that we are well fixed financially.

Such complicated and apparently unnecessary behavior leads philosophers, both amateur and professional, to ask over and over again, "Why can't human beings live simply and naturally?" Perhaps, unconsciously, they would like to escape the complexity of human life for the relative simplicity of such lives as dogs and cats lead. But the symbolic process, which makes possible the absurdities of human conduct, also makes possible language and therefore all the human achievements dependent upon language. The fact that more things can go wrong with motorcars than with wheelbarrows is no reason for going back to wheelbarrows. Similarly, the fact that the symbolic process makes complicated follies possible is no reason for wanting to return to a cat-and-dog existence.

Language as Symbolism

Of all forms of symbolism, language is the most highly developed, most subtle, and most complicated. It has been pointed out that human beings, by agreement, can make anything stand for anything. Now, human beings have agreed, in the course of centuries of mutual dependency, to let the various noises that they can produce with their lungs, throats, tongues, teeth, and lips systematically stand for specified happenings in their nervous systems. We call that system of agreements *language*. For example, we who speak English have been so trained that when our nervous systems register the presence of a certain kind of animal, we may make the following noise: "There's a cat." Anyone hearing us would expect to find that by looking in the same direction, he would experience a similar event in his nervous system—one that would have led him to make an almost identical noise. Again, we have been so trained that when we are conscious of wanting food, we make the noise, "I'm hungry."

There is, as has been said, *no necessary connection between the symbol and that which is symbolized*. Just as men can wear yachting costumes without ever having been near a yacht, so they can make the noise, "I'm hungry," without being hungry. Furthermore, just as social rank can be symbolized by feathers in the hair, by tattooing on the breast, by gold ornaments on the watch chain, by a thousand different devices according to the culture we live in, so the fact of being hungry can be symbolized by a thousand different noises according to the culture we live in: "J'ai faim," or "Es hungert mich," or "Ho appetito," or "Hara ga hetta," and so on.

Linguistic Naïveté

However obvious these facts may appear at first glance, they are actually not so obvious as they seem except when we take special pains to think about the subject. Symbols and things symbolized are independent of each other; nevertheless, all of us have a way of feeling as if, and sometimes acting as if, there were necessary connections. For example, there is the vague sense that we all have that foreign languages are inherently absurd. Foreigners have "funny names" for things: why can't they call things by their "right names"? This feeling exhibits itself most strongly in those American and English tourists who seem to believe that they can make the natives of any country understand English if they shout it at them loud enough. They feel, that is, that the symbol *must necessarily* call to mind the thing symbolized.

Anthropologists report similar attitudes among primi-

tive peoples. In talking with natives, they frequently
come across unfamiliar words in the native language.
When they interrupt the conversation to ask, *"Guglu?
What is a guglu?"* the natives laugh, as if to say, "Imagine not knowing what a *guglu* is! What amazingly silly
people!" When an answer is insisted upon, they explain,
when they can get over laughing, "Why, a *guglu* is a
GUGLU, of course!" Very small children think in this respect the way primitive people do; often when policemen say to a whimpering lost child, "All right, little
girl, we'll find your mother for you. Who is your mother?
What's your mother's name?" the child can only bawl,
"My muvver is *mummy*. I want *mummy!*" This leaves
the police, as they say in murder mysteries, baffled. Again,
there is the little boy who is reported to have said, "Pigs
are called pigs because they are such *dirty* animals."

Similar naïveté regarding the symbolic process is illustrated by an incident in the adventures of a theatrical
troupe playing melodramas to audiences in the western
ranching country. One night, at a particularly tense moment in the play, when the villain seemed to have the
hero and the heroine in his power, an overexcited cowpuncher in the audience suddenly rose from his seat and
shot the villain. The cowpuncher of this story, however,
is no more ridiculous than those thousands of people
today, many of them adults, who write fan letters to a
ventriloquist's dummy, or those goodhearted but impres-

sionable people who send presents to the broadcasting station when two characters in a radio serial get married, or those astonishing patriots who rushed to recruiting offices to help defend the nation when the United States was "invaded" by an "army from Mars."

These, however, are only the more striking examples of primitive and infantile attitudes towards symbols. There would be little point in mentioning them if we were uniformly and permanently aware of the independence of symbols from things symbolized. But we are not. Most of us retain many habits of evaluation ("thinking habits") more appropriate to life in the jungle than to life in modern civilization. Moreover, all of us are capable of reverting to them, especially when we are overexcited or when subjects about which we have special prejudices are mentioned. Worst of all, various people who have easy access to such instruments of public communication as the press, the radio, the lecture platform, and the pulpit actively encourage primitive and infantile attitudes towards symbols. Political and journalistic charlatans, advertisers of worthless or overpriced goods, and promoters of religious bigotry stand to profit either in terms of money or power or both, if the majority of people can be kept thinking like savages or children.

The Word-Deluge We Live In

The interpretation of words is a never-ending task for any citizen in modern society. We now have, as the result of modern means of communication, hundreds of thousands of words flung at us daily. We are constantly being talked at, by teachers, preachers, salesmen, public officials, and moving-picture sound tracks. The cries of the hawkers of soft drinks, soap chips, and laxatives pursue us into our very homes, thanks to the radio—and in some houses the radio is never turned off from morning to night. Daily the newsboy brings us, in large cities, from thirty to fifty enormous pages of print, and almost three times that amount on Sundays. The mailman brings magazines and direct-mail advertising. We go out and get more words at bookstores and libraries. Billboards confront us on the highways, and we even take portable radios with us to the seashore. Words fill our lives.

This word-deluge in which we live is by no means entirely to be regretted. It is to be expected that we should become more dependent on mutual intercommunications as civilization advances. But, with words being flung about as heedlessly of social consequences as they now are, it is obvious that if we approach them with primitive habits of evaluation, or even with a tendency to revert occasionally to primitive habits of evaluation, we cannot do otherwise than run into error, confusion, and tragedy.

Why Is the World a Mess? One Theory

But, the reader may say, surely educated people don't think like savages! Unfortunately they do—some about one subject, some about another. The educated are frequently quite as naïve about language as the uneducated, although the ways in which they exhibit their naïveté may be less easily discernible. Indeed, many are worse off than the uneducated, because while the uneducated often realize their own limitations, the educated are in a position to refuse to admit their ignorance and conceal their limitations from themselves by their skill at word-juggling. After all, education as it is still understood in many circles is principally a matter of learning facility in the manipulation of words.

Such training in word-manipulation cannot but lead to an unconscious assumption that if any statement *sounds* true, it must be true—or, if not true, at least passable. This assumption (always unconscious) leads even learned men to make beautiful "maps" of "territories" that do not exist—without ever suspecting their nonexistence. Indeed, it can safely be said that whenever people are more attached to their verbal "maps" than to the factual "territories" (that is, whenever they are so attached to pet theories that they cannot give them up in the face of facts to the contrary), they are exhibiting serious linguistic naïveté. Some educated and extremely intelligent people are so attached to the verbal "maps" they have created that, when they can find no territories in the known world to correspond to them, they create "supersensory" realms of "transcendental reality," so that they will not have to admit the uselessness of their maps.[1] Such people are often in a position to impose their notions on others, in beautifully written books and in eloquent lectures, and they thus spread the results of linguistic naïveté wherever their influence can reach.

As this is being written, the world is becoming daily a worse madhouse of murder, hatred, and destruction. It would seem that the almost miraculous efficiency achieved by modern instruments of communication should enable nations to understand each other better and co-operate more fully. But, as we know too well, the opposite has been the case; the better the communications, the bloodier the quarrels.

Linguistic naïveté—our tendency to think like savages about practically all subjects other than the purely technological—is not a factor to be ignored in trying to account for the mess civilization is in. By using the radio and the newspaper as instruments for the promotion of political, commercial, and sectarian balderdash, rather than as instruments of public enlightenment, we seem to have increased the infectiousness of savagery of

[1] See Eric Temple Bell, *The Search for Truth;* also Thurman W. Arnold, *The Folklore of Capitalism.*

thought. Men react to meaningless noises, maps of non-existent territories, as if they stood for actualities, and never suspect that there is anything wrong with the process. Political leaders hypnotize themselves with the babble of their own voices and use words in a way that shows not the slightest concern with the fact that if language, the basic instrument of man's humanity, finally becomes as meaningless as they would make it, co-operation will not be able to continue, and society itself will fall apart.

But to the extent that we too think like savages and babble like idiots, we all share the guilt for the mess in which human society finds itself. To cure these evils, we must first go to work on ourselves. An important beginning step is to understand how language works, what we are doing when we open these irresponsible mouths of ours, and what it is that happens, or should happen, when we listen or read.

Applications

The following hobby is suggested for those who wish to follow the argument of this book. In a scrapbook or, perhaps better, on 5 x 7 filing cards, start a collection of quotations, newspaper clippings, editorials, anecdotes, bits of overheard conversation, advertising slogans, etc., that illustrate in one way or another linguistic naïveté. The ensuing chapters of this book will suggest many different kinds of linguistic naïveté and confusion to look for, and the methods for classifying the examples found will also be suggested. The simplest way to start will be to look for those instances in which people seem to think that there are *necessary* connections between symbols and things symbolized—between words and what words stand for. Innumerable examples can be found in books on cultural anthropology, especially in those sections dealing with word-magic. After a few such examples are chosen and studied, the reader will be able to recognize readily similar patterns of thought in his contemporaries and friends. Here are a few items with which such a collection might be begun:

1. "The Malagasy soldier must eschew kidneys, because in the Malagasy language the word for kidney is the same as that for 'shot'; so shot he would certainly be if he ate a kidney."— J. G. FRAZER, *The Golden Bough* (one-volume abridged edition), p. 22.

2. [A child is being questioned.] "Could the sun have been called 'moon' and the moon 'sun'?—*No.*—Why not?—*Because the sun shines brighter than the moon. . . .* But if everyone had called the sun 'moon,' and the moon 'sun,' would we have known it was wrong?—*Yes, because the sun is always bigger, it always stays like it is and so does the moon.*—Yes, but the sun isn't changed, only its name. Could it have been called . . . etc.?—*No. . . . Because the moon rises in the evening, and the sun in the day.*"—PIAGET, *The Child's Conception of the World*, pp. 81-82.

3. The City Council of Cambridge, Massachusetts, unani-

mously passed a resolution (December, 1939) making it illegal "to possess, harbor, sequester, introduce or transport, within the city limits, any book, map, magazine, newspaper, pamphlet, handbill or circular containing the words Lenin or Leningrad."

4. The gates of the 1933 Century of Progress Exposition at Chicago were opened, through the use of the photoelectric cell, by the light of the star Arcturus. It is reported that a woman, on being told of this, remarked, *"Isn't it wonderful how those scientists know the names of all those stars!"*

5. "State Senator John McNaboe of New York bitterly opposed a bill for the control of syphilis in May, 1937, because 'the innocence of children might be corrupted by a widespread use of the term. . . . This particular word creates a shudder in every decent woman and decent man.' "—STUART CHASE, *The Tyranny of Words,* p. 63.

6. A picture in the magazine *Life* (October 28, 1940) shows the backs of a sailor's hands, with the letters "H-O-L-D F-A-S-T" tattooed on the fingers. The caption explains, "This tattoo was supposed to keep sailors from falling off yardarm."

3. REPORTS

Vague and insignificant forms of speech, and abuse of language, have so long passed for mysteries of science; and hard or misapplied words with little or no meaning have, by prescription, such a right to be mistaken for deep learning and height of speculation, that it will not be easy to persuade either those who speak or those who hear them, that they are but the covers of ignorance and hindrance of true knowledge.

JOHN LOCKE

FOR THE purposes of the interchange of information, the basic symbolic act is the *report* of what we have seen, heard, or felt: "There is a ditch on each side of the road." "You can get those at Smith's hardware store for $2.75." "There aren't any fish on that side of the lake, but there are on this side." Then there are reports of reports: "The longest waterfall in the world is Victoria Falls in Rhodesia." "The Battle of Hastings took place in 1066." "The papers say that there was a big smash-up on Highway 41 near Evansville." Reports adhere to the following rules: first, they are capable of verification; secondly, they exclude, so far as possible, judgments, inferences, and the use of "loaded" words.

Verifiability

Reports are verifiable. We may not always be able to verify them ourselves, since we cannot track down the evidence for every piece of history we know, nor can we all go to Evansville to see the remains of the smash-up before they are cleared away. But if we are roughly agreed on the names of things, on what constitutes a "foot," "yard," "bushel," and so on, and on how to measure time, there is relatively little danger of our misunderstanding each other. Even in a world such as we have today, in which everybody seems to be fighting everybody else, *we still to a surprising degree trust each other's reports*. We ask directions of total strangers when we are traveling. We follow directions on road signs without being suspicious of the people who put the signs up. We read books of information about science, mathematics, automotive engineering, travel, geography, the history of costume, and other such factual matters, and we usually assume that the author is doing his best to tell us as truly as he can what he knows. And we are safe in so assuming most of the time. With the emphasis that is being given today to the discussion of biased newspapers, propagandists, and the general untrustworthiness of many of the communications we receive, we are likely to forget that we still have an enormous amount of reliable information available and that deliberate misinformation, except in warfare, still is more the exception than the rule. The desire for self-preservation that compelled men to evolve means for the exchange of information also compels them to regard the giving of false information as profoundly reprehensible.

At its highest development, the language of reports is known as science. By "highest development" we mean greatest general usefulness. Presbyterian and Catholic, workingman and capitalist, German and Englishman, *agree* on the meanings of such symbols as $2 \times 2 = 4$, $100°$ *C., HNO₃, 8:35* A.M., *1940* A.D., *5000 r.p.m., 1000 kilowatts, pulex irritans,* and so on. But how, it may be asked, can there be agreement even about this much among people who are at each other's throats about practically everything else? The answer is that circumstances *compel them to agree,* whether they wish to or not. If, for example, there were a dozen different religious sects in the United States, each insisting on its own way of naming the time of the day and the days of the year, the mere necessity of having a dozen different calendars, a dozen different kinds of watches, and a dozen sets of schedules for business hours, trains, and radio programs, to say nothing of the effort that would be required for translating terms from one nomenclature to another, would make life as we know it impossible.

The language of reports, then, including the more accurate reports of science, is "map" language, and because it gives us reasonably accurate representations of the "territory" it enables us to get work done. Such language may often be what is commonly termed "dull" or "uninteresting" reading; one does not usually read logarithmic tables or telephone directories for entertainment. But we could not get along without it. There are numberless occasions in the talking and writing we do in everyday life that require that we state things *in such a way that everybody will agree with our formulation.*

Some Writing Exercises: The Exclusion of Judgments

The reader will find that practice in writing reports is a quick means of increasing his linguistic awareness. It is an excellent exercise, one which will constantly provide him with his own examples of the principles of language and interpretation under discussion. The reports should be about first-hand experience—scenes the reader has witnessed himself, meetings and social events he has taken part in, people he knows well. They should be of such a nature that they can be *verified* and *agreed upon.*

This is not a simple task. A report must exclude all expressions of the writer's approval or disapproval of the occurrences, persons, or objects he is describing. For example, a report cannot say, "It was a wonderful car," but must say something like this: "It has been driven 50,000 miles and has never required any repairs." Again, statements like "Jack lied to us" must be suppressed in favor of the more verifiable statement, "Jack told us he didn't have the keys to his car with him. However, when he pulled a handkerchief out of his pocket a few minutes later, the keys fell out." Also, a report may not say, "The senator was stubborn, defiant, and unco-operative," or "The senator courageously stood by his principles"; it must say instead, "The senator's vote was the only one against the bill." Most people regard statements like the following as statements of fact: "He is a *thief*." "He is a *bad boy*." These again must be excluded in favor of statements of the more verifiable kind: "He was convicted of theft and served two years at Waupun." "His mother, his father, and most of the neighbors say he is a bad boy." After all, to say of a man that he is a "thief" is to say in effect, "He has stolen *and will steal again*"—which is more a prediction than a report. Even to say, "He has stolen," is to pass a judgment on an act about which there may be difference of opinion among different observers. But to say that he was "convicted of theft" is to make a statement capable of being agreed upon through verification in court and prison records.

Scientific verifiability rests upon the external observation of facts, not upon the heaping up of judgments. If one person says, "Peter is a deadbeat," and another says, "I think so too," the statement has not been verified. In court cases, considerable trouble is sometimes caused by witnesses who cannot distinguish their judgments from the facts upon which those judgments are based. Cross-examinations under these circumstances go something like this:

Witness. That dirty double-crosser Jacobs ratted on me!
Defense Attorney. Your honor, I object.
Judge. Objection sustained. [Witness's remark is stricken from the record.] Now, try to tell the court exactly what happened.
Witness. He *double-crossed* me, the dirty, lying rat!
Defense Attorney. Your honor, I object!
Judge. Objection sustained. [Witness's remark is again stricken from the record.] Will the witness try to stick to the facts.
Witness. But I'm telling you the facts, your honor. He did *double-cross* me.

This can continue indefinitely unless the cross-examiner exercises some ingenuity in order to get at the facts behind the judgment. To the witness it is a "fact" that he was "double-crossed." Often hours of patient questioning are required before the factual bases of the judgment are revealed.

The Exclusion of Inferences

Another requirement of reports is that they must make no guesses as to what is going on in other people's minds. When we say, "He was angry," we are not reporting, we are making an *inference* from such observable facts as the following: "He pounded his fist on the table; he swore; he threw the telephone directory at his stenographer." In this particular example, the inference appears to be fairly safe; nevertheless, it is important to remember, especially for the purposes of training oneself, that it is an inference. Such expressions as "He thought a lot of himself," "He was scared of girls," "She always wants nothing but the best," should be avoided in favor of the more verifiable "He showed evidences of annoyance when people did not treat him politely," "He stammered when he asked girls to dance with him," "She frequently declared that she wanted nothing but the best."

The Exclusion of "Loaded" Words

In short, the process of reporting is the process of keeping one's personal feelings out. In order to do this, one must be constantly on guard against "loaded" words that reveal or arouse feelings. Instead of "sneaked in," one should say "entered quietly"; instead of "politicians," "congressmen" or "aldermen"; instead of "officeholder," "public official"; instead of "tramp," "homeless unemployed"; instead of "Chinaman," "Chinese"; instead of "dictatorial set-up," "centralized authority"; instead of "crackpots," "holders of uncommon views." A newspaper reporter, for example, is not permitted to write, "A bunch of fools who are suckers enough to fall for Senator Smith's ideas met last evening in that rickety firetrap that disfigures the south edge of town." Instead he says, "Between seventy-five and a hundred people were present last evening to hear an address by Senator Smith at the Evergreen Gardens near the South Side city limits."

Second Stage of the Writing Exercise: Slanting

In the course of writing reports of personal experiences, it will be found that in spite of all endeavors to keep judgments out, some will creep in. An account of a man, for example, may go like this: "He had apparently not shaved for several days, and his face and hands were covered with grime. His shoes were torn, and his coat, which was several sizes too small for him, was spotted with dried clay." Now, in spite of the fact that no judgment has been stated, a very obvious one is implied. Let us contrast this with another description of the same man. "Although his face was bearded and neglected, his eyes were clear, and he looked straight ahead as he walked rapidly down the road. He looked very tall; perhaps the fact that his coat was too small for him emphasized that impression. He was carrying a book under his left arm, and a small terrier ran at his heels." In this example, the impression about the same man is considerably changed, simply by the inclusion of new details and the subordination of unfavorable ones. *Even if explicit judgments are kept out of one's writing, implied judgments will get in.*

How, then, can we ever give an impartial report? The answer is, of course, that we cannot attain complete impartiality while we use the language of everyday life. Even with the very impersonal language of science, the task is sometimes difficult. Nevertheless, we can, by being aware of the favorable or unfavorable feelings that certain words and facts can arouse, attain enough impartiality for practical purposes. Such awareness enables us *to balance the implied favorable and unfavorable judgments against each other.* To learn to do this, it is a good idea to write *two* essays at a time on the same subject, both strict reports, to be read side by side: the first to contain facts and details likely to prejudice the reader in favor of the subject, the second to contain those likely to prejudice the reader against it. For example:

FOR	AGAINST
He had white teeth.	His teeth were uneven.
His eyes were blue, his hair blond and abundant.	He rarely looked people straight in the eye.
He had on a clean blue shirt.	His shirt was frayed at the cuffs.
He often helped his wife with the dishes.	He rarely got through drying dishes without breaking a few.
His pastor spoke very highly of him.	His grocer said he was always slow about paying his bills.

Slanting Both Ways at Once

This process of selecting details favorable or unfavorable to the subject being described may be termed *slanting*. Slanting gives no explicit judgments, but it differs from reporting in that it deliberately makes certain judgments inescapable. The writer striving for impartiality will, therefore, take care to slant *both for and against* his subject, trying as conscientiously as he can to keep the balance even. The next stage of the exercise, then, should be to rewrite the parallel essays into a single coherent essay in which details on both sides are included:

His teeth were white, but uneven; his eyes were blue, his hair blond and abundant. He did not often look people straight in the eye. His shirt was slightly frayed at the cuffs, but it was clean. He frequently helped his wife with the dishes, but he broke many of them. Opinion about him in the community was divided. His grocer said he was slow about paying his bills, but his pastor spoke very highly of him.

This example is, of course, oversimplified and admittedly not very graceful. But practice in writing such essays will first of all help to prevent one from slipping unconsciously from observable facts to judgments; that is, from "He was a member of the Ku Klux Klan" to "the dirty scoundrel!" Next, it will reveal how little we really want to be impartial anyway, especially about our best friends, our parents, our alma mater, our own children, our country, the company we work for, the product we sell, our competitor's product, or anything else in which our interests are deeply involved. Finally, we will discover that, even if we have no wish to be impartial, we write more clearly, more forcefully, and more convincingly by this process of sticking as close as possible to observable facts. There will be less "hot air" and more substance.

How Judgments Stop Thought

A judgment ("He is a fine boy," "It was a beautiful service," "Baseball is a healthful sport," "She is an awful bore") is a *conclusion,* summing up a large number of previously observed facts. The reader is probably familiar with the fact that students, when called upon to write "themes," almost always have difficulty in writing papers of the required length, because their ideas give out after a paragraph or two. The reason for this is that those early paragraphs contain so many such judgments that there is little left to be said. When the conclusions are carefully excluded, however, and observed facts are given instead, there is never any trouble about the length of papers; in fact, they tend to become too long, since inexperienced writers, when told to give facts, often give far more than are necessary, because they lack discrimination between the important and the trivial. This, however, is better than the literary constipation with which most students are afflicted as soon as they get a writing assignment.

Still another consequence of judgments early in the course of a written exercise—and this applies also to hasty judgments in everyday thought—is the temporary blindness they induce. When, for example, an essay starts with the words, "He was a real Wall Street executive," or "She was a typical cute little co-ed," if we continue writing at all, we must make all our later statements consistent with those judgments. The result is that all the individual characteristics of this particular "executive" or this particular "co-ed" are lost sight of entirely; and the rest of the essay is likely to deal not with observed facts, but with the writer's *private notion* (based on previously read stories, movies, pictures, etc.) of what "Wall Street executives" or "typical co-eds" look like. The premature judgment, that is, often prevents us from seeing what is directly in front of us. Even if the writer feels sure at the beginning of a written exercise that the man he is describing is a "loafer" or that the scene he is describing is a "beautiful residential suburb," he will conscientiously keep such notions out of his head, lest his vision be obstructed.

A few weeks of practice in writing reports, slanted reports, and reports slanted both ways will improve powers of observation, as well as ability to recognize soundness of observation in the writings of others. A sharpened sense for the distinction between facts and judgments, facts and inferences, will reduce susceptibility to the flurries of frenzied public opinion which certain people find it to their interest to arouse. Alarming judgments and inferences can be made to appear inevitable by means of skillfully slanted reports. A reader who is aware of the technique of slanting, however, cannot be stampeded by such methods. He knows too well that there may be other relevant facts which have been left out. Who worries now about the "Twenty-one Days Left to Save the American Way of Life" of the 1936 presidential campaign? Who worries now about the "snooping into private lives" and the "establishment of an American Gestapo" that were supposed to result from the 1940 census? Yet people worry about such things at the time.

Applications

1. Here are a number of statements which the reader may attempt to classify as judgments, inferences, or reports. Since the distinctions are not always clear-cut, a one-word answer will not ordinarily be adequate. If the reader finds himself in disagreement with others as to the classification of some of the statements, he is advised to remember the Social Worker and the Advertising Man and not to argue. Note that we are concerned here with the *nature* of the statements, not their truth or falsity;

for example, the statement, "Water freezes at 10° Cen-
tigrade," is, although inaccurate, a report.

a. She goes to church only in order to show off her clothes.
b. A penny saved is a penny earned.
c. Loveliest of trees, the cherry now
   Is hung with bloom along the bough.
                    A. E. HOUSMAN
d. In the old days, newspapers used to tell the truth.
e. The German-American Bund is a Nazi propaganda agency.
f. Belgium has been called the Niobe of nations.
g. "Italy's would-be invaders can't blitzkrieg through country
   which is crisscrossed by a whole series of mountain ranges
   and whose narrow passes and extremely few serpentine
   roads are guarded by large and determined Greek forces."
                    Chicago *Daily News*
h. Senator Smith has for a long time secretly nursed presidential ambitions.
i. Piping down the valleys wild,
   Piping songs of pleasant glee,
   On a cloud I saw a child,
   And he laughing said to me:

   "Pipe a song about a Lamb!"
   So I piped with merry cheer.
   "Piper, pipe that song again;"
   So I piped: he wept to hear.
                    WILLIAM BLAKE
j. "But the liberals needn't be feared if you understand them.
   The thing to do is to keep constantly posted on what they
   are up to and treat them as something that got on your
   shoe. They are mostly noise, and an honest man has the
   advantage, because truth and tolerance simply are not in
   them."
                    WESTBROOK PEGLER

k. "And Adam lived an hundred and thirty years, and begat a son in his own likeness, after his image; and called his name Seth: And the days of Adam after he had begotten Seth were eight hundred years: and he begat sons and daughters: And all the days that Adam lived were nine hundred and thirty years: and he died."—Genesis 5:3-5

2. In addition to trying such exercises in report writing and the exclusion of judgments and inferences as are suggested in this chapter, it is suggested that the reader try writing (a) reports heavily slanted *against* persons or events he *likes,* and (b) reports heavily slanted *in favor of* persons or events he thoroughly *dislikes.* For example, the ardent Democrat might show a Republican rally in a favorable light and a Democratic rally in an unfavorable light; the ardent Republican might reverse this procedure. This is a necessary preliminary to "slanting both ways at once," which is obviously an impossible task for anyone who can see things only in one way. Incidentally, the "Reporter at Large" department and the "Profiles" department of *The New Yorker* often offer good examples of the report technique: explicit judgments are few, and a real effort is made to give at least the appearance of "slanting both ways at once."

4. CONTEXTS

*Dictionary definitions frequently offer verbal sub-
stitutes for an unknown term which only conceal a lack of real understanding. Thus a person
might look up a foreign word and be quite satisfied with the meaning "bullfinch" without the
slightest ability to identify or describe this bird.
Understanding does not come through dealings
with words alone, but rather with the things for
which they stand. Dictionary definitions permit
us to hide from ourselves and others the extent
of our ignorance.*　　H. R. HUSE

How Dictionaries Are Made

IT IS an almost universal belief that every word has a
"correct meaning," that we learn these meanings principally from teachers and grammarians (except that most
of the time we don't bother to, so that we ordinarily
speak "sloppy English"), and that dictionaries and grammars are the "supreme authority" in matters of meaning
and usage. Few people ask by what authority the writers
of dictionaries and grammars say what they say. The
docility with which most people bow down to the dictionary is amazing, and the person who says, "Well, the
dictionary is wrong!" is looked upon with smiles of pity

and amusement which say plainly, "Poor fellow! He's really quite sane otherwise."

Let us see how dictionaries are made and how the editors arrive at definitions. What follows applies, incidentally, only to those dictionary offices where first-hand, original research goes on—not those in which editors simply copy existing dictionaries. The task of writing a dictionary begins with the reading of vast amounts of the literature of the period or subject that it is intended to cover. As the editors read, they copy on cards every interesting or rare word, every unusual or peculiar occurrence of a common word, a large number of common words in their ordinary uses, *and also the sentences in which each of these words appears,* thus:

> pail
> The dairy *pails* bring home increase of milk
> Keats, *Endymion*
> I, 44-45

That is to say, the *context* of each word is collected, along with the word itself. For a really big job of dictionary writing, such as the *Oxford English Dictionary* (usually bound in about twenty-five volumes), millions of such cards are collected, and the task of editing occupies decades. As the cards are collected, they are alphabetized and sorted. When the sorting is completed, there will be for each word anywhere from two or three to several hundred illustrative quotations, each on its card.

To define a word, then, the dictionary editor places before him the stack of cards illustrating that word; each of the cards represents an actual use of the word by a writer of some literary or historical importance. He reads the cards carefully, discards some, re-reads the rest, and divides up the stack according to what he thinks are the several senses of the word. Finally, he writes his definitions, following the hard-and-fast rule that each definition *must* be based on what the quotations in front of him reveal about the meaning of the word. The editor cannot be influenced by what *he* thinks a given word *ought* to mean. He must work according to the cards, or not at all.

The writing of a dictionary, therefore, is not a task of setting up authoritative statements about the "true meanings" of words, but a task of *recording,* to the best of one's ability, what various words *have meant* to authors in the distant or immediate past. *The writer of a dictionary is a historian, not a law-giver.* If, for example, we had been writing a dictionary in 1890, or even as late as 1919, we could have said that the word "broadcast" means "to scatter," seed and so on; but we could not have decreed that from 1921 on, the commonest meaning of the word should become "to disseminate audible messages, etc., by wireless telephony." To regard the dictionary as an "authority," therefore, is to credit the dictionary writer with gifts of prophecy which neither he nor anyone else possesses. In choosing our words when we speak or write, we can be *guided* by the historical record afforded us by the dictionary, but we cannot be *bound* by it, because new situations, new experiences, new inventions, new feelings, are always compelling us to give new uses to old words. Looking under a "hood," we should ordinarily have found, five hundred years ago, a monk; today, we find a motorcar engine.

Verbal and Physical Contexts

The way in which the dictionary writer arrives at his definitions is merely the systematization of the way in which we all learn the meanings of words, beginning at infancy, and continuing for the rest of our lives. Let us say that we have never heard the word "oboe" before, and we overhear a conversation in which the following sentences occur:

He used to be the best *oboe* player in town. . . . Whenever they came to that *oboe* part in the third movement, he used to get very excited. . . . I saw him one day at the music shop, buying a new reed for his *oboe*. . . . He never liked to play the clarinet after he started playing the *oboe*. He said it wasn't so much fun, because it was too easy.

Although the word may be unfamiliar, its meaning becomes clear to us as we listen. After hearing the first sentence, we know that an "oboe" is "played," so that it must be either a game or a musical instrument. With the second sentence the possibility of its being a game is eliminated. With each succeeding sentence the possibilities as to what an "oboe" may be are narrowed down until we get a fairly clear idea of what is meant. This is how we learn by *verbal context*.

But even independently of this, we learn by *physical and social context*. Let us say that we are playing golf and that we have hit the ball in a certain way with certain unfortunate results, so that our companion says to us, "That's a bad *slice*." He repeats this remark every time our ball fails to go straight. If we are reasonably bright, we learn in a very short time to say, when it happens again, "That's a bad slice." On one occasion, however, our friend says to us, "That's not a *slice* this time; that's a *hook*." In this case we consider what has happened, and we wonder what is different about the last stroke from those previous. As soon as we make the distinction, we have added still another word to our vocabulary. The result is that after nine holes of golf, we can use both these words accurately—and perhaps several others as well, such as "divot," "number-five iron," "approach shot," *without ever having been told what they mean.* Indeed, we may play golf for years without ever being able to give a dictionary definition of "to slice": "To strike (the ball) so that the face of the club draws inward across the face of the ball, causing it to curve toward the right in flight (with a right-handed player)" (*Webster's New International Dictionary*). But even without being able to give such a definition, we should still be able to use the word accurately whenever the occasion demanded.

We learn the meanings of practically all our words (which are, it will be remembered, merely complicated noises), not from dictionaries, not from definitions, but from hearing these noises as they accompany actual situations in life and learning to associate certain noises with certain situations. Even as dogs learn to recognize "words," as for example by hearing "biscuit" at the same time as an actual biscuit is held before their noses, so do we all learn to interpret language by being aware of the happenings that accompany the noises people make at us—by being aware, in short, of contexts.

The "definitions" given by little children in school show clearly how they associate words with situations; they almost always define in terms of physical and social contexts: "Punishment is when you have been bad and they put you in a closet and don't let you have any supper." "Newspapers are what the paper boy brings and you wrap up the garbage with it." These are good definitions. The main reason that they cannot be used in dictionaries is that they are *too* specific; it would be impossible to list the myriads of situations in which every word has been used. For this reason, dictionaries give definitions on a high level of abstraction; that is, with particular references left out for the sake of conciseness. This is another reason why it is a great mistake to regard a dictionary definition as "telling us all about" a word.

Extensional and Intensional Meaning

From this point on, it will be necessary to employ some special terms in talking about meaning: *extensional meaning,* which will also be referred to as *denotation,* and *intensional meaning*—note the *s*—which will also be referred to as *connotation.*[1] Briefly explained, the extensional meaning of an utterance is that which it *points to* or denotes in the extensional world, referred to in Chapter 3 above. That is to say, the extensional meaning is something that *cannot be expressed in words,* because it is that which words stand for. An easy way to remember this is to put your hand over your mouth and point whenever you are asked to give an extensional meaning.

[1] The words *extension* and *intension* are borrowed from logic; *denotation* and *connotation* are borrowed from literary criticism. The former pair of terms will ordinarily be used, therefore, when we are talking about people's "thinking habits"; the latter, when we are talking about words themselves.

The *intensional meaning* of a word or expression, on the other hand, is that which is *suggested* (connoted) inside one's head. Roughly speaking, whenever we express the meaning of words by uttering more words, we are giving intensional meaning, or connotations. To remember this, put your hand over your eyes and let the words spin around in your head.

Utterances may have, of course, both extensional and intensional meaning. If they have no intensional meaning at all—that is, if they start no notions whatever spinning about in our heads—they are meaningless noises, like foreign languages that we do not understand. On the other hand, it is possible for utterances to have no extensional meaning at all, in spite of the fact that they may start many notions spinning about in our heads. Since this point will be discussed more fully in Chapter 5, perhaps one example will be enough: the statement, "Angels watch over my bed at night," is one that has intensional but no extensional meaning. This does not mean that there are no angels watching over my bed at night. When we say that the statement has no extensional meaning, we are merely saying that we cannot see, touch, photograph, or in any scientific manner detect the presence of angels. The result is that, if an argument begins on the subject whether or not angels watch over my bed, *there is no way of ending the argument to the satisfaction of all disputants,* the Christians and the non-

Christians, the pious and the agnostic, the mystical and the scientific. Therefore, whether we believe in angels or not, knowing in advance that any argument on the subject will be both endless and futile, we can avoid getting into fights about it.

When, on the other hand, statements have extensional content, as when we say, "This room is fifteen feet long," arguments can come to a close. No matter how many guesses there are about the length of the room, all discussion ceases when someone produces a tape measure. This, then, is the important difference between extensional and intensional meanings: namely, when utterances have extensional meanings, discussion can be ended and agreement reached; when utterances have intensional meanings only and no extensional meanings, arguments may, and often do, go on indefinitely. Such arguments can result only in irreconcilable conflict. Among individuals, they may result in the breaking up of friendships; in society, they often split organizations into bitterly opposed groups; among nations, they may aggravate existing tensions so seriously as to become contributory causes of war.

Arguments of this kind may be termed "non-sense arguments," because they are based on utterances about which no sense data can be collected. Needless to say, there are occasions when the hyphen may be omitted— that depends on one's feelings toward the particular argument under consideration. The reader is requested to provide his own examples of "non-sense arguments." Even the foregoing example of the angels may give offense to some people, in spite of the fact that no attempt is made to deny or affirm the existence of angels. He can imagine, therefore, the uproar that might result from giving a number of examples, from theology, politics, law, economics, literary criticism, and other fields in which it is not customary to distinguish clearly sense from non-sense.

The "One Word, One Meaning" Fallacy

Everyone, of course, who has ever given any thought to the meanings of words has noticed that they are always shifting and changing in meaning. Usually, people regard this as a misfortune, because it "leads to sloppy thinking" and "mental confusion." To remedy this condition, they are likely to suggest that we should all agree on "one meaning" for each word and use it only with that meaning. Thereupon it will occur to them that we simply cannot make people agree in this way, even if we could set up an ironclad dictatorship under a committee of lexicographers who could place censors in every newspaper office and dictaphones in every home. The situation, therefore, appears hopeless.

Such an impasse is avoided when we start with a new

premise altogether—one of the premises upon which modern linguistic thought is based: namely, *that no word ever has exactly the same meaning twice*. The extent to which this premise fits the facts can be demonstrated in a number of ways. First, if we accept the proposition that the contexts of an utterance determine its meaning, it becomes apparent that since no two contexts are ever *exactly* the same, no two meanings can ever be exactly the same. How can we "fix the meaning" even for as common an expression as "to believe in" when it can be used in such sentences as the following?

I *believe in* you (I have confidence in you).
I *believe in* democracy (I accept the principles implied by the term democracy).
I *believe in* Santa Claus (It is my opinion that Santa Claus exists).

Secondly, we can take for example a word of "simple" meaning like "kettle." But when John says "kettle," its intensional meanings to him are the common characteristics of all the kettles John remembers. When Peter says "kettle," however, its intensional meanings to him are the common characteristics of all the kettles he remembers. *No matter how small or how negligible the differences may be between John's "kettle" and Peter's "kettle," there is some difference.*

Finally, let us examine utterances in terms of extensional meanings. If John, Peter, Harold, and George each say "my typewriter," we would have to point to *four different typewriters* to get the extensional meaning in each case: John's new Underwood, Peter's old Corona, Harold's L. C. Smith, and the undenotable intended "typewriter" that George plans some day to buy: "My typewriter, when I buy one, will be a noiseless." Also, if John says "my typewriter" today, and again "my typewriter" tomorrow, the extensional meaning is different in the two cases, because the typewriter is not *exactly* the same from one day to the next (nor from one minute to the next): slow processes of wear, change, and decay are going on constantly. Although we can say, then, that the differences in the meanings of a word on one occasion, on another occasion a minute later, and on still another occasion another minute later, are *negligible,* we cannot say that the meanings are *exactly* the same.

To say dogmatically that we "know what a word means" *in advance of its utterance* is nonsense. All we can know in advance is *approximately* what it *will* mean. After the utterance, we interpret what has been said in the light of both verbal and physical contexts, and act according to our interpretation. An examination of the verbal context of an utterance, as well as the examination of the utterance itself, directs us to the intensional meanings; an examination of the physical context directs us to the extensional meanings. When John says to James, "Bring me that book, will you?" James looks in the direction of John's pointed finger (physical context) and sees a desk with several books on it (physical context); he thinks back over their previous conversation (verbal context) and knows which of those books is being referred to.

Interpretation *must* be based, therefore, on the totality of contexts. If it were otherwise, we should not be able to account for the fact that even if we fail to use the right (customary) words in some situations, people can very frequently understand us. For example:

A. Gosh, look at that second baseman go!
B (looking). You mean the shortstop?
A. Yes, that's what I mean.

A. There must be something wrong with the oil line; the engine has started to balk.
B. Don't you mean "gas line"?
A. Yes—didn't I say gas line?

Contexts sometimes indicate so clearly what we mean that often we do not even have to say what we mean in order to be understood.

The Ignoring of Contexts

It is clear, then, that the ignoring of contexts in any act of interpretation is at best a stupid practice. At its worst, it can be a vicious practice. A common example is the sensational newspaper story in which a few words by a public personage are torn out of their context and made the basis of a completely misleading account. There is the incident of an Armistice Day speaker, a university teacher, who declared before a high-school assembly that the Gettysburg Address was "a powerful piece of propaganda." The context clearly revealed that "propaganda" was being used according to its dictionary meanings rather than according to its popular meanings; it also revealed that the speaker was a very great admirer of Lincoln's. However, the local newspaper, completely ignoring the context, presented the account in such a way as to convey the impression that the speaker had called Lincoln a liar. On this basis, the newspaper began a campaign against the instructor. The speaker remonstrated with the editor of the newspaper, who replied, in effect, *"I don't care what else you said.* You said the Gettysburg Address was propaganda, didn't you?" This appeared to the editor complete proof that Lincoln had been maligned and that the speaker deserved to be discharged from his position at the university. Similar practices may be found in advertisements. A reviewer may be quoted on the jacket of a book as having said, "A brilliant work," while reading of the context may reveal that what he really said was, "It just falls short of being a brilliant work." There are some people who will always be able to find a defense for such a practice in saying, "But he did use the words, 'a brilliant work,' didn't he?"

People in the course of argument very frequently complain about words meaning different things to different people. Instead of complaining, they should accept it as a matter of course. It would be startling indeed if the word "justice," for example, were to have the same meaning to the nine justices of the United States Supreme Court; we should get nothing but unanimous decisions. It would be even more startling if "justice" meant the same to Fiorello La Guardia as to Josef Stalin. If we can get deeply into our consciousness the principle that no word ever has the same meaning twice, we will develop the habit of automatically examining contexts, and this enables us to understand better what others are saying. As it is, however, we are all too likely to have signal reactions to certain words and read into people's remarks meanings that were never intended. Then we waste energy in angrily accusing people of "intellectual dishonesty" or "abuse of words," when their only sin is that they use words in ways unlike our own, as they can hardly help doing, especially if their background has been widely different from ours. There are cases of intellectual dishonesty and of the abuse of words, of course, but they do not always occur in the places where people think they do.

In the study of history or of cultures other than our own, contexts take on special importance. To say, "There was no running water or electricity in the house," does not condemn an English house in 1570, but says a great deal against a house in Chicago in 1941. Again, if we wish to understand the Constitution of the United States, it is not enough, as our historians now tell us, merely to look up all the words in the dictionary and to read the interpretations written by Supreme Court justices. We must see the Constitution in its *historical context:* the conditions of life, the current ideas, the fashionable prejudices, and the probable interests of the people who drafted the Constitution. After all, the words "The United States of America" stood for quite a different-sized nation and a different culture in 1790 from what they stand for today. When it comes to very big subjects, the range of contexts to be examined, verbal, social, and historical, may become very large indeed.

The Interaction of Words

All this is not to say, however, that the reader might just as well throw away his dictionary, since contexts are so important. Any word in a sentence—any sentence in a paragraph, any paragraph in a larger unit—whose meaning is revealed by its context, *is itself part of the context of the rest of the text.* To look up a word in a dictionary, therefore, frequently explains not only the word itself, but the rest of the sentence, paragraph, conversation, or essay in which it is found. *All words within a given context interact upon one another.*

Realizing, then, that a dictionary is a historical work, we should understand the dictionary thus: "The word *mother* has most frequently been used in the past among English-speaking people to indicate *a female parent.*" From this we can safely infer, "If that is how it has been used, that is what it probably means in the sentence I am trying to understand." This is what we normally do, of course; after we look up a word in the dictionary, *we re-examine the context to see if the definition fits.*

A dictionary definition, therefore, is an invaluable guide to interpretation. Words do not have a single "correct meaning"; they apply to *groups* of similar situations, which might be called *areas of meaning.* It is for definition in terms of areas of meaning that a dictionary is useful. In each use of any word, we examine the particular context and the extensional events denoted (if possible) to discover the *point* intended within the area of meaning.

Applications

1. It has been said in this chapter that to say that one word should have one meaning or that we can know the meaning of a word in advance of its utterance is non-

sense. Here are some examples of the uses of the word *air*. To see how different they actually are, translate the sentences into other words.

She had an *air* of triumph.
John left the casting director's office walking on *air*.
On summer nights the *air* was warm and fragrant.
He gave her the *air*.
Want some *air* in your tires, Mister?
She certainly does give herself *airs!*
There was a suspicious *air* about the whole thing.
Slum children benefit from getting out into the *air* and sunlight.
A gentle *air* was moving the curtains at the open window.
In 1789 change was in the *air*.
At that she just went up in the *air*.
High up in the *air* a hawk was circling.
The doctors say he needs a change of *air*.
It would be better if this whole dirty business were brought out into the open *air*. . . . There's nothing better in such cases than the free *air* of public discussion.
Jonathan was always building castles in the *air*.
As they left the theater, half of the audience was whistling the catchy *air*.
When he got across the border he filled his lungs with the *air* of freedom.
The Philharmonic is on the *air* every Sunday afternoon.

2. Provide contexts, in this case sentences, which illustrate some of the various areas of meaning you can find in the following words:

arm   dog   flight   frog   date   people   rich   free

3. Sitting where you are, say the words, "Come here." Now after moving to another seat, say "Come here" again. Is the extensional meaning of the words still the same? Has the intensional meaning been affected?

Take a blank sheet of paper and sign your name ten or a dozen times. There are now before you ten or a dozen examples of the extensional meaning of the words "my signature." Compare them. You might cut them apart and match them up against a light. Are the extensional meanings in any two cases the same? Would they be the same if they were printed?

"To make roasted potatoes, first wash the potatoes and peel them. After the potatoes have been peeled, parboil them and place them in the pan with the roast to brown. When done, serve the potatoes with gravy made from the juices of the meat." What can you say about the extensional meanings of "potatoes" throughout this passage?

5. WORDS THAT DON'T INFORM

Are words in Phatic Communion ["*a type of speech in which ties of union are created by a mere exchange of words*"] *used primarily to convey meaning, the meaning which is symbolically theirs? Certainly not! They fulfil a social function and that is their principal aim, but they are neither the result of intellectual reflection, nor do they necessarily arouse reflection in the listener.*

B. MALINOWSKI

Noises as Expression

WHAT complicates the problems of interpretation above all is that often words are not used informatively at all. In fact, we have every reason to believe that the ability to use noises as symbols was developed only recently in the course of our evolution. Long before we developed language as we know it, we probably made, like the lower animals, all sorts of animal cries, expressive of such internal conditions as hunger, fear, triumph, and sexual desire. We can recognize a variety of such noises and the conditions they indicate in our domestic animals. Gradually these noises seem to have become more and more differentiated: consciousness expanded. Grunts and gibberings became symbolic language. But, although we developed symbolic language, the habit of making noises *expressing,* rather than *reporting,* our internal conditions has remained. The result is that we use language in *presymbolic* ways; that is, as the equivalent of screams, howls, purrs, and gibbering. These presymbolic uses of language coexist with our symbolic systems, and we still have constant recourse to them in the talking we do in everyday life.

The presymbolic character of much of our talk is most clearly illustrated in cries expressive of strong feeling of any kind. If, for example, we carelessly step off a curb when a car is coming, it doesn't much matter whether someone yells, "Look out!" or "Kiwotsuke!" or "Hey!" or "Prends garde!" or simply utters a scream, so long as whatever noise is made is uttered loud enough to alarm us. It is the fear expressed in the *loudness* and the *tone* of the cry that conveys the necessary sensations, and not the words. Similarly, commands given sharply and angrily usually produce quicker results than the same commands uttered tonelessly. The quality of the voice itself, that is to say, has a power of expressing feelings that is almost independent of the symbols used. We can say, "I hope you'll come to see us again," in a way that clearly indicates that we hope the visitor never comes back. Or again, if a young lady with whom we are strolling says, "The moon is bright tonight," we are able to tell by the tone whether she is making a meteorological observation or indicating that she wants to be kissed.

Snarl-Words and Purr-Words

The making of noises with the vocal organs is a muscular activity. Many of our muscular activities are involuntary. Many of our speeches—especially exclamations— are likewise involuntary. Our responses to powerful stimuli, such as to something that makes us very angry, are a complex of muscular and physiological activities: the contraction of fighting muscles, the increase of blood pressure, the tearing of hair, and so on, *and* the making of noises, such as growls and snarls. Human beings, however, probably because they consider it beneath their dignity to express their anger in purely animalistic noises, do not ordinarily growl like dogs, but substitute series of words, such as "You dirty double-crosser!" "You filthy scum!" Similarly, instead of purring or wagging the tail, the human being again substitutes speeches such as "She's the sweetest girl in all the world!" "Oh, dear, what a cute baby!"

Speeches such as these are, therefore, complicated human equivalents of snarling and purring and are not symbolic in the same sense that the statement, "Chicago is in the state of Illinois," is symbolic. That is to say, "She's the sweetest girl in all the world" is not a statement about the girl, but a revelation of the speaker's feelings—a revelation such as is made among lower animals by wagging the tail or purring. Similarly, the ordinary oratorical and editorial denunciation of "Reds," "Wall Street," "corporate interests," "radicals," "economic royalists," and "fifth columnists," are often only protracted snarls, growls, and yelps, with, however, the surface appearance of logical and grammatical articulation. These series of "snarl-words" and "purr-words," as it will be convenient to call them, are not reports describing conditions in the extensional world, but *symptoms of disturbance,* unpleasant or pleasant, in the speaker.

Indeed, what we have called "judgments" in Chapter 3 —words expressive of our likes and dislikes—are extremely complicated snarls and purrs. Their principal function is to indicate the approval or disapproval felt by the speaker, although, to be sure, they often indicate at the same time the reasons for those feelings. To call judgments snarls and purrs may seem to be unduly disrespectful of the human race, but such disrespect is not intended. The terminology is used merely to emphasize the fact that judgments, like snarls and purrs, do not as such have extensional content. This is an important point to remember in controversy.

For example, let us suppose that Smith has said, "Senator Booth is a fourflusher," and that Jones has said, "Senator Booth is a great statesman." The question most likely to be argued, under what are now normal circumstances, will be, "Is Senator Booth a fourflusher or a great statesman?" The progress of such an argument is fairly predictable: Smith cites facts to "prove" that the senator is a "fourflusher"; Jones comes right back with other facts to "prove" the contrary. Each will deny or belittle the facts advanced by the other. Their voices will become louder; they will start to gesticulate wildly; they will start shaking their fists under each other's noses. Finally, their friends may have to separate them. Such a conclusion, as we have seen, is inevitable when questions without extensional content, or non-sense questions, are argued.

Disputes about presymbolic utterances should therefore be avoided. Often such snarls and purrs are not merely a matter of a few words, but of paragraphs, of entire editorials or speeches, and sometimes of entire books. The question to be discussed should never take the form, "Is Hitler really a beast as the speaker says?" but rather, "Why does the speaker feel as he does?" Once we know why the judgment has been made, we may follow the speaker in the judgment or make a different one of our own.

All this is not to say that we should not snarl or purr. In the first place, we couldn't stop ourselves if we wanted to; and in the second, there are many occasions that demand good violent snarls, as well as soft purrs of delight. Subtle and discriminating judgments, made by sensitive and intelligent individuals, are well worth listening to, since they contribute to our moral sensitivity. But we *must* guard ourselves against mistaking these for reports.

Noises for Noise's Sake

There are, of course, other presymbolic uses of language. Sometimes we talk simply for the sake of hearing ourselves talk; that is, for the same reason that we play golf or dance. The activity gives us a pleasant sense of being alive. Children prattling, adults singing in the bathtub, are alike enjoying the sound of their voices. Sometimes large groups make noises together, as in group singing, group recitation, or group chanting, for similar presymbolic reasons. In all this, the significance of the words used is almost completely irrelevant. We often, for example, may chant the most lugubrious words about a desire to be carried back to a childhood home in old Virginia, when in actuality we have never been there and haven't the slightest intention of going.

What we call "social conversation" is again presymbolic in character. When we are at a tea or dinner party, for example, we all have to talk—about anything: the weather, the performance of the Chicago White Sox, Thomas Mann's latest book, or Myrna Loy's last picture. It is typical of these conversations that, except among very good friends, few of the remarks made on these subjects are ever important enough to be worth making for their informative value. Nevertheless, it is regarded as "rude" to remain silent. Indeed, in such matters as greetings and farewells: "Good morning"—"Lovely day"— "And how's your family these days?"—"It was a pleasure meeting you"—"Do look us up the next time you're in town"—it is regarded as a social error not to say these things even if we do not mean them. There are numberless daily situations in which we talk simply because it would be impolite not to. Every social group has its own form of this kind of talking—"the art of conversation," "small talk," or the mutual "kidding" that Americans love so much. From these social practices it is possible to infer, as a general principle, that *the prevention of silence is itself an important function of speech,* and that it is completely impossible for us in society to talk only when we "have something to say."

This presymbolic talk for talk's sake is, like the cries of animals, a form of activity. We talk together about nothing at all and thereby establish friendships. The purpose of the talk is not the communication of information, as the symbols used would seem to imply ("I see the Dodgers are out in the lead again"), but the establishment of communion. Human beings have many ways of establishing communion among themselves: breaking bread together, playing games together, working together. But talking together is the most easily arranged of all these forms of collective activity. The *togetherness* of the talking, then, is the most important element in social conversation; the subject matter is only secondary.

Presymbolic Language in Ritual

Sermons, political caucuses, conventions, "pep rallies," and other ceremonial gatherings illustrate the fact that all groups—religious, political, patriotic, scientific, and occupational—like to gather together at intervals for the purpose of sharing certain accustomed activities, wearing special costumes (vestments in religious organizations, regalia in lodges, uniforms in patriotic societies, and so on), eating together (banquets), displaying the flags, ribbons, or emblems of their group, and marching in processions. Among these ritual activities is always included a number of speeches, either traditionally worded or specially composed for the occasion, whose principal function is *not* to give the audience information it did not have before, *not* to create new ways of feeling, but something else altogether.

What this something else is, we shall analyze more fully in Chapter 7 on "Directive Language." We can analyze now, however, one aspect of language as it appears in ritual speeches. Let us look at what happens at a "pep rally" such as precedes college football games. The members of "our team" are "introduced" to a crowd that already knows them. Called upon to make speeches, the players mutter a few incoherent and often ungrammatical remarks, which are received with wild applause. The leaders of the rally make fantastic promises about the mayhem to be performed on the opposing team the next day. The crowd utters "cheers," which normally consist of animalistic noises arranged in extremely primitive rhythms. *No one comes out any wiser or better informed than he was before he went in.*

To some extent religious ceremonies are equally puzzling at first glance. The priest or clergyman in charge utters set speeches, *often in a language incomprehensible to the congregation* (Hebrew in orthodox Jewish synagogues, Latin in the Roman Catholic Church, Sanskrit in Chinese and Japanese temples), with the result that, as often as not, no information whatsoever is communicated to those present.

If we approach these linguistic events as students of language trying to understand what is happening and if we examine our own reactions when we enter into the spirit of such occasions, we cannot help observing that, whatever the words used in ritual utterance may signify, we often do not think very much about their signification during the course of the ritual. Most of us, for example, have often repeated the Lord's Prayer or sung "The Starspangled Banner" without thinking about the words at all. As children we are taught to repeat such sets of words before we can understand them, and many of us continue to say them for the rest of our lives without bothering about their signification. Only the superficial, however, will dismiss these facts as "simply showing what fools human beings are." We cannot regard such utterances as "meaningless," because they have a genuine effect upon us. We may come out of church, for example, with no clear memory of what the sermon was about, but with a sense nevertheless that the service has somehow "done us good."

Ritualistic utterances, therefore, whether made up of words that have symbolic significance at other times, of words in foreign or obsolete tongues, or of meaningless syllables, may be regarded as consisting in large part of presymbolic uses of language: that is, *accustomed sets of noises* which convey no information, but to which feelings (in this case group feelings) are attached. Such utterances rarely make sense to anyone not a member of the group. The abracadabra of a lodge meeting is absurd to anyone but a member of the lodge. When language becomes ritual, that is to say, its effect becomes to a considerable extent independent of whatever significations the words once possessed.

The Importance of Understanding the Presymbolic Uses of Language

Presymbolic uses of language have this characteristic in common: their functions can be performed, if necessary, without the use of grammatically and syntactically articulated symbolic words. They can even be performed without recognizable speech at all. Group feeling may be established, for example, among animals by collective barking or howling, and among human beings by college cheers, community singing, and such collective noise-making activities. Indications of friendliness such as we give when we say "Good morning" or "Nice day, isn't it?" can be given by smiles, gestures, or, as among animals, by nuzzling or sniffing. Frowning, laughing, smiling, jumping up and down, can satisfy a large number of needs for expression, without the use of verbal symbols. But the use of verbal symbols is more customary among human beings, so that instead of expressing our feelings by knocking a man down, we often verbally blast him to perdition; instead of drowning our sorrows in drink, we perhaps write poems.

To understand the presymbolic elements that enter into our everyday language is extremely important. We cannot restrict our speech to the giving and asking of factual information; we cannot confine ourselves strictly to statements that are literally true, or we should often be unable to say even "Pleased to meet you" when the occasion demanded. The intellectually persnickety are always telling us that we "ought to say what we mean" and "mean what we say," and "talk only when we have something to talk about." These are, of course, impossible prescriptions.

Ignorance of the existence of these presymbolic uses of language is not so common among uneducated people (who often perceive such things intuitively) as it is among those "educated" people who, having a great contempt for the stupidity of others, have a correspondingly high opinion of their own perspicacity. Such "enlightened" people listen to the chatter at teas and receptions and conclude from the triviality of the conversation that all the guests except themselves are fools. They may discover that people often come away from church services without any clear memory of the sermon and conclude that church-goers are either fools or hypocrites. They may hear the political oratory of the opposition party, wonder "how anybody can believe such rot," and conclude therefrom that people in general are so unintelligent that it would be impossible for democracy to be made to work. (They will overlook the fact, of course, that similar conclusions could be drawn from the speeches *they* applaud at their own party conventions.) Almost all such gloomy conclusions about the stupidity or hypocrisy of our friends and neighbors are unjustifiable on such evidence, because they usually come from applying the standards of symbolic language to linguistic events that are either partly or wholly presymbolic in character.

One further illustration may make this clearer. Let us suppose that we are on the roadside struggling with a flat tire. A not-very-bright-looking but friendly youth comes up and asks, "Got a flat tire?" If we insist upon interpreting his words literally, we will regard this as an extremely silly question and our answer may be, "Can't you see I have, you dumb ox?" If we pay no attention to what the words say, however, and understand his meaning, we will return his gesture of friendly interest by showing equal friendliness, and in a short while he may be helping us to change the tire. In a similar way, many situations in life as well as in literature demand that we pay no attention to what the words say, since the meaning may often be a great deal more intelligent and intelligible than the surface *sense* of the words themselves. It is probable that a great deal of our pessimism about the world, about humanity, and about democracy may be due in part to the fact that unconsciously we apply the standards of symbolic language to presymbolic utterances.

Applications

Try to live a whole day without any presymbolic uses of language, restricting yourself solely to (1) specific statements of fact which contribute to the hearer's information; (2) specific requests for needed information or services. This exercise is recommended only to those whose devotion to science and the experimental method is greater than their desire to keep their friends.

6. CONNOTATIONS

Tens of thousands of years have elapsed since we shed our tails, but we are still communicating with a medium developed to meet the needs of arboreal man. . . . We may smile at the linguistic illusions of primitive man, but may we forget that the verbal machinery on which we so readily rely, and with which our metaphysicians still profess to probe the Nature of Existence, was set up by him, and may be responsible for other illusions hardly less gross and not more easily eradicable?

OGDEN AND RICHARDS

The Double Task of Language

REPORT language, as we have seen, is *instrumental* in character—that is, instrumental in getting work done; presymbolic language expresses the feelings of the speaker and is *an activity in itself,* pleasurable or not, as the case may be. Considering language from the point of view of the hearer, we can say that report language *informs* us and that presymbolic language *affects* us—that is, affects our feelings. When language is affective, it has the character of a kind of force. A spoken insult, for example, provokes a return insult, just as a blow provokes a return blow; a loud and peremptory command compels, just as a push compels; talking and shouting are as much a display of energy as the pounding of the chest.

Now, if someone screams in a loud piercing voice, "THE HOUSE IS ON FIRE!!" two tasks are performed: first, insofar as this utterance is a report, it *informs* us of a fact; secondly, insofar as the loudness and the screaming quality of the voice express the speaker's feelings, it *affects* our feelings. That is to say, informative and affective elements are often present at once in the same utterance.[1] And the first of the affective elements in speech, as this example illustrates, is the tone of voice, its loudness or softness, its pleasantness or unpleasantness, its variations during the course of the utterance in volume and intonation.

Another affective element in language is rhythm. *Rhythm* is the name we give to the effect produced by the repetition of auditory (or kinesthetic) stimuli at fairly regular intervals. From the primitive beat of the tomtom to the most subtle delicacies of civilized poetry and music, there is a continuous development and refinement of man's responsiveness to rhythm. To produce rhythm is to arouse attention and interest; so affective is

[1] Such terms as "emotional" and "emotive," which imply misleading distinctions between the "emotional appeals" and "intellectual appeals" of language, should be carefully avoided. In any case, "emotional" applies too specifically to strong feelings. The word "affective," however, in such an expression as "the affective uses of language," describes not only the way in which language can arouse strong feelings, but also the way in which it arouses extremely subtle, sometimes unconscious, responses. "Affective" has the further advantage of introducing no inconvenient distinctions between "physical" and "mental" responses.

rhythm, indeed, that it catches our attention even when we do not want our attention distracted. *Rhyme* and *alliteration* are, of course, ways of emphasizing rhythm in language, through repetition of similar sounds at regular intervals. Political slogan-writers and advertisers therefore have a special fondness for rhyme and alliteration: "Tippecanoe and Tyler Too," "Keep Cool with Coolidge," "Order from Horder," "Better Buy Buick"—totally absurd slogans so far as informative value is concerned, but by virtue of their sound capable of setting up small rhythmic echoes in one's head that make such phrases difficult to forget.

In addition to tone of voice and rhythm, another extremely important affective element in language is the aura of feelings, pleasant or unpleasant, that surrounds practically all words. It will be recalled that in Chapter 4, a distinction was made between denotations (or extensional meaning) pointing to things, and connotations (or intensional meaning) "ideas," "notions," "concepts," and feelings suggested in the mind. These connotations can be divided into two kinds, the *informative* and the *affective*.

Informative Connotations

The informative connotations of a word are its socially agreed upon, "impersonal" meanings, *insofar as meanings can be given at all by additional words*. For example, if we talk about a "pig," we cannot readily give the extensional meaning (denotation) of the word unless there happens to be an actual pig around for us to point at; but we can give the informative connotations: "mammalian domestic quadruped of the kind generally raised by farmers to be made into pork, bacon, ham, lard . . ." —which are connotations upon which everybody can agree. Sometimes, however, the informative connotations of words used in everyday life differ so much from place to place and from individual to individual that a special substitute terminology with more fixed informative connotations has to be used when special accuracy is desired. The scientific names for plants and animals are an example of terminology with such carefully established informative connotations.

Affective Connotations

The affective connotations of a word, on the other hand, are the aura of personal feelings it arouses, as, for example, "pig": "Ugh! Dirty, evil-smelling creatures, wallowing in filthy sties," and so on. While there is no necessary agreement about these feelings—some people like pigs and others don't—it is the existence of these feelings that enables us to use words, under certain circumstances, *for their affective connotations alone,* without regard to their informative connotations. That is to

say, when we are strongly moved, we express our feelings by uttering words with the affective connotations
appropriate to our feelings, without paying any attention
to the informative connotations they may have. We
angrily call people "reptiles," "wolves," "old bears,"
"skunks," or lovingly call them "honey," "sugar," "duck,"
and "apple dumpling." Indeed, all verbal expressions of
feeling make use to some extent of the affective connotations of words.

All words have, according to the uses to which they are
put, some affective character. There are many words that
exist more for their affective value than for their informative value; for example, we can refer to "that man"
as "that gentleman," "that individual," "that person,"
"that gent," "that guy," "that hombre," "that bird," or
"that bozo"—and while the person referred to may be
the same in all these cases, each of these terms reveals a
difference in our feelings toward him. Dealers in antiques
frequently write "Gyfte Shoppe" over the door, hoping
that such a spelling carries, even if their merchandise
does not, the flavor of antiquity. Affective connotations
suggestive of England and Scotland are often sought in
the choice of brand names for men's suits and overcoats:
"Glenmoor," "Regent Park," "Bond Street." Sellers of
perfume choose names for their products that suggest
France—"Mon Désir," "Indiscret," "Evening in Paris"—
and expensive brands always come in "flacons," never in

bottles. Consider, too, the differences among the following expressions:

I have the honor to inform Your Excellency . . .
This is to advise you . . .
I should like to tell you, sir . . .
I'm telling you, Mister . . .
Cheez, boss, git a load of dis . . .

The parallel columns below also illustrate how affective
connotations can be changed while extensional meanings
remain the same:

Finest quality filet mignon.	First-class piece of dead cow.
Cubs trounce Giants 5-3.	Score: Cubs 5, Giants 3.
McCormick Bill steam-rollered through Senate.	Senate passes McCormick Bill over strong opposition.
Japanese divisions advance five miles.	Japs stopped cold after five-mile advance.
French armies in rapid retreat!	The retirement of the French forces to previously prepared positions in the rear was accomplished briskly and efficiently.
The governor appeared to be gravely concerned and said that a statement would be issued in a few days after careful examination of the facts.	The governor was on the spot.

The story is told that during the Boer War, the Boers
were described in the British press as "sneaking and

skulking behind rocks and bushes." The British forces, when they finally learned from the Boers how to employ tactics suitable to veldt warfare, were described as "cleverly taking advantage of cover."

A Note on Verbal Taboo

The affective connotations of some words create peculiar situations. In some circles of society, for example, it is "impolite" to speak of eating. A maid answering the telephone has to say, "Mr. Jones is at dinner," and not, "Mr. Jones is eating dinner." The extensional meaning is the same in both cases, but the latter form is regarded as having undesirable connotations. The same hesitation about referring too baldly to eating is shown in the economical use made of the French and Japanese words meaning "to eat," *manger* and *taberu;* a similar delicacy exists in many other languages. Again, when creditors send bills, they practically never mention "money," although that is what they are writing about. There are all sorts of circumlocutions: "We would appreciate your early attention to this matter." "May we look forward to an immediate remittance?" "There is a balance in our favor which we are sure you would like to clear up." Furthermore, we ask movie ushers and filling-station attendants where the "lounge" or "rest room" is, although we usually have no intention of lounging or resting; indeed, it is impossible in polite society to state, without having to resort to a medical vocabulary, what a "rest room" is for. The word "dead" likewise is used as little as possible by many people, who substitute such expressions as "gone west," "passed away," "gone to his reward," and "departed." In every language there is a long list of such carefully avoided words whose affective connotations are so unpleasant or so undesirable that people cannot say them, even when they are needed.

Words having to do with physiology and sex—and words even vaguely suggesting physiological and sexual matters—have, especially in American culture, remarkable affective connotations. Ladies of the last century could not bring themselves to say "breast" or "leg"—not even of chicken—so that the terms "white meat" and "dark meat" were substituted. It was deemed inelegant to speak of "going to bed," and "to retire" was used instead. Such verbal taboos are very numerous and complicated, especially on the radio today. Scientists and physicians asked to speak on the radio have been known to cancel their speeches in despair when they discovered that ordinary physiological terms, such as "stomach" and "bowels," are forbidden on some stations. Indeed, there are some words, well known to all of us, whose affective connotations are so powerful that if they were printed here, even for the purposes of scientific analysis, this book would be excluded from all public schools and libraries, and anyone placing a copy of it in the United States mails would be subject to Federal prosecution!

The stronger verbal taboos have, however, a genuine social value. When we are extremely angry and we feel the need of expressing our anger in violence, the uttering of these forbidden words provides us with a relatively harmless verbal substitute for going berserk and smashing furniture; that is, they act as a kind of safety valve in our moments of crisis.

Why some words should have such powerful affective connotations while others *with the same informative connotations* should not is difficult to explain fully. Some of our verbal taboos, especially the religious ones, obviously originate in our earlier belief in word-magic; the names of gods, for example, were often regarded as too holy to be spoken. But all taboos cannot be explained in terms of word-magic. According to some psychologists, our verbal taboos on sex and physiology are probably due to the fact that we all have certain feelings of which we are so ashamed that we do not like to admit even to ourselves that we have them. We therefore resent words which remind us of those feelings, and get angry at the utterer of such words. Such an explanation would confirm the fairly common observation that those fanatics who object most strenuously to "dirty" books and plays do so not because their minds are especially pure, but because they are especially morbid.

Everyday Uses of Language

The language of everyday life, then, differs from "reports" such as those discussed in Chapter 3. As in reports, we have to be accurate in choosing words that have the informative connotations we want; otherwise the reader or hearer will not know what we are talking about. But in addition, we have to give those words the affective connotations we want in order that he will be interested or moved by what we are saying and feel towards things the way we do. This double task confronts us in almost all ordinary conversation, oratory, persuasive writing, and literature. Much of this task, however, is performed intuitively; without being aware of it, we choose the tone of voice, the rhythms, and the affective connotations appropriate to our utterance. Over the informative connotations of our utterances we exercise somewhat more conscious control. Improvement in our ability to understand language, as well as in our ability to use it, depends, therefore, not only upon sharpening our sense for the informative connotations of words, but also upon the sharpening of our intuitive perceptions.

The following, finally, are some of the things that can happen in any given speech event:

1. The informative connotations may be inadequate or misleading, but the affective connotations may be suffi-

ciently well directed so that we are able to interpret correctly. For example, when someone says, "Imagine who I saw today! Old What's-his-name—oh, you know who I mean—Whoosis, that old buzzard that lives on, oh—what's the name of that street!" there are means, certainly not clearly informative, by which we manage to understand who is being referred to.

2. The informative connotations may be correct enough and the extensional meanings clear, but the affective connotations may be inappropriate, misleading, or ludicrous. This happens frequently when people try to write elegantly: "Jim ate so many bags of *Arachis hypogaea,* commonly known as peanuts, at the ball game today that he was unable to do justice to his evening repast."

3. Both informative and affective connotations may "sound all right," but there may be no "territory" corresponding to the "map." For example: "He lived for many years in the beautiful hill country just south of Chicago." There is no hill country just south of Chicago.

4. Both informative and affective connotations may be used *consciously* to create "maps" of "territories" that do not exist. There are many reasons why we should wish on occasion to do so. Of these, only two need be mentioned now. First, we may wish to give pleasure:

> Yet mark'd I where the bolt of Cupid fell:
> It fell upon a little western flower,
> Before milk-white, now purple with love's wound,

And maidens call it Love-in-idleness.
Fetch me that flower; the herb I show'd thee once:
The juice of it on sleeping eyelids laid
Will make or man or woman madly dote
Upon the next live creature that it sees.

Midsummer Night's Dream

A second reason is to enable us to plan for the future. For example, we can say, "Let us suppose there is a bridge at the foot of this street; then the heavy traffic on High Street would be partly diverted over the new bridge; shopping would be less concentrated on High Street. . . ." Having visualized the condition that would result, we can recommend or oppose the bridge according to whether or not we like the probable results. The relationship of present words to future events is a subject we must leave for the next chapter.

Applications

1. The relative absence of information and the deluge of affective connotations in advertising is notorious. Nevertheless, it is revealing to analyze closely specimens like the following, separating informative and affective connotations into two parallel columns for contrast:

You'll enjoy *different* tomato juice made from *aristocrat* tomatoes.

A new kind of shirt has been born! A shirt as advanced in concept and performance as today's speediest, most luxurious

planes! A shirt that borrows its perfection from tomorrow—
that offers a COMBINATION of features unmatched by any other
shirt of today! Not *one* superiority—BUT THE SUM OF MANY—
make the new PHILADELPHIAN the most completely satisfactory
shirt your money can buy! Words cannot describe the way it
FITS, FEELS AND LOOKS on you! You've got to see it and wear
it to understand.

You'll sense this subtle feeling of young adventure the first
time you go for a Westwind *glider ride!* This car is built for
skimming over the roughest roads with the quiet smoothness
of a glider in flight. Cradled on long, liquidlike springs, cush-
ioned in chair-high seats "amidships," where riding is best,
you're billowed along while tremendous twelve-cylinder power
whispers and flows and surges and recedes as softly and gently
as the rise and fall of the tide.

The rich smoothness of Kingsway is the result of the re-
discovering of the almost lost art of BULKING—an old-fashioned,
slow, deliberate method for mellowing fine tobaccos. In BULK-
ING, an unhurried miracle of nature transpires; harsh qualities
grow mild, delicate aromas emerge, permeating every shred of
the superb Kingsway tobaccos. The result is a mellower, really
smoother smoke.

2. As we have seen, the statement, "His manner is rude
and uncultivated," can also be made by one who ap-
proaches the situation in a more friendly light: "His manner is simple and unspoiled." Try altering the following
statements so that they could still be applied to the same
situations, yet convey more favorable judgments:

The party bigwigs were reactionary.
Mrs. Smith was always prying into other people's affairs.
He is prejudiced against labor unions.

She is noisy and talkative.

He was flunked out of school.

They spend every cent he makes.

He is a renegade communist.

He was a spy during the World War.

The new government ruthlessly suppressed all opposition.

The crowd which welcomed the candidate was rowdy and hysterical.

Congressman Blank is a demagogue.

Polonius was a sententious old fool.

He had a one-track mind on the subject of calendar reform.

A small group of willful men obstructed the vital legislation.

She never has to be asked twice to show off her piano-playing at a party.

Men fall for her because she always acts cute and helpless.

7. DIRECTIVE LANGUAGE

The effect of a parade of sonorous phrases upon human conduct has never been adequately studied.

THURMAN W. ARNOLD

Making Things Happen

THE MOST interesting and perhaps least understood of the relations between words and things is the relation between words and future events. When we say, for example, "Come here!" we are not describing the extensional world about us, nor are we merely expressing our feelings; we are trying to *make something happen*. What we call "commands," "pleas," "requests," and "orders" are the simplest ways we have of making things happen by means of words. There are, however, more roundabout ways. When we say, for example, "Our candidate is a great American," we are of course making an enthusiastic purr about him, but we may also be influencing other people to vote for him. Again, when we say, "Our war against the enemy is God's war. God wills that we must triumph," we are saying something that is incapable of scientific verification; nevertheless, it may influence others to help in the prosecution of the war. Or if we merely state as a fact, "Milk contains vitamins," we may be influencing others to buy milk.

Consider, too, such a statement as "I'll meet you tomorrow at two o'clock in front of the Palace Theater." Such a statement about *future* events can only be made, it will be observed, in a system in which symbols are independent of things symbolized. That is to say, a map can be made, in spite of the fact that the territory it stands for is not yet an actuality. Guiding ourselves by means of such maps of territories-to-be, we can impose a certain predictability upon future events.

With words, therefore, we influence and to an enormous extent *control future events*. It is for this reason that writers write; preachers preach; employers, parents, and teachers scold; propagandists send out news releases; statesmen give addresses. All of them, for various reasons, are trying to influence our conduct—sometimes for our own good, sometimes for their own. These attempts to control, direct, or influence the future actions of fellow human beings with words may be termed *directive uses of language*.

Now it is obvious that if directive language is going to direct, it cannot be dull or uninteresting. If it is to influence our conduct, it *must* make use of every affective element in language: dramatic variations in tone of voice, rhyme and rhythm, purring and snarling, words with strong affective connotations, endless repetition. If mean-ingless noises will move the audience, meaningless noises must be made; if facts move them, facts must be given; if noble ideals move them, we must make our proposals appear noble; if they will respond only to fear, we must scare them stiff.

The nature of the affective means used in directive lan-guage is limited, of course, by the nature of our aims. If we are trying to direct people to be more kindly toward each other, we obviously do not want to arouse feelings of cruelty or hate. If we are trying to direct people to think and act more intelligently, we obviously should not use subrational appeals. If we are trying to direct people to lead better lives, we use affective appeals that arouse their finest feelings. Included among directive utterances, therefore, are many of the greatest and most treasured works of literature: the Christian and Buddhist scrip-tures, the writings of Confucius, Milton's *Areopagitica,* and Lincoln's Gettysburg Address.

There are, however, occasions when it is felt that lan-guage is not sufficiently affective by itself to produce the results wanted. We supplement directive language, there-fore, by *nonverbal affective appeals* of many kinds. We supplement the words "Come here" by gesturing with our hands. Advertisers are not content with saying in words how beautiful their products will make us; they supplement their words by the use of colored inks and by pictures. A newspaper is not content with saying that the New Deal is a "menace"; it supplies political cartoons depicting New Dealers as criminally insane people placing sticks of dynamite under a magnificent building labeled "American way of life." The affective appeal of sermons and religious exhortations may be supplemented by costumes, incense, processions, choir music, and church bells. A political candidate seeking office reinforces his speechmaking with a considerable array of nonverbal affective appeals: brass bands, flags, parades, picnics, barbecues, and free cigars.

Now, if we want people to do certain things and are indifferent as to *why they do them,* then no affective appeals are excluded. Some political candidates want us to vote for them regardless of our reasons for doing so. Therefore, if we hate the rich, they will snarl at the rich for us; if we dislike strikers, they will snarl at strikers; if we like clambakes, they will throw clambakes; if the majority of us like hillbilly music, they may say nothing about the problems of government and travel among their constituencies with hillbilly bands. Again, most business firms want us to buy their products regardless of our reasons for doing so; therefore if delusions and fantasies will lead us to buy their products, they will seek to produce delusions and fantasies; if we want to be popular with the other sex, they will promise us popularity; if we like pretty girls in bathing suits, they will associate pretty

girls in bathing suits with their products, whether they
are selling shaving cream, automobiles, summer resorts,
ice-cream cones, house paint, or hardware. Only the law
keeps them from presenting pretty girls without bathing suits. The records of the Federal Trade Commission,
as well as the advertising pages of any big-circulation
magazine, show that some advertisers will stop at practically nothing.

The Implied Promises of Directive Language

Aside from the affective elements, verbal and nonverbal,
accompanying directive utterances that are intended simply to attract attention or to create pleasant sensations—
that is, repetition, beauty of language, the pretty colors
in advertisements, brass bands in political parades, girl
pictures, and so on—*practically all directive utterances say
something about the future.* They are "maps," either explicitly or by implication, of *"territories" that are to be.*
They direct us to do certain things with the stated or implied promise that if we do these things, certain consequences will follow: "If you adhere to the Bill of Rights,
your civil rights too will be protected." "If you vote for
me, I will have your taxes reduced." "Live according to
these religious principles, and you will have peace in your
soul." "Read this magazine, and you will keep up with
important current events." "Take McCarter's Liver Pills

and enjoy that glorious feeling that goes with regularity." Needless to say, some of these promises are kept, and some are not. Indeed, we encounter promises daily that are obviously incapable of being kept.

There is no sense in objecting as some people do to advertising and political propaganda—the only kind of directives they worry about—on the ground that they are based on "emotional appeals." Unless directive language has affective power of some kind, it is useless. We do not object to campaigns that tell us, "Give to the Community Chest and enable poor children to enjoy better care," although that is an "emotional appeal." Nor do we resent being reminded of our love of home, friends, and nation when people issue moral or patriotic directives at us. The important question to be asked of any directive utterance is, "Will things happen as promised if I do as I am directed? If I accept your philosophy, shall I achieve peace of mind? If I vote for you, will my taxes be reduced? If I use Lifeguard Soap, will my boy friend come back to me?"

We rightly object to advertisers who make false or misleading claims and to politicians who ignore their promises, although it must be admitted that, in the case of politicians, they are sometimes forced by their constituents against their will to make promises they know they cannot keep. Life being as uncertain and as unpredictable as it is, we are constantly trying to find out what is going to happen next, so that we may prepare ourselves. Directive utterances undertake to tell us how we can bring about certain desirable events and how we can avoid undesirable events. If we can rely upon what they tell us about the future, the uncertainties of life are reduced. When, however, directive utterances are of such a character that things do *not* happen as predicted—when, after we have done as we were told, the peace in the soul has not been found, the taxes have not been reduced, the boy friend has not returned, and the nationally advertised gelatine has not given us a surge of "quick energy," there is disappointment. Such disappointments may be trivial or grave; in any event, they are so common that we do not even bother to complain about some of them. They are all serious in their implications, nevertheless. Each of them serves, in greater or less degree, to break down that mutual trust that makes co-operation possible and knits people together into a society.

Every one of us, therefore, who utters directive language, with its concomitant promises, stated or implied, is morally obliged to be as certain as he can, since there is no absolute certainty, that he is arousing no false expectations. Politicians promising the immediate abolition of poverty, national advertisers suggesting that tottering marriages can be restored to bliss by a change in the brand of laundry soap used in the family, newspapers threatening the collapse of the nation if the party they favor is not elected—all such utterers of nonsense are, for the reasons stated, menaces to the social order. It does not matter much whether such misleading directives are uttered in ignorance and error or with conscious intent to deceive, because the disappointments they cause are all similarly destructive of mutual trust among human beings.

The Foundations of Society

However, preaching, no matter how noble, and propaganda, no matter how persuasive, do not create society. We can, if we wish, ignore such directives. We come now to directive utterances that we cannot ignore if we wish to remain organized in our social groups.

What we call society is a vast network of mutual agreements. We agree to refrain from murdering our fellow citizens, and they in turn agree to refrain from murdering us; we agree to drive on the right-hand side of the road, and others agree to do the same; we agree to deliver specified goods, and others agree to pay us for them; we agree to observe the rules of an organization, and the organization agrees to let us enjoy its privileges. This complicated network of agreements, into which almost every detail of our lives is woven and upon which most of our expectations in life are based, consists essentially of *statements about future events which we are supposed, with our own efforts, to bring about.* Without such agreements, there would be no such thing as society. All of us would be huddling in miserable and lonely caves, not daring to trust anyone. With such agreements, and a will on the part of the vast majority of people to live by them, behavior begins to fall into relatively predictable patterns; co-operation becomes possible; peace and freedom are established.

Therefore, in order that we shall continue to exist as human beings, we *must* impose patterns of behavior on each other. We must make citizens conform to social and civic customs; we must make husbands dutiful to their wives; we must make soldiers courageous, judges just, priests pious, and teachers solicitous for the welfare of their pupils. In early stages of culture the principal means of imposing patterns of behavior was, of course, physical coercion. But such control can also be exercised, as human beings must have discovered extremely early in history, by *words*—that is, by directive language. Therefore, directives about matters which society as a whole regards as essential to its own safety are made especially powerful, so that no individual in that society will fail to be impressed with a sense of his obligations. To make doubly sure, the words are further reinforced by the assurance that punishment, possibly including torture and death, will be visited upon those who fail to heed them.

Directive Utterances with Collective Sanction

These directive utterances with collective sanction, which try to impose patterns of behavior upon the individual in the interests of the whole group, are among the most interesting of linguistic events. Not only are they usually accompanied by ritual; they are usually the central purpose of ritual. There is probably no kind of utterance that we take more seriously, that affects our lives more deeply, that we quarrel about more bitterly. Constitutions of nations and of organizations, legal contracts, and oaths of office are utterances of this kind; in marriage vows, confirmation exercises, induction ceremonies, and initiations, they are the essential constituent. Those terrifying verbal jungles called laws are simply the systematization of such directives, accumulated and modified through the centuries. In its laws, society makes its mightiest collective effort to impose predictability upon human behavior.

Directive utterances made under collective sanction may exhibit any or all of the following features:

1. Such language is almost always phrased in words that have affective connotations, so that people will be appropriately impressed and awed. Archaic and obsolete vocabulary or stilted phraseology quite unlike the language of everyday life is employed. For example: "Wilt thou, John, take this woman for thy lawful wedded

wife?" "This lease, made this tenth day of July, A.D. One Thousand Nine Hundred and Forty, between Samuel Smith, hereinafter called the Lessor, and Jeremiah Johnson, hereinafter called Lessee, WITNESSETH, that Lessor, in consideration of covenants and agreements hereinafter contained and made on the part of the Lessee, hereby leases to Lessee for a private dwelling, the premises known and described as follows, to wit . . ."

2. Such directive utterances are often accompanied by appeals to supernatural powers, who are called upon to help carry out the vows, or to punish us if we fail to carry them out. An oath, for example, ends with the words, "So help me God." Prayers, incantations, and invocations accompany the utterance of important vows in practically all cultures, from the most primitive to the most civilized. These further serve, of course, to impress our vows on our minds.

3. If God does not punish us for failing to carry out our agreements, it is made clear either by statement or implication that our fellow men will. For example, we all realize that we can be imprisoned for desertion, nonsupport, or bigamy; sued for "breach of contract"; "unfrocked" for activities contrary to priestly vows; "cashiered" for "conduct unbecoming an officer"; "impeached" for "betrayal of public trust"; shot for "treason."

4. The formal and public utterance of the vows may be preceded by preliminary disciplines of various kinds:

courses of training in the meaning of the vows one is undertaking; fasting and self-mortification, as before entering the priesthood; initiation ceremonies involving physical torture, as before being inducted into the warrior status among savage peoples or membership in college fraternities.

5. The utterance of the directive language may be accompanied by other activities or gestures, all calculated to impress the occasion on the mind. For example, everybody in a courtroom stands up when a judge is about to open a court; huge processions and extraordinary costumes accompany coronation ceremonies; academic gowns are worn for commencement exercises; for many weddings, an organist and a soprano are procured and special clothes are worn.

6. The uttering of the vows may be immediately followed by feasts, dancing, and other joyous manifestations. Again the purpose seems to be to reinforce still further the effect of the vows. For example, there are wedding parties and receptions, graduation dances, banquets for the induction of officers, and, even in the most modest social circles, some form of "celebration" when a member of the family enters into a compact with society. In primitive cultures, initiation ceremonies for chieftains may be followed by feasting and dancing that last for several days or weeks.

7. In cases where the first utterance of the vows is not

made a special ceremonial occasion, the effect on the memory is usually achieved by frequent repetition. The flag ritual ("I pledge allegiance to the flag of the United States . . .") is repeated daily in some schools. Mottoes, which are briefly stated general directives, are repeated frequently; sometimes they are stamped on dishes, sometimes engraved on a warrior's sword, sometimes inscribed in prominent places such as gates, walls, and doorways, where people can see them and be reminded of their duties.

The common feature of all these activities that accompany directive utterances, as well as of the affective elements in the language of directive utterances, is the deep effect they have on the memory. Every kind of sensory impression from the severe pain of initiation rites to the pleasures of banqueting, music, splendid clothing, and ornamental surroundings may be employed; every emotion from the fear of divine punishment to pride in being made the object of special public attention may be aroused. This is done in order that the individual who enters into his compact with society—that is, the individual who utters the "map" of the not-yet-existent "territory"—shall never forget to try to bring that "territory" into existence.

For these reasons, such occasions as when a cadet receives his commission, when a Jewish boy has his *bar mizvah,* when a priest takes his vows, when a policeman receives his badge, when a foreign-born citizen is sworn in as a citizen of the United States, or when a president takes his oath of office—these are events one never forgets. Even if, later on, a person realizes that he has not fulfilled his vows, he cannot shake off the feeling that he should have done so. All of us, of course, use and respond to these ritual directives. The phrases and speeches to which we respond reveal our deepest religious, patriotic, social, professional, and political allegiances more accurately than do the citizenship papers or membership cards that we may carry in our pockets or the badges that we may wear on our coats. A man who has changed his religion after reaching adulthood will, on hearing the ritual he was accustomed to hearing in childhood, often feel an urge to return to his earlier form of worship. In such ways, then, do human beings use words to reach out into the future and control each other's conduct.

Four Footnotes

Four notes may be added before we leave the subject of directive language. First, it should be remembered that, since words cannot "say all" about anything, the promises implied in directive language are never more than "outline maps" of "territories-to-be." The future will fill in those outlines, often in unexpected ways. Sometimes the future will bear no relation to our "maps" at all, in spite of all our endeavors to bring about the promised events.

We swear always to be good citizens, always to do our duty, and so on, but we never quite succeed in being good citizens *every* day of our lives or in performing *all* our duties. A realization that directives cannot *fully* impose any pattern on the future saves us from having impossible expectations and therefore from suffering needless disappointments.

Secondly, one should distinguish between the directive "is" and the informative "is." Such statements as "A Boy Scout is clean and chivalrous and brave" or "Policemen are defenders of the weak" *set up goals* and do not necessarily describe the present situation. This is extremely important, because all too often people understand such definitions as being descriptive and are thereupon shocked, horrified, and disillusioned upon encountering a Boy Scout who is not chivalrous or a policeman who is a bully. They decide that they are "through with all Boy Scouts" or "through with all policemen," which, of course, is nonsense.

Thirdly, it should be remarked that definitions, when they are not descriptive statements about language, as is explained more fully in Chapter 8, are almost always *directives about language*. Definitions do not tell us anything about the things for which a word stands; they merely direct us to use words in certain ways. For example, if someone says to us, "Conscription may be defined as the organized trampling down of human rights," he is telling us nothing directly about conscription, but merely telling us to talk about conscription in the same way we would talk about anything else to which the expression "the organized trampling down of human rights" would be applicable. Often such definitions are addressed to us with the air of revealing the "real nature" of that which is defined: "That's what conscription really is!" Even this book, perhaps, has sometimes sounded as if it were revealing the "real nature" of certain linguistic processes. The reader is hereby warned that no such purpose is intended. It merely urges the reader to *talk about* linguistic events in specified ways, using, for example, such terms as "report," "symbolic process," "directive language," and "affective connotation." The implied promise behind this exhortation is that if the reader does as he is told, he will find certain problems clarified. Similar directives about what words to use under what conditions are to be found in practically all expositions.

Finally, it should be remarked that many of our social directives and many of the rituals with which they are accompanied are antiquated and somewhat insulting to adult minds. Rituals that originated in times when people had to be scared into good behavior are unnecessary to people who already have a sense of social responsibility. For example, a five-minute marriage ceremony performed at the city hall for an adult, responsible couple may "take" much better than a full-dress church ceremony performed for an infantile couple. In spite of the fact that the strength of social directives obviously lies in the willingness, the maturity, and the intelligence of the people to whom the directives are addressed, there is still too much tendency to rely upon the efficacy of ceremonies as such. This tendency is due, of course, to a lingering belief in word-magic, the notion that, by *saying* things repeatedly or in specified ceremonial ways, we can cast a spell over the future and force events to turn out the way we said they would—"There'll always be an England!" An interesting manifestation of this superstitious attitude towards words and rituals is to be found in some of our school boards and educators faced with the problem of "educating students for democracy." Instead of increasing the time allotted for the factual study of democratic institutions, enlarging the opportunities for the day-to-day exercise of democratic practices, and thereby trying to develop the political insight and maturity of their students, such educators content themselves by staging bigger and better flag-saluting ceremonies and trebling the occasions for singing "God Bless America." If, because of such "educational" activities, the word "democracy" finally becomes a meaningless noise to some students, the result is hardly to be wondered at.

Applications

Most, but not all, of the following passages are directives. What kind of directives are they, and what are their implied promises?

Blessed are the meek: for they shall inherit the earth.

A stitch in time saves nine.

There is no conflict between capital and labor.

Should auld acquaintance be forgot
And never brought to mind?

No parking.

A man's best friend is his dog.

We hold these truths to be self-evident, that all men are created equal, that they are endowed by their Creator with certain unalienable Rights, that among these are life, liberty, and the pursuit of happiness.

Gentlemen of the jury! Let us recognize this dastardly crime for what it is—a cruel, cold-blooded murder!

A straight line is the shortest distance between two points.

Blow, winds, and crack your cheeks! rage! blow!
You cataracts and hurricanoes, spout
Till you have drench'd our steeples, drown'd the cocks!
King Lear

"Surely goodness and mercy shall follow me all the days of my life: and I will dwell in the house of the Lord forever."
Psalms 23:6

THIS CERTIFIES THAT THERE IS ON DEPOSIT IN THE TREASURY OF
THE UNITED STATES OF AMERICA
ONE DOLLAR
IN SILVER PAYABLE TO THE BEARER ON DEMAND

I hereby will and bequeath to my sister, Mary Anderson Jones, and to her heirs and assigns, the sum of ten thousand dollars . . .

I do solemnly swear to tell the truth, the whole truth, and nothing but the truth, so help me God.

Are we downhearted? No!

And remember, ladies and gentlemen of the radio audience, whenever you say "Blotto Coffee" to your grocer, you are saying "Thank you" to us.

8. HOW WE KNOW WHAT WE KNOW

The syllogism consists of propositions, propositions consist of words, words are symbols of notions. Therefore if the notions themselves, which is the root of the matter, are confused and overhastily abstracted from the facts, there can be no firmness in the superstructure.

FRANCIS BACON

Bessie, the Cow

THE UNIVERSE is in a perpetual state of flux. The stars are in constant motion, growing, cooling, exploding. The earth itself is not unchanging; mountains are being worn away, rivers are altering their channels, valleys are deepening. All life is also a process of change, through birth, growth, decay, and death. Even what we used to call "inert matter"—chairs and tables and stones—is not inert, as we now know, for, at the submicroscopic level, they are whirls of electrons. If a table looks today very much as it did yesterday or as it did a hundred years ago, it is not because it has not changed, but because the changes have been too minute for our coarse perceptions. To modern science there is no "solid matter." If matter looks "solid" to us, it does so only because its motion is too rapid or too minute to be felt. It is "solid" only in the sense that a rapidly rotating color chart is "white" or a rapidly spinning top is "standing still." Our senses are extremely limited, so that we constantly have to use instruments such as microscopes, telescopes, speedometers, stethoscopes, and seismographs to detect and record occurrences which our senses are not able to record directly. The way in which we happen to see and feel things is the result of the peculiarities of our nervous systems. There are "sights" we cannot see, and, as even children know today with their high-frequency dog whistles, "sounds" that we cannot hear. It is absurd, therefore, to imagine that we ever perceive anything "as it really is."

Inadequate as our senses are, with the help of instruments they tell us a great deal. The discovery of micro-organisms with the use of the microscope has given us a measure of control over bacteria; we cannot see, hear, or feel radio waves, but we can create and transform them to useful purpose. Most of our conquest of the external world, in engineering, in chemistry, and in medicine, is due to our use of mechanical contrivances of one kind or another to increase the capacity of our nervous systems. In modern life, our unaided senses are not half enough to get us about in the world. We cannot even obey speed laws or compute our gas and electric bills without mechanical aids to perception.

To return, then, to the relations between words and

what they stand for, let us say that there is before us "Bessie," a cow. Bessie is a living organism, constantly changing, constantly ingesting food and air, transforming it, getting rid of it again. Her blood is circulating, her nerves are sending messages. Viewed microscopically, she is a mass of variegated corpuscles, cells, and bacterial organisms; viewed from the point of view of modern physics, she is a perpetual dance of electrons. What she is in her entirety, we can never know; even if we could at any precise moment say what she was, at the next moment she would have changed enough so that our description would no longer be accurate. It is impossible to say completely what Bessie or anything else really *is*. Bessie is no static "object," but a dynamic *process*.

The Bessie that we experience, however, is something else again. We experience only a small fraction of the total Bessie: the lights and shadows of her exterior, her motions, her general configuration, the noises she makes, and the sensations she presents to our sense of touch. *And because of our previous experience, we observe resemblances in her to certain other animals to which, in the past, we have applied the word "cow."*

The Process of Abstracting

The "object" of our experience, then, is not the "thing in itself," but *an interaction between our nervous systems* (*with all their imperfections*) *and something outside them*. Bessie is unique—there is nothing else in the universe exactly like her in all respects. But our nervous systems, automatically *abstracting* or selecting from the process-Bessie those features of hers in which she resembles other animals of like size, functions, and habits, *classify* her as "cow."

When we say, then, that "Bessie is a cow," we are only noting the process-Bessie's resemblances to other "cows" and *ignoring differences*. What is more, we are leaping a huge chasm: from the dynamic process-Bessie, a whirl of electro-chemico-neural eventfulness, to a relatively static "idea," "concept," or *word*, "cow." The reader is referred to the diagram entitled "The Abstraction Ladder," which he will find on page 126.

As the diagram illustrates, the "object" we see is an abstraction of the lowest level, but it is still an abstraction, since it leaves out characteristics of the process that is the real Bessie. The *word* "Bessie" (cow_1) is the lowest *verbal* level of abstraction, leaving out further characteristics—the differences between Bessie yesterday and Bessie today, between Bessie today and Bessie tomorrow—and selecting only the similarities. The word "cow" selects only the similarities between Bessie (cow_1), Daisy (cow_2), Rosie (cow_3), and so on, and therefore leaves out still more about Bessie. The word "livestock" selects or abstracts only the features that Bessie has in common with pigs, chickens, goats, and sheep. The term "farm asset" abstracts only the features Bessie has in common with barns, fences, livestock, furniture, generating plants, and tractors, and is therefore on a very high level of abstraction. A branch line has been drawn in the diagram to indicate the fact that in discussing Bessie for different purposes abstracting may be done in different ways. This point will be discussed more fully in Chapter 10.

Why We Must Abstract

This process of abstracting, of leaving characteristics out, is an indispensable convenience. To illustrate by still another example, suppose that we live in an isolated village of four families, each owning a house. A's house is referred to as *maga;* B's house is *biyo;* C's is *kata,* and D's is *pelel.* This is quite satisfactory for ordinary purposes of communication in the village, unless a discussion arises about building a new house—a spare one, let us say. We cannot refer to the projected house by any one of the four words we have for the existing houses, since each of these has too specific a meaning. We must find a *general* term, at a higher level of abstraction, that means "something that has certain characteristics in common with *maga, biyo, kata,* and *pelel,* and yet is not A's, B's, C's, or D's." Since this is much too complicated to say each time, an *abbreviation* must be invented. Let us say we choose the

THE ABSTRACTION LADDER [1]

Start Reading from Bottom *UP*

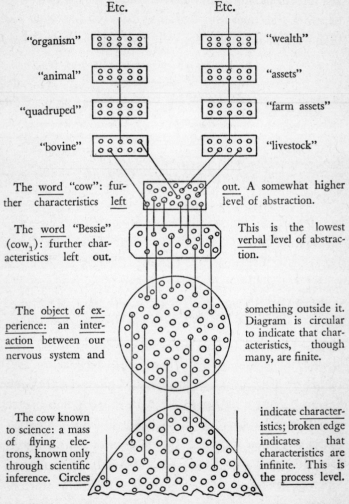

Etc.   Etc.

"organism"   "wealth"

"animal"   "assets"

"quadruped"   "farm assets"

"bovine"   "livestock"

The word "cow": fur-ther characteristics left out. A somewhat higher level of abstraction.

The word "Bessie" (cow_1): further characteristics left out. This is the lowest verbal level of abstraction.

The object of experience: an interaction between our nervous system and something outside it. Diagram is circular to indicate that characteristics, though many, are finite.

The cow known to science: a mass of flying electrons, known only through scientific inference. Circles indicate characteristics; broken edge indicates that characteristics are infinite. This is the process level.

[1] Adapted, by kind permission, from the "Structural Differential," of A. Korzybski.

noise, *house*. Out of such needs do our words come—they are a form of shorthand. The invention of a new abstraction is a great step forward, since it *makes discussion possible*—as, in this case, not only the discussion of a fifth

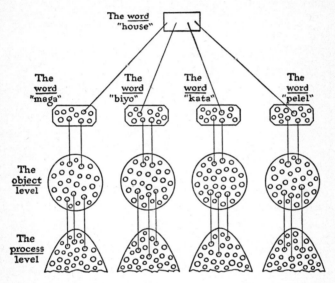

house, but of all future houses we may build or see in our travels or dream about. There is no such *thing* as "a house." "A house" is an abstraction. There are only houses —house$_1$, house$_2$, house$_3$, and so on—each one distinct, each with characteristics not possessed by other houses.

The indispensability of this process of abstracting can again be illustrated by what we do when we "calculate." The word "calculate" originates from the Latin word *calculus,* meaning "pebble," and comes to have its present meaning from such ancient practices as that of putting a pebble into a box for each sheep as it left the fold, so that one could tell, by checking the sheep returning at night against the pebbles, whether any had been lost. Primitive as this example of calculation is, it will serve to show why mathematics works. Each pebble is, in this example, an abstraction representing the "oneness" of each sheep—its numerical value. And because we are abstracting from extensional events on clearly understood and uniform principles, the numerical facts about the pebbles are also, barring unforeseen circumstances, numerical facts about the sheep. Our x's and y's and other mathematical symbols are similar abstractions, although of still higher level. And they are useful in predicting occurrences and in getting work done because, since they are abstractions properly and uniformly made from starting points in the extensional world, the relations revealed by the symbols will be, again barring unforeseen circumstances, relations existing in the extensional world.

On Definitions

Definitions, contrary to popular opinion, tell us nothing about things. They only describe people's linguistic habits; that is, they tell us what noises people make under what conditions. Definitions should be understood as *statements about language.*

House. This is a word, at the next higher level of abstraction, that can be substituted for the more cumbersome expression, "Something that has characteristics in common with Bill's bungalow, Jordan's cottage, Mrs. Smith's tourist home, Dr. Jones's mansion . . ."

Red. A feature that rubies, roses, ripe tomatoes, robins' breasts, uncooked beef, and lipsticks have in common is abstracted, and this word expresses that abstraction.

Kangaroo. Where the biologist would say "herbivorous mammal, a marsupial of the family Macropodidae," ordinary people say "kangaroo."

Now it will be observed that while the definitions of "house" and "red" given here point *down* the abstraction ladder (see the charts) to *lower* levels of abstraction, the definition of "kangaroo" remains at the same level. That is to say, in the case of "house," we could if necessary go and *look* at Bill's bungalow, Jordan's cottage, Mrs. Smith's tourist home, and Dr. Jones's mansion, and figure out for ourselves what features they seem to have in common; in this way, we might begin to understand under what conditions to use the word "house." But all we know about "kangaroo" from the above is that where some people say one thing, other people say another. That is, when we stay at the *same* level of abstraction in giving a definition, we do not give any information, unless, of course, the listener or reader is already sufficiently familiar with the defining words so that he can work himself down the abstraction ladder. Dictionaries, in order to save space, have to assume in many cases such familiarity with the language on the part of the reader. But where the assumption is unwarranted, definitions at the same level of abstraction are worse than useless. Looking up "indifference" in some cheap pocket dictionaries, we find it defined as "apathy"; we look up "apathy" and find it defined as "indifference."

Even more useless, however, are the definitions that go *up* the abstraction ladder to *higher* levels of abstraction—the kind most of us tend to make automatically. Try the following experiment on an unsuspecting friend:

"What is meant by the word *red?*"
"It's a color."
"What's a *color?*"
"Why, it's a quality things have."
"What's a *quality?*"
"Say, what are you trying to do, anyway?"

You have pushed him into the clouds. He is lost.

If, on the other hand, we habitually go *down* the abstraction ladder to *lower* levels of abstraction when we are asked the meaning of a word, we are less likely to get lost in verbal mazes; we will tend to "have our feet on the ground" and know what we are talking about. This habit displays itself in an answer such as this:

"What is meant by the word *red?*"
"Well, the next time you see a bunch of cars stopped at an intersection, look at the traffic light facing them. Also, you might go to the fire department and see how their trucks are painted."

Chasing Oneself in Verbal Circles

In other words, the kind of "thinking" we must be extremely wary of is that which *never* leaves the higher verbal levels of abstraction, the kind that never points *down* the abstraction ladder to lower levels of abstraction and from there to the extensional world:

"What do you mean by *democracy?*"
"Democracy means the preservation of human rights."
"What do you mean by *rights?*"
"By rights I mean those privileges God grants to all of us—I mean man's inherent privileges."
"Such as?"
"Liberty, for example."
"What do you mean by *liberty?*"
"Religious and political freedom."
"And what does that mean?"
"Religious and political freedom is what we have when we do things the democratic way."

Of course it is possible to talk meaningfully about democracy, as Jefferson and Lincoln have done, as Charles and Mary Beard do in *The Rise of American Civilization,* as Frederick Jackson Turner does in *The Frontier in American History,* as Lincoln Steffens does in his *Autobiography,* as Thurman Arnold does in *The Bottlenecks of Business*—to name only the first examples that come to mind—but such a sample as the above is not the way to do it. The trouble with speakers who never leave the higher levels of abstraction is not only that they fail to notice when they are saying something and when they are not; they also produce a similar lack of discrimination in their audiences. Never coming down to earth, they frequently chase themselves around in verbal circles, unaware that they are making meaningless noises.

This is by no means to say, however, that we must never make extensionally meaningless noises. When we use directive language, when we talk about the future, when we utter ritual language or engage in social conversation, and when we express our feelings, we are usually making utterances that have no extensional verifiability. It must not be overlooked that our highest ratiocinative and imaginative powers are derived from the fact that symbols *are* independent of things symbolized, so that we are free not only to go quickly from low to extremely high levels of abstraction (from "canned peas" to "groceries" to "commodities" to "national wealth") and to manipulate symbols even when the things they stand for cannot be so manipulated ("If all the freight cars in the country were hooked up to each other in one long line . . ."), but we are also free to manufacture symbols at will even if they stand only for abstractions made from other abstractions and not for anything in the extensional world. Mathematicians, for example, often play with symbols that have no extensional content, just to find out what can be done with them; this is called "pure mathematics." And pure mathematics is far from being a useless pastime, because mathematical systems that are elaborated with no extensional application in mind often prove later to be applicable in useful and unforeseen ways. Mathematicians, however, when they are dealing with extensionally meaningless symbols, usually know what they are doing. We likewise *must* know what we are doing.

Nevertheless, all of us (including mathematicians), when we speak the language of everyday life, often make meaningless noises without knowing that we are doing so. We have already seen what confusions this can lead to. The fundamental purpose of the abstraction ladder, as shown both in this chapter and the next, is to make us aware of the process of abstracting.

Applications

1. Arrange the following words in order of increasing abstraction, starting as nearly as possible at the bottom of the abstraction ladder.

a. Man, male, Herbert F. Jackson, human being, American, Iowan, "redhead."

b. Fruit, orchard crop, apple, agricultural product, pome, article of international trade, article of export, Winesap.

c. Paul Robeson, artist, basso, singer, Negro, man, Phi Beta Kappa, athlete, football player. Use as many branch lines in your diagram as you find you need.

d. Retail business, our distribution system, McGreevy's Drug Store, business, the economic life of the nation, the drug business.
e. Newspaper, the New York *Times,* a daily, channel of public information, the press, a publication.

2. The foregoing examples of the abstracting process have all of necessity begun with the verbal levels of abstraction. Starting with some object that you have at hand, a book, pencil, chair, window—something that you can see, touch, or hear—make some abstraction ladders beginning with the object level. Note carefully what characteristics you are leaving out as you abstract.

3. Apply the following terms to events in the extensional world—i.e., go down the abstraction ladder: American standard of living, college, human nature, national honor, an insult.

9. THE LITTLE MAN WHO WASN'T THERE

> *Everybody is familiar with the fact that the ordinary man does not see things as they are, but only sees certain* fixed types. . . . *Mr. Walter Sickert is in the habit of telling his pupils that they are unable to draw any individual arm because they think of it as an arm; and because they think of it as an arm they think they know what it ought to be.*
>
> T. E. HULME

How Not to Start a Car

THERE was recently a story in the newspapers about a man who, having trouble with his car, got angry at it and "poked it one in the eye"—that is, he smashed his fist through one of the headlights. (The newspapers learned about it when he turned up at a hospital to get his hand bandaged.) He got angry at the car just as he might have got angry at a person, horse, or mule that was stubborn and unco-operative. He thereupon proceeded to "teach" that car "a lesson." He may be said to have had a signal reaction to the behavior of the car—a complete, unreflective, automatic reaction.

Savages, of course, often behave in similar ways. When crops fail or rocks fall upon them, they "make a deal with"—offer sacrifices to—the "spirits" of vegetation or the "spirits" of the rocks, in order to obtain better treatment from them in the future. All of us, however, have certain reactions of similar kinds: sometimes, tripping over a chair, we kick it and call it names; some people, indeed, when they fail to get letters, get angry at the postman. In all such behavior, we *confuse* the abstraction which is *inside* our heads with that which is *outside* and act as if the abstraction *were* the event in the outside world. We create in our heads an imaginary chair that maliciously trips us and then "punish" the extensional chair that bears ill will to nobody; we create an imaginary postman who is "holding back our mail" and bawl out the extensional postman who would gladly bring us letters if he had any to bring.

The Confusion of Lower Levels of Abstraction

In a wider sense, however, we are confusing levels of abstraction—confusing that which is inside our heads with that which is outside—all the time. For example, we talk about the yellowness of a pencil as if the yellowness were a "property" of the pencil and not a product, as we have seen, of the *interaction* of something outside our skins with our nervous systems. We confuse, that is to say, the two lowest levels of the abstraction ladder (see page 126) and treat them as one. Properly speaking, we should not say, "The pencil is yellow," which is a statement that places the yellowness in the pencil; we should say instead, "That which has an effect on me which leads me to say 'pencil' also has an effect on me which leads me to say 'yellow.'" We don't have to be that precise, of course, in the language of everyday life, but it should be observed that the latter statement takes into consideration the part our nervous systems play in creating whatever pictures of reality we may have in our heads, while the former statement does not.

Now this habit of confusing that which is inside our skins and that which is outside is essentially that naïve reaction of children and savages, although it persists in "grown-ups." The more advanced civilization becomes, the more conscious we must be that our nervous systems *automatically leave out characteristics* of the events before us. If we are not aware of characteristics left out, if we are not conscious of the process of abstracting, we make *seeing and believing a single process.* If, for example, you react to the twenty-second rattlesnake you have seen in your life as if it were identical with the abstraction you have in your head as the result of the last twenty-one rattlesnakes you have seen, you may not be far out in your reactions. But civilized life provides our nervous systems with more complicated problems than rattlesnakes to deal with. There is a case cited by Korzybski in *Science and Sanity* of a man who suffered from hay fever whenever there were roses in the room. In an experiment, a bunch of roses was produced unexpectedly in front of him, and he immediately had a violent attack of hay fever, despite the fact that the "roses" in this case were *made of paper*. That is, his nervous system saw-and-believed in one operation.

Confusing Higher Levels of Abstraction

But words, as we have seen by means of the abstraction ladder, are still higher levels of abstraction than the "objects" of experience. The more words at extremely high levels of abstraction we have, then, the more conscious we must be of this process of abstracting. For example, the word "rattlesnake" leaves out every important feature of the actual rattlesnake. But if the word is vividly remembered as part of a whole complex of terrifying experiences with an actual rattlesnake, the word itself is capable of arousing the same feelings as an actual rattlesnake. There are people, therefore, who turn pale at the *word*.

This, then, is the origin of word-magic. The word "rattlesnake" and the actual creature are felt to be *one and the same thing,* because they arouse the same feelings. This sounds like nonsense, of course, and it is nonsense. But from the point of view of a childish logic, it has its justification. As Lévy-Bruhl explains in his *How Natives Think,* primitive "logic" works on such a principle. The

creature frightens us; the word frightens us; therefore
the creature and the word are "the same"—not actually
the same, perhaps, but there is a "mystic connection" between the two. This sense of "mystic connection" is
Lévy-Bruhl's term for what we have called "necessary
connection" in our discussion of linguistic naïveté. In
this way, "mystical power" is attributed to words. There
come to be "fearful words," "forbidden words," "un-
speakable words"—words taking on the characteristics of
the things they stand for. Such feelings as these about the
power of words are, as we have already seen, probably in
part responsible for such social phenomena as the strenu-
ous campaign in the early 1930's to bring back prosperity
through frequent reiteration of the *words,* "Prosperity is
around the corner!"

The commonest form of this confusion of levels of abstraction, however, is illustrated by our reacting to the
twenty-second Republican we encounter in our lives as if
he were identical with the abstraction "Republican" inside our heads. "If he's Republican, he must be O.K.—
or terrible," we are likely to say, confusing the extensional
Republican with our abstraction "Republican," which is
the product not only of the last twenty-one "Republicans"
we have met, but also of all that we have been *told* about
"Republicans."

"Jews"

To make the principles clearer, we shall use an example that is loaded with prejudices for many people: "Mr. Miller is a *Jew*." To such a statement, some "Christians" have a marked signal reaction, which may take such forms as these: automatically deciding that Mr. Miller is not the kind of person one likes to meet socially, although, of course, one cannot help running into "Jews" in business; automatically excluding him from tenancy in the apartment house one owns or from membership in the fraternity or country club one belongs to; automatically putting oneself on guard against his expected sharp financial practices; automatically suspecting his political views of being "tinged with communism"; automatically shrinking away.

That is to say, a "Christian" of this kind confuses his high-level abstraction, "Jew," with the extensional Mr. Miller and behaves towards Mr. Miller as if he were identical with that abstraction. (See the abstraction ladder, page 126.)

Now it happens that the word "Jew," as the result of a number of historical accidents, has powerful affective connotations in Christian culture. Jews, a small minority in medieval Christendom, were the only people legally permitted to lend money at interest because of the Christian proscriptions against usury. They were excluded from agriculture and from most professions because they were "non-Christians." As non-Christians they were regarded by the ignorant and the superstitious with terror. Nevertheless, a few Jews *had* to be tolerated, because moneylenders were necessary to the development of business. It became the standard practice of Christians, therefore, to borrow money from Jews to satisfy their business requirements, meanwhile calling them names to satisfy their consciences—just as, during Prohibition in the United States, it was a fairly common practice to patronize bootleggers to satisfy one's thirst, meanwhile denouncing them for "lawlessness" on all public occasions to satisfy one's conscience. Furthermore, many princes and noblemen who owed large sums of money to Jews made the happy discovery that it was easy to avoid the payment of their debts by arousing the superstitious populace to torturing and massacring the Jews on the pretext of "holy crusades." After such incidents, the Jews would be either dead or willing to cancel the debts owed them in order to save their lives. Such business risks would further increase the interest rates, even as the risk of police raids increased the price of bootleg liquor. The increased interest rates would further infuriate the Christians. The word "Jew," therefore, came to have increasingly powerful affective connotations, expressing at once the terror felt by Christians toward non-Christians and the resentment felt by people everywhere toward money-lenders, who are always felt to be "grasping," "unscrupulous," and "cunning." The moral objections to money-lending disappeared, of course, especially after people began to found new forms of Christianity, partly in order that they might freely engage in that profession. Nevertheless, the affective connotations of the word "Jew" survived and have remained, even to this day. They reveal their continued existence in such uses of the term as these: "He *jewed* me out of ten dollars," "Go on and give him some money; don't be such a *Jew*," "He *jewed* down the price." In some circles, it is not uncommon for mothers to discipline disobedient children by saying to them, "If you don't behave, I'll sell you to the *Jew man.*"

Let us return now to our hypothetical Mr. Miller, who has been introduced as a "Jew." To a person for whom these affective connotations are very much alive—and there are many such—and who habitually confuses that which is inside his nervous system with that which is outside, Mr. Miller is a man "not to be trusted." If Mr. Miller succeeds in business, that "proves" that "Jews are smart"; if Mr. Johansen succeeds in business, it only proves that Mr. Johansen is smart. If Mr. Miller fails in business, it is alleged that he nevertheless has "money salted away somewhere." If Mr. Miller is strange or foreign in his habits, that "proves" that "Jews don't assimilate." If he is thoroughly American—i.e., indistinguishable from other natives—he is "trying to pass himself off as one of us." If Mr. Miller fails to give to charity, that is because "Jews are tight"; if he gives generously, he is "trying to buy his way into society." If Mr. Miller lives in the Jewish section of town, that is because "Jews are so clannish"; if he moves to a locality where there are no other Jews, that is because "they try to horn in everywhere." In short, Mr. Miller is automatically condemned, no matter who he is or what he does.

But Mr. Miller may be, for all we know, rich or poor, a wife beater or a saint, a stamp collector or a violinist, a farmer or a physicist, a lens grinder or an orchestra leader. If, as the result of our signal reactions, we put ourselves on guard about our *money* immediately upon meeting Mr. Miller, we may offend a man from whom we might have profited financially, morally, or spiritually, or we may fail to notice his attempts to flirt with our wife —that is, we shall act with complete inappropriateness to the *actual* situation at hand. Mr. Miller is not identical with our notion of "Jew," *whatever our notion of "Jew" may be*. The "Jew," created by intensional definition of the *word, simply is not there*.

John Doe, the "Criminal"

Another instance of the confusion of levels of abstraction is to be found in cases like this: Let us say that here is a man, John Doe, who is introduced as one "who has just been released after three years in the penitentiary." This is already on a fairly high level of abstraction, but it is nevertheless a *report*. From this point, however, many people *immediately and unconsciously* climb to still higher levels of abstraction: "John Doe is an *ex-convict* . . . he's a *criminal!*" But the word "criminal" is not only on a much higher level of abstraction than "the man who spent three years in the penitentiary," but it is also, as we have seen before in Chapter 3, a *judgment,* with the implication, "He has committed a crime in the past and will probably commit more crimes in future." The result is that when John Doe applies for a job and is forced to state that he has spent three years in the penitentiary, prospective employers, automatically confusing levels of abstraction, may say to him, "You can't expect me to give jobs to criminals!"

John Doe, for all we know from the report, may have undergone a complete reformation or, for that matter, may have been unjustly imprisoned in the first place; nevertheless, he may wander in vain, looking for a job. If, in desperation, he finally says to himself, "If everybody is going to treat me like a criminal, I might as well become one," and goes out and commits a robbery, who is responsible for his act? Yet, if John Doe gets caught, those who refused to employ him say, on reading the papers about the robbery, "There, I told you so! Lucky I didn't hire that criminal!"

The reader is familiar with the way in which rumor grows as it spreads. Many of the exaggerations of rumor are again due to this inability on the part of some people to refrain from climbing to higher levels of abstraction—from reports to inferences to judgments—and then confusing the levels. According to this kind of "reasoning":

Report. "Mary Smith didn't get in until two last Saturday night."
Inference. "I bet she was out tearing around!"
Judgment. "She's a worthless hussy. I never did like the looks of her. I knew it the moment I first laid eyes on her."

Basing our actions towards our fellow human beings on such hastily abstracted judgments, it is no wonder that we frequently make life miserable not only for others, but for ourselves.

As a final example of this type of confusion, *notice the difference between what happens when a man says to himself, "I have failed three times," and what happens when he says, "I am a failure!" It is the difference between sanity and self-destruction.*

Delusional Worlds

Consciousness of abstracting prepares us in advance for the fact that things that look alike are *not* alike, for the fact that things that have the same name are *not* the same, for the fact that judgments are *not* reports. In short, it prevents us from acting like fools. Without consciousness of abstracting—or rather, without the habit of *delaying reactions,* which is the product of a deep awareness that seeing is not believing—we are completely unprepared for the differences between roses and paper roses, between the intensional "Jew" and the extensional Mr. Miller, between the intensional "criminal" and the extensional John Doe.

Such delayed reactions are a sign of adulthood. It happens, however, that as the result of miseducation, bad training, frightening experiences in childhood, obsolete traditional beliefs, propaganda, and other influences in our lives, all of us have what might be termed "areas of insanity" or, perhaps better, "areas of infantilism." There are certain subjects about which we can never, as we say, "think straight," because we are "blinded by prejudice." Some people, for example, as the result of a childhood experience, cannot help being frightened by the mere sight of a policeman—any policeman; the terrifying "policeman" inside their heads "is" the extensional policeman outside, who probably has no designs that anyone could regard as terrifying. Some people turn pale at the sight of a spider—any spider—even a nice, harmless one safely enclosed in a bottle. Some people automatically become hostile at the *words* "un-American," "Nazi," or "communist."

The picture of reality created inside our heads by such unconsciousness of abstracting is not at all a "map" of any existing "territory." It is a delusional world. In this never-never land, all "Jews" are out to cheat you; all "capitalists" are overfed tyrants, smoking expensive cigars and gnashing their teeth at labor unions; all "WPA workers" idly "lean on shovels," meanwhile "living on the fat of the land." In this world, too, all snakes are poisonous, automobiles can be disciplined by a well-directed sock in the eye, and every stranger with a foreign accent is a spy. Some of these people who spend too much of their time in such delusional worlds eventually get locked up, but, needless to say, there are many of us still at large.

How do we reduce such areas of infantilism in our thought? One way is to know deeply that there is no "necessary connection" between words and what they stand for. For this reason, the study of a foreign language is always good for us, even if it has no other uses. Other ways have already been suggested: to be aware of the process of abstracting and *to realize fully that words never "say all" about anything*. The abstraction ladder—an adaptation of a diagram originated by Alfred Korzybski to illustrate visually the relationship between words, "objects," and events—is designed to help us understand and remain conscious of the process of abstracting. It should be looked at often. In its original form, made out of pieces of wood joined with string so that it can be *felt* as well as seen, it is used today by some psychiatrists in the treatment of many types of maladjustment and insanity.

Applications

The reader who wishes practice in analyzing the disordered reactions described in this book is urged to make for himself a collection of "case histories" in which he describes and attempts to find the source of the mental blockages involved. He will probably find no lack of examples among his own acquaintance, as well as among speakers, writers, and other people in public life. He may even, it might be added, find some in himself.

10. CLASSIFICATIONS

> *For of course the true meaning of a term is to be found by observing what a man does with it, not by what he says about it.*
>
> P. W. BRIDGMAN

Giving Things Names

THE FIGURE below shows eight objects, let us say animals, four large and four small, a different four with round heads and another four with square heads, and still another four with curly tails and another four with

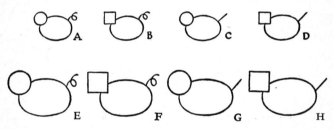

straight tails. These animals, let us say, are scampering about your village, but since at first they are of no importance to you, you ignore them. You do not even give them a name.

One day, however, you discover that the little ones eat up your grain, while the big ones do not. A differentiation sets itself up, and, abstracting the common characteristics of A, B, C, and D, you decide to call these *gogo;* E, F, G, and H you decide to call *gigi.* You chase away the *gogo,* but leave the *gigi* alone. Your neighbor, however, has had a different experience; he finds that those with square heads bite, while those with round heads do not. Abstracting the common characteristics of B, D, F, and H, he calls them *daba,* and A, C, E, and G he calls *dobo.* Still another neighbor discovers, on the other hand, that those with curly tails kill snakes, while those with straight tails do not. He differentiates them, abstracting still another set of common characteristics: A, B, E, and F are *busa,* while C, D, G, and H are *busana.*

Now imagine that the three of you are together when E runs by. You say, "There goes the *gigi*"; your first neighbor says, "There goes the *dobo*"; your other neighbor says, "There goes the *busa.*" Here immediately a great controversy arises. What is it *really,* a *gigi,* a *dobo,* or a *busa?* What is its *right name?* You are quarreling violently when along comes a fourth person from another village who calls it a *muglock,* an edible animal, as opposed to *uglock,* an inedible animal—which doesn't help matters a bit.

Of course, the question, "What is it *really? What is its right name?"* is a nonsense question. By a nonsense question is meant one that is not capable of being answered. Things can have "right names" only if there is a necessary connection between symbols and things symbolized, and we have seen that there is not. That is to say, in the light of your interest in protecting your grain, it may be necessary for you to distinguish the animal E as a *gigi;* your neighbor, who doesn't like to be bitten, finds it practical to distinguish it as a *dobo;* your other neighbor, who likes to see snakes killed, distinguishes it as a *busa.* What we call things and where we draw the line between one class of things and another depend upon the interests we have and the purposes of the classification. For example, animals are classified in one way by the meat industry, in a different way by the leather industry, in another different way by the fur industry, and in a still different way by the biologist. None of these classifications is any more final than any of the others; each of them is useful for its purpose.

This holds, of course, regarding everything we perceive. A table "is" a table to us, because we can understand its relationship to our conduct and interests; we eat at it, work on it, lay things on it. But to a person living in a culture where no tables are used, it may be a very big stool, a small platform, or a meaningless structure. If our culture and upbringing were different, that is to say, our world would not even look the same to us.

Many of us, for example, cannot distinguish between pickerel, pike, salmon, smelts, perch, croppies, halibut, and mackerel; we say that they are "just fish, and I don't like fish." To a seafood connoisseur, however, these distinctions are real, since they mean the difference to him between one kind of good meal, a very different kind of good meal, or a poor meal. To a zoologist, even finer distinctions become of great importance, since he has other and more general ends in view. When we hear the statement, then, "This fish is a specimen of the small porgy, *Lagodon rhomboides,*" we accept this as being "true," even if we don't care, not because that is its "right name," but because that is how it is *classified* in the most complete and most general system of classification which people most deeply interested in fish have evolved.

When we name something, then, we are classifying. *The individual object or event we are naming, of course, has no name and belongs to no class until we put it in one.* To illustrate again, suppose that we were to give the extensional meaning of the word "Korean." We would have to point to all "Koreans" living at a particular moment and say, "The word 'Korean' denotes at the present moment these persons: A_1, A_2, A_3, . . . A_n." Now, let us say, a child, whom we shall designate as Z, is born among these "Koreans." *The extensional meaning of the word "Korean," determined prior to the existence of Z, does not include Z.* Z is a new individual belonging to no classification, since all classifications were made without taking Z into account. Why, then, is Z also a "Korean"? *Because we say so.* And, saying so—fixing the classification—we have determined to a considerable extent future attitudes toward Z. For example, Z will always have certain rights in Korea; he will always be regarded in other nations as an "alien" and will be subject to laws applicable to "aliens"; he will never be permitted to enter the U. S. except under very limited conditions.

In matters of "race" and "nationality," the way in which classifications work is especially apparent. For example, the present writer is by "race" a "Japanese," by "nationality" a "Canadian," but, his friends say, "essentially" an "American," since he thinks, talks, behaves, and dresses much like other Americans. Because he is "Japanese," he is excluded by law from becoming a citizen of the United States; because he is "Canadian," he has certain rights in all parts of the British Empire; because he is "American," he gets along with his friends and teaches in an American institution of higher learning without any noticeable special difficulties. Are these classifications "real"? Of course they are, and *the effect that each of them has* upon what he may do and what he may not do constitutes their "reality."

There was, again, the story some years ago of the immigrant baby whose parents were "Czechs" and eligible to enter the United States by quota. The child, however, because it was born on what happened to be a "British" ship, was a "British subject." The quota for Britishers was full for that year, with the result that the newborn infant was regarded by immigration authorities as "not admis-

sible to the United States." How they straightened out
this matter, the writer does not know. The reader can
multiply instances of this kind at will. When, to take another example, is a person a "Negro"? By the definition
accepted in the United States, any person with even a
small amount of "Negro blood"—that is, whose parents
or ancestors were classified as "Negroes"—is a "Negro."
*Logically, it would be exactly as justifiable to say that
any person with even a small amount of "white blood"
is "white."* Why do they say one rather than the other?
Because the former system of classification *suits the convenience of those making the classification.*

There are few complexities about classifications at the
level of dogs and cats, knives and forks, cigarettes and
candy, but when it comes to classifications at high levels
of abstraction, for example, those describing conduct, social institutions, philosophical and moral problems, serious difficulties occur. When one person kills another, is
it an act of murder, an act of temporary insanity, an act
of homicide, an accident, or an act of heroism? As soon
as the process of classification is completed, our attitudes
and our conduct are to a considerable degree determined.
We hang the murderer, we lock up the insane man, we
free the victim of circumstances, we pin a medal on the
hero.

The Blocked Mind

Unfortunately, people are not always aware of the way in which they arrive at their classifications. Unaware of the characteristics of the extensional Mr. Miller not covered by classifying him as "a Jew" and attributing to Mr. Miller all the characteristics *suggested* by the affective connotations of the term with which he has been classified, they pass final judgment on Mr. Miller by saying, "Well, a Jew's a Jew. There's no getting around that!"

We need not concern ourselves here with the injustices done to "Jews," "Roman Catholics," "Republicans," "WPA workers," "New Deal proposals," and so on, by such hasty judgments or, as it is better to call them, signal reactions. "Hasty judgments" suggests that such errors can be avoided by thinking more slowly; this, of course, is not the case, for some people think very slowly with no better results. What we are concerned with is the way in which we block the development of our own minds by such signal reactions.

To continue with our example of the people who say, "A Jew's a Jew. There's no getting around that!"—they are, as we have seen, confusing the denoted, extensional Jew with the fictitious "Jew" inside their heads. Such persons, the reader will have observed, can usually be made to admit, on being reminded of certain "Jews" whom they admire—perhaps Albert Einstein, perhaps Hank Greenberg, perhaps Jascha Heifetz, perhaps Benny Goodman—that "there are exceptions, of course." They have been compelled by experience, that is to say, to take cognizance of at least a few of the multitude of "Jews" who do not fit their preconceptions. At this point, however, they continue triumphantly, "But exceptions only prove the rule!" [1]—which is another way of saying, "Facts don't count." In extremely serious cases of people who "think" in this way, it can sometimes be observed that the best friends they have may be Isaac Cohens, Isidor Ginsbergs, and Abe Sinaikos; nevertheless, in explaining this, they will say, "I don't think of them as Jews at all. They're just friends." In other words, the fictitious "Jew" inside their heads remains unchanged *in spite of their experience*.

People like this *cannot learn from experience*. They continue to vote "Republican" or "Democratic," no matter what the Republicans or Democrats do. They continue to object to "socialists," no matter what the socialists propose. They continue to regard "mothers" as sacred, no matter which mother. A woman who had been given up both by physicians and psychiatrists as hopelessly insane was being considered by a committee whose task it was

---

[1] This extraordinarily fatuous saying originally meant, "The exception *tests* the rule"—"Exceptio probat regulam." This older meaning of the word "prove" survives in such an expression as "automobile proving ground," for testing automobiles.

to decide whether or not she should be committed to an asylum. One member of the committee doggedly refused to vote for commitment. "Gentlemen," he said in tones of deepest reverence, "you must remember that this woman is, after all, a mother." Similarly such people continue to hate "Protestants," no matter which Protestant. Unaware of characteristics left out in the process of classification, they overlook, when the term "Republican" is applied to both the party of Abraham Lincoln and the party of Warren Harding, the rather important differences between them: "If the Republican party was good enough for Abe Lincoln, it's good enough for me!"

Cow_1 Is Not Cow_2

How do we prevent ourselves from getting into such intellectual blind alleys, or, finding we are in one, how do we get out again? One way is to remember that practically all statements in ordinary conversation, debate, and public controversy taking the form, "Jews are Jews," "Republicans are Republicans," "Business is business," "Boys will be boys," "Woman drivers are woman drivers," and so on, are *not true*. Let us put one of these back into a context in life.

"I don't think we should go through with this deal, Bill. Is it altogether fair to the railroad company?"
"Aw, forget it! *Business is business,* after all."

Such an assertion, although it looks like a "simple statement of fact," is not simple and is not a statement of fact. The first "business" *denotes* the transaction under discussion; the second "business" invokes the *connotations* of the word. The sentence says, therefore, "Let us treat this transaction with complete disregard for considerations of honor, sentiment, or justice, as the word 'business' suggests." Similarly, when a father tries to excuse the mischief done by his sons, he says, "Boys will be boys"; in other words, "Let us regard the actions of my sons with that indulgent amusement customarily extended toward those whom we call 'boys,'" though the angry neighbor will say, of course, "Boys, my eye! They're little hoodlums; that's what they are!" These are not informative statements but *directives, directing us to classify the object or event under discussion in given ways, in order that we may feel or act in the ways suggested by the terms of the classification.*

There is a simple technique for preventing such directives from having their harmful effect on our thinking. It is the suggestion made by Korzybski that we add "index numbers" to our terms, thus: Englishman$_1$, Englishman$_2$ . . . ; cow$_1$, cow$_2$, cow$_3$ . . . ; Frenchman$_1$, Frenchman$_2$, Frenchman$_3$, . . . ; communist$_1$, communist$_2$, communist$_3$ . . . The terms of the classification tell us what the individuals in that class have in common; THE INDEX NUMBERS REMIND US OF THE CHARACTER-

ISTICS LEFT OUT. *A rule can then be formulated as a general guide in all our thinking and reading: Cow$_1$ IS NOT cow$_2$; Jew$_1$ IS NOT Jew$_2$; politician$_1$ IS NOT politician$_2$, and so on. This rule, if remembered, prevents us from confusing levels of abstraction and forces us to consider the facts on those occasions when we might otherwise find ourselves leaping to conclusions which we may later have cause to regret.*

"Truth"

Most intellectual problems are, ultimately, problems of classification and nomenclature. There is a debate still going on at the present time between the American Medical Association and the Anti-Trust Division of the Department of Justice as to whether the practice of medicine is a "profession" or "trade." The American Medical Association *wants* immunity from laws prohibiting the "restraint of trade"; therefore, it insists that medicine *is* a "profession." The Anti-Trust Division *wants* to stop certain economic practices connected with the practice of medicine, and therefore it insists that medicine *is* a "trade." Partisans of either side will accuse the other of "perverting the meanings of words" and of "not being able to understand plain English." Who is right?

The usual way in which such questions are settled is by appeals to etymological dictionaries to discover the "real meanings" of the words "trade" and "profession," by consultation of past legal decisions and learned treatises of various kinds. The decision finally rests, however, not upon appeals to past authority, but upon *what society wants.* If it wants the A.M.A. to be immune from anti-trust prosecution, it will finally get the Supreme Court to "define" medicine as a "profession." If it wants the A.M.A. prosecuted, it will get a decision that medicine is a "trade." In either case society will get the decision it wants, even if it has to wait until the present members of the Supreme Court are dead and an entirely new court is appointed. When the desired decision is handed down, people will say, "Truth has triumphed." *Society, in short, regards as "true" those systems of classification that produce the desired results.*

The scientific test of "truth," like the social test, is strictly practical, except for the fact that the "desired results" are more severely limited. The results desired by society may be irrational, superstitious, selfish, or humane, but the results desired by scientists are only that our systems of classification produce predictable results. Classifications, as has already been indicated, determine our attitudes and behavior toward the object or event classified. When lightning was classified as "evidence of divine wrath," no courses of action other than prayer were suggested to prevent one's being struck by lightning. As soon, however, as it was classified as "electricity," Benjamin Franklin achieved a measure of control over it by his invention of the lightning rod. Certain physical disorders were formerly classified as "demonic possession," and this suggested that we "drive the demons out" by whatever spells or incantations we could think of. The results were uncertain. But when those disorders were classified as "bacillus infections," courses of action were suggested that led to more predictable results. Science seeks only the *most generally useful* systems of classification; these it regards for the time being, until more useful classifications are invented, as "true."

Applications

1. The applications of this chapter are so numerous that it is possible here only to suggest a few.

a. What is meant when someone says, "What people ordinarily call rabbits are really hares, and what they call hares are really rabbits"?

b. What takes place when a judge renders a decision that a given firm is or is not "engaged in interstate commerce"? Is a "corporation" a "person," or isn't it?

c. What is the difference between a "Pullman *porter*" and an "airline *hostess*" (1) from the point of view of services performed, and (2) from the point of view of social status? And why the difference?

d. What differences in criminological theory are implied when a place to put social offenders is called (1) a prison, (2) a reformatory, and (3) an institute for social rehabilitation, and what are the resulting differences in such matters as the choice of staff, the treatment of inmates, the design, furniture, and arrangement of the buildings and grounds?

e. When is an athlete an "amateur"?

f. What is the difference between "relief" and "social insurance"?

g. Is Britain (July, 1941) a "democracy," or is she not—and what follows from the answer we give to this question?

h. We are sometimes told that the problems of the world are "economic," sometimes that they are "political," and sometimes that they are "spiritual." What do people mean by such statements?

2. Another subject to be considered in the light of our study of classifications is humor. Is not much of humor the result of changing accustomed classifications so that things appear in unexpected lights?

> I loved thee beautiful and kind,
> And plighted an eternal vow:
> So altered are thy face and mind,
> 'Twere perjury to love thee now!
>
> ROBERT, EARL NUGENT
> (1702-1788)

Would this, then, be the reason that people who see things only in their accustomed classifications are usually looked upon as dull, and that people with "single-track minds," who see life in terms of one dominating interest, are usually said to lack a sense of humor?

Many other applications, in science, in ethics, in law, in business, and in everyday life, will suggest themselves to the thoughtful reader.

11. THE TWO-VALUED ORIENTATION

> *And the admired art of disputing hath added much to the natural imperfection of languages. . . . This is unavoidably to be so where men's parts and learning are estimated by their skill in disputing. And if reputation and reward shall attend these conquests . . . 'tis no wonder if the wit of man so employed should perplex, involve, and subtilize the signification of sounds; so as never to want something to say in opposing or defending any question—the victory being adjudged not to him who had truth on his side, but the last word in the dispute.*
>
> JOHN LOCKE

IN SUCH an expression as "We must listen to *both* sides of every question," there is an assumption, frequently unexamined, that every question has, fundamentally, only two sides. We tend to think in opposites, to feel that what is not "good" must be "bad" and that what is not "bad" must be "good." This feeling is heightened when we are excited or angry. During war times, for example, it is often felt that whoever is not a "100 per cent patriot" *must* be a "foreign agent." Children manifest this same tendency. When they are taught English history, for example, the first thing they want to know about every ruler is whether he was a "good king" or a "bad king." In popular literature and movie scenarios written for childish mentalities, there are always "heroes" on the one hand, to be cheered, and "villains" on the other, to be hissed. Much popular political thought is based upon the opposition of "Americanism" (whatever that may mean) against "foreign -isms" (whatever that may mean). This tendency to see things in terms of two values only, affirmative and negative, good and bad, hot and cold, love and hate, may be termed the *two-valued orientation*.

The Two-Valued Orientation and Combat

Now, in terms of a single desire, there are only two values, roughly speaking: things that gratify or things that frustrate that desire. If we are starving, there are only two kinds of things in the world so far as we are concerned at the moment: edible things and inedible things. If we are in danger, there are the things that we fear and the things that may help and protect us. At primitive levels of existence, in our absorption in self-defense or food-seeking, there are, in terms of those limited desires, only two categories possible: things that give us pain and things that give us pleasure. Life at such levels can be folded neatly down the middle, with all good on one side, all bad on the other, and *everything is accounted for,* because things that are irrelevant to our interests escape our notice altogether.

When we are fighting, moreover, we are reduced at once to such a two-valued orientation. For the time being, nothing in the world exists except ourselves and our opponent. Dinner tomorrow, the beauties of the landscape, the interested bystanders—all are forgotten. We fight, therefore, with all the intensity we are capable of; our muscles are tense, our hearts beat much faster than usual, our veins swell, and the supply of white corpuscles in our blood stream increases to take care of possible damage. Indeed, the two-valued orientation, which under conditions of great excitement shows as many "physical" manifestations as "mental," may be regarded as an inevitable accompaniment to combat. If we fight, we develop the two-valued orientation; if we develop the two-valued orientation, we begin to want to fight. Under the influence of the two-valued orientation, we have in place of our normal reactions elaborate sets of signal reactions, lumping together all evils as one Evil, all good things as one Good.

To savages, whose life is a perpetual fight with the elements, with enemies, with wild animals, or with hostile spirits supposed to reside in natural objects, the two-valued orientation appears to be the normal orientation. Every act of a man's life in a primitive, superstitious society is strictly governed by ritual necessity or tabu. There is, as anthropology has shown, no freedom in savage existence, since strict compulsions about "good" and "bad" govern every detail of life. One must, for example, hunt and fish in specified ways with specified ceremonies in order to achieve success; one must avoid walking on people's shadows; one must avoid stirring the pot from right to left instead of from left to right; one must avoid calling people by their given names lest the name be overheard by evil spirits. A bird flying over the village is either "good luck" or "bad luck." Nothing is meaningless or accidental to a savage, because everything he sees, if he notices it at all, *must* be accounted for under one of the two values.

The trouble with such thought, of course, is that there is never any way of evaluating any new experience, process, or object other than by such terms as "good magic" or "bad magic." Any departure from custom is discouraged on the ground that it is "unprecedented" and therefore "bad magic." For this reason, many primitive peoples have apparently static civilizations in which each generation duplicates almost exactly the ways of life of previous generations—hence they become what is known as "backward" peoples. They have in their language no means of progressing towards new evaluations, since all things are viewed only in terms of two sets of values.[1]

[1] This is not to say that primitive peoples are "not intelligent." It simply means that lack of cultural intercommunication has deprived them of the opportunity to pool their knowledge with other peoples, so that they have had little occasion to develop the linguistic machinery

Oppositions

But, the objection may arise, doesn't everything have its opposite: hot and cold, love and hate, life and death, black and white, sane and insane, thick and thin, clean and dirty? This objection would be at least plausible if all kinds of opposition were alike—but they are not. The simplest kind of opposition is, of course, opposition in terms of a single interest: edible vs. inedible things; we vs. they; Americans vs. foreigners (everybody else). This kind of opposition may be illustrated by the following diagram:

not-A   not-A

A

not-A   not-A

But the opposition between "white" and "black" is another kind of opposition. White and black are the extreme *limits of a scale,* and between them there is a continuous range of deepening shades of gray:

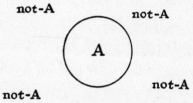

which would offer finer evaluations needed for the accurate pooling of knowledge. Civilized people, insofar as they are civilized, have advanced not because of superior native intelligence, but because they have inherited the products of centuries of widest cultural intercommunication.

Again, the oppositions between "hot" and "cold" and between "up" and "down" are relationships made with reference to a selected *point* in a scale:

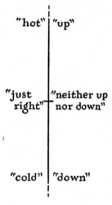

There are also further types of opposition, such as *complementary* oppositions, such as the positive and negative of a photograph or the right and left hands, and *directional* oppositions, like east and west, to and fro, coming and going.

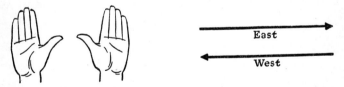

These are, of course, only a few of the types of opposition, but this is enough to indicate not only the inadequacy of an orientation based on two values, but also the falsity of treating all oppositions as if they were alike.

The Political Use of the Two-
Valued Orientation

The two-valued orientation is most clearly illustrated today by a regressive tendency now fashionable in the modern world—the tendency which has achieved its fullest expression in the Germany of Adolf Hitler. Here, as even a cursory examination of official Nazi party propaganda shows, the two-valued orientation is relied upon almost exclusively. Hunger, famine, unemployment, crooked capitalism, defeat in the first World War, bad smells, immorality, treachery, selfishness, and all things offensive are lined up on the "bad" side with "Jewish-dominated plutocracy." Anyone or anything that stands in the way of Hitler's wishes is "Jewish," "degenerate," "corrupt," "democratic," "internationalist," and, as a crowning insult, "non-Aryan." On the other hand, everything that Hitler chooses to call "Aryan" is noble, virtuous, heroic, and altogether glorious. Courage, self-discipline, honor, beauty, health, and joy are "Aryan." Everything he calls upon people to do, they are to do "to fulfill their Aryan heritage." In the light of this two-valued orientation of "Aryanism" vs. "non-Aryanism," everything is examined and appraised: art, books, people, philosophies, music, mathematics, physics, dogs, cats, calisthenics, architecture, morals, cookery, religion. If

Hitler approves, it is "Aryan." If he disapproves, it is "non-Aryan" or "Jewish-dominated." The absurdity of classifying the Japanese as "Aryan," just because Japan and Germany have friendly understandings, and President Roosevelt as "Jewish," of classifying pointed roofs as "Aryan" and flat roofs as "international" and therefore "Jewish," or of classifying one branch of physics as "Aryan" and another as "Jewish," does not in the least deter Hitler or his propaganda minister.

The connection between the two-valued orientation and combat is again apparent in the history of Nazism. From the very beginning, Hitler kept telling his followers that they were "surrounded by enemies." Germany, ever since Hitler came to power, has been on constant war footing against real or imagined enemies. Long before the present war started, everyone, including women and children, was being pressed into "war" service of one kind or another. In order to keep the combative sense growing and in order to prevent its fizzling out for want of tangible enemies before the start of actual warfare, the German people were kept fighting at home against alleged "enemies within the gates": the Jews, most of all, and anybody else who opposed the Nazis in any way. The brutalities inflicted upon dissenting German citizens, Jewish, Catholic, and Protestant, even in so-called peace times, show the characteristic war hysteria: the feeling that nothing is too good for the "good," and nothing is too bad for the "bad," and *that there is no middle ground*. "Whoever is not for us is against us."

The Multi-Valued Orientation

Except in quarrels and violent controversies, the language of everyday life shows what may be termed a multi-valued orientation. We have *scales* of judgment. Instead of "good" and "bad," we have "very bad," "bad," "not bad," "fair," "good," "very good"; instead of "sane" and "insane," we have "quite sane," "sane enough," "mildly neurotic," "neurotic," "almost psychotic," "psychotic." If we have only two values, for example, "law-abiding" and "law-breaking," we have only two ways of acting toward a given legal situation; the former are freed, and the latter are, let us say, executed. The man who rushes a traffic light is, of course, under such a dispensation, "just as much a law-breaker as a murderer" and will therefore have to get the same punishment. If this seems absurd, one has only to recall the medieval heresy trials in which the "orthodox" were freed and the "heretics" put to death—with the result that pious men who made slight theological errors through excess of Christian zeal were burned to as black a crisp as infidels or desecrators of the church. As soon as additional distinctions between *degrees* of offense are established, additional possibilities are thrown open, so that a minor traffic violation may mean a one dollar fine; vagrancy, ten days; smuggling, two to five years in prison; grand larceny, five to fifteen years—that is, as many *degrees* of punishment as there are *degrees* of guilt recognized.

The greater the number of distinctions, the greater becomes the number of courses of action suggested to us. This means that we become increasingly capable of reacting *appropriately* to the many complex situations life presents. The physician does not lump all people together into the two classes of the "healthy" and the "ill"; he distinguishes an indefinite number of conditions that may be described as "illness" and has an indefinite number of treatments or combinations of treatments. But the primitive witch-doctor did one song and dance for all illnesses.

The two-valued orientation is an orientation based ultimately, as we have seen, on a single interest. But human beings have many interests: they want to eat, to sleep, to have friends, to publish books, to sell real estate, to build bridges, to listen to music, to maintain peace, to conquer disease. Some of these desires are stronger than others, and life presents a perpetual problem of weighing one set of desires against others and making choices: "I like having the money, but I think I would like having that car even better than having the money." "I'd like to fire the strikers, but I think it's more important to obey the laws of the land." "I'd like to obey the laws, but I think it's more important that those strikers be taught a lesson." "I don't like standing in line for tickets, but I do want to see that show." For the weighing of the various and complicated desires that civilization gives rise to, an increasingly finely graduated scale of values is necessary, as well as foresight, lest in satisfying one desire we frustrate even more important ones. The ability to see things in terms of more than two values may be referred to as a *multi-valued orientation*.

The Multi-Valued Orientation and Democracy

The multi-valued orientation shows itself, of course, in almost all intelligent and even moderately intelligent public discussion. The editors of responsible papers, such as the New York *Times, PM,* Kansas City *Star,* Chicago *Daily News,* Milwaukee *Journal*—to name only a few— and the writers for reputable magazines, such as *Fortune, The New Republic, Common Sense,* or *Atlantic Monthly* have a way of instinctively avoiding the unqualified two-valued orientation. They may condemn Hitler, but they remind one at the same time of the external causes that produced Hitlerism and of the fascistic tendencies in our own nation. They may attack a political administration, but they do not forget its positive achievements. They may even recommend war, but they remind us of the limitations of war as a method of solving problems. From our point of view here, it does not matter whether it is from other motives, such as timidity, that they avoid speaking in terms of angels and devils, pure "good" and pure "evil." The important thing is that they do, and by so doing they keep open the possibility of adjusting differences, reconciling conflicting interests, and arriving at just estimates. There are people who object to this "shilly-shallying" and insist on "an outright yes or no." They are the Gordian knot cutters; they may undo the knot, but they ruin the rope.

Indeed, many features of the democratic process presuppose the multi-valued orientation. Even that most ancient of judicial procedures, the trial by jury, restricted to the conclusions "guilty" and "not guilty," is not as two-valued as it looks, since in the very selection of the charge to be brought against the prisoner a choice is made among many possibilities, and also, in the jury's verdict as well as in the judge's sentence, guilt is often modified by recognition of "extenuating circumstances." Modern administrative tribunals and boards of mediation, not tied down by the necessity of arriving at clear verdicts of "guilty" and "not guilty" and empowered to issue "consent decrees" and to close agreements between litigants, are even more multi-valued than the trial by jury and therefore, for some purposes, considerably more efficient.

To take another example, very few bills ever pass a democratic parliamentary body in exactly the form in which they were proposed. Opposing parties argue back and forth, make bargains and compromises with each other, and by such a process tend to arrive at decisions that are more exactly adjusted to the needs of everyone in the community than the original proposals. The more fully developed a democracy, the more flexible become its orientations, and the more fully does it reconcile the conflicting desires of the people.

Even more multi-valued is the language of science. Instead of saying "hot" and "cold," we give the temperature in *degrees on a fixed or agreed-upon scale:* —20° F., 37° C., and so on. Instead of saying "strong" and "weak," we give strength in *horse-power* or *voltage;* instead of "fast" and "slow," we give speed in miles per hour or feet per second. Instead of being limited to two possible answers or even to several, we have an infinite number when we use these numerical methods. The language of science, therefore, can be said to offer an *infinite-valued orientation*. Having at its command the means to adjust one's action in an infinite number of ways according to the exact situation at hand, science travels rapidly and gets things done.

The Affective Power of the Two-Valued Orientation

In spite of all that has been said to recommend multi- and infinite-valued orientation, it must not be overlooked that in the *expression of feelings,* the two-valued orientation is almost unavoidable. There is a profound "emotional" truth in the two-valued orientation that accounts for its adoption in strong expressions of feeling, especially those that call for sympathy, pity, or help in a struggle. "Down with slums and up with better housing." "A ship ticket NOW is a passage to life! Thousands of stanch anti-fascists face death this winter from disease and starvation." The more spirited the expression, indeed, the more sharply will things be dichotomized into the "good" and the "bad."

As an expression of feeling and therefore as an affective element in speaking and writing, the two-valued orientation almost always appears. It is hardly possible to express strong feelings or to arouse the interest of an apathetic listener without conveying to some extent this sense of conflict. Everyone who is trying to promote a cause, therefore, shows the two-valued orientation somewhere in the course of his writing. It will be found, however, that the two-valued orientation is *qualified* in all conscientious attempts at presenting what is believed to be truth—qualified sometimes, in the ways explained above, by pointing out what can be said against the "good" and what can be said for the "bad"—qualified at other times by the introduction, elsewhere in the text, of a multi-valued approach to the problems.

The two-valued orientation, in short, can be compared to a paddle, which performs the functions, in primitive methods of navigation, both of starter and steering apparatus. In civilized life the two-valued orientation may be the starter, since it arouses our interest with its affective power, but the multi-valued or infinite-valued orientation is our steering apparatus that directs us to our destination.

"The Hydrostatic Paradox of Controversy"

One of the principal points at which the two-valued orientation can seriously upset our thinking is in controversy. If *one* of the debaters has a two-valued orientation which leads him to feel that the New Deal, for example, is "entirely good" and the Republicans "entirely bad," he unconsciously forces his opponent into the position of maintaining that the New Deal is "entirely bad" and the Republicans "entirely good." If we argue with such a person at all, there is hardly any way to escape being put into a position as extreme on one side as his is on the other. This fact was well stated by Oliver Wendell

Holmes in his *Autocrat of the Breakfast-Table,* where he speaks of "the hydrostatic paradox of controversy":

Don't you know what that means?—Well, I will tell you. You know that, if you had a bent tube, one arm of which was of the size of a pipe-stem, and the other big enough to hold the ocean, water would stand at the same height in one as in the other. Controversy equalizes fools and wise men in the same way—*and the fools know it.*

Disputes in which this "equalization" is likely to occur are, of course, a waste of time. The *reductio ad absurdum* of this kind of discussion is often to be found in the high school and college "debate," as still practiced in many localities. Since both the "affirmative" and "negative" can do little other than exaggerate their own claims and belittle the claims of the opposition, the net intellectual result of such encounters is usually almost negligible, and decisions as to who "won" the debate must be made on such irrelevant points as skill of presentation and the pleasing personalities of the contestants. Parliaments and congresses, it will be observed, do not try to conduct much of their serious discussion on the floor. Speeches are made principally for the constituents back home and not for the other legislators. The main work of government is done in the committee room, where the traditional atmosphere of debate is absent. Freed from the necessity of standing resolutely on "affirmative" or "negative" positions, legislators in committee are able to thresh out

problems, investigate facts, and arrive at workable conclusions that represent positions in between the possible
extremes. It would seem that in training students to become citizens in a democracy, practice in sitting on and
testifying before committees of inquiry would be more
suitable than debating, after the fashion of medieval
school-men, for "victory."

The Two-Valued Orientation and the Mob Spirit

The use of the two-valued orientation in political and
social discussion is not confined, of course, to Hitler. It
is customary for all those whom we call "spread-eagle
orators" and "demagogues" to rely upon it as their principal argumentative technique. As in Germany, it produces here the results of intoxication, fanaticism, and
brutality. "What do they care," roars an orator of this
kind, "those international bankers and great corporate
warmongers, their fellow conspirators, the atheistic Jews
and communists, and their hireling politicians and editors—what do they care in their insatiable lust for power
for the right of the workingman to the fruits of his
labor, the right of a farmer to a decent living on the soil
he tills, and the right of the small businessman to the
modest rewards of his enterprise? We have been long-
suffering. We have been patient. But the time has come

when we must put a stop to these forces of international anarchy! The time has come for Americans to ARISE!" Listeners who uncritically permit themselves to be carried away by such oratory week after week almost invariably find their pulses rising, their fists clenching, and the desire to act violently accumulating within them.

This, of course, is what changes a peaceful assembly into a mob. It must be admitted, however, that the speaker cannot be held entirely to blame, since the tendency towards the two-valued orientation must exist in the listeners prior to the haranguing. The internal disturbance produced by such speeches is so great that an outlet must be found in some kind of activity. If, therefore, people in this condition are not restrained by the police, they are as likely as not to start rioting in the streets, throwing bricks in shop windows, and beating up strangers. Such intoxications are also responsible for lynching bees. Every kind of cruelty is inflicted upon anyone suspected of being on the "bad" side.

Accompanying such conduct, and indeed enabling it, is a tremendous sense of self-righteousness. People in whom a strict two-valued orientation has been inculcated ordinarily have no compunctions about any of the brutalities they commit, because they feel that "the dirty rats have it coming to them." They come to believe themselves to be instruments of divine justice. To be able to satisfy one's most primitive blood lusts and to be able at the same time to regard oneself as an instrument of justice is a rare combination of pleasures. Those who succumb frequently to this form of self-indulgence are likely, therefore, to become incurably addicted to brutality, as SS Guards are said to be in Germany and some policemen are said to be in this country.

Intoxications of this kind usually have alleged religious or patriotic motives. Sometimes the excuse for them is "the maintenance of law and order." The principal objection to them from a practical point of view is that they notoriously fail to achieve their objectives. The mobs that descend upon dissenting pacifistic or religious groups in order to compel them by force to kiss the flag do not advance the cause of national defense, but weaken it by creating burning resentments among those minorities. Southern lynch mobs do not solve the Negro problem; they simply make it worse. In short, the two-valued orientation produces the combative spirit, *but nothing else.* When guided by it for any purpose other than fighting, we practically always achieve results opposite from those intended.

Nevertheless, some orators and editorial writers employ the crude, unqualified two-valued orientation with extraordinary frequency, although in the alleged interests of peace, prosperity, good government, and other laudable aims. Do such writers and speakers do this because they know no better? Or are they so contemptuous of their audiences that they feel that a qualified statement such as "The opposition party's good points are outweighed by its bad points" would be too subtle for the public's comprehension? Another possibility is that they are sincere; they cannot help having signal reactions whenever certain hated subjects come into their minds. A final possibility, even less pleasant to think about, is that some of them are deliberately trying, under the cover of laudable objectives, to produce unrest, hatred, confusion, and civil disobedience, for obscure purposes of their own.

Applications

The two-valued orientation appears in each of the following passages, in crude form (accompanied by confusion of levels of abstraction), as well as at higher levels of feeling; qualified as well as unqualified. Analyze each of them carefully, especially in the light of the questions: "How much confidence can I safely repose in the judgment of the author of this passage? A great deal? None at all? Or is there not enough evidence to be able to say?" Be on guard against the assumption that the two-valued orientation is always a "bad" thing.

1. "Blessed is the man that walketh not in the counsel of the ungodly, nor standeth in the way of sinners, nor sitteth in the seat of the scornful. But his delight is in the law of the

Lord; and in his law doth he meditate day and night. And he shall be like a tree planted by the rivers of water, that bringeth forth his fruit in his season; his leaf also shall not wither; and whatsoever he doeth shall prosper.

"The ungodly are not so: but are like the chaff which the wind driveth away. Therefore the ungodly shall not stand in the judgment, nor sinners in the congregation of the righteous.

"For the Lord knoweth the way of the righteous: but the way of the ungodly shall perish."—Psalms 1

2. "I warn John L. Lewis and his communistic cohorts that no second carpetbag expedition into the Southland, under the Red banner of Soviet Russia and concealed under the slogans of the CIO, will be tolerated. If the minions of the CIO attempt to carry through the South their lawless plan of organization, if they attempt to demoralize our industry, to corrupt our colored citizens, to incite race hatreds and race warfare, I warn him here and now that they will be met by the flower of Southern manhood and they will reap the bitter fruits of their folly." [Quotation from Representative E. E. Cox of Georgia.]—STUART CHASE, *The Tyranny of Words*

3. "As a way of life democracy has now become synonymous with civilization: it is democracy, rather than communism, that is the real alternative to fascist barbarism. Evils of all sorts exist in democratic countries: exhibitions of arbitrary power, class exploitation, local outbreaks of collective sadism. . . . But, unlike fascism, democracy is not based upon the existence of these evils; nor does it exult in them and proclaim them to be the new virtues.

"So it comes to this. There is nothing that civilized men anywhere have developed and cherished that a democratic polity, as such, rejects: rather, it gives free play to all the forces and institutions and ideas that have led to the humanization of man: if fascism has contributed anything to the sum total of human knowledge or human development, democracy must be ready to include these lessons in its own synthesis.

"Fascism, on the other hand, distrusts civilization as such: under the impact of its monstrous collective demonism, it deliberately, as a necessary part of its mechanism of defense, tramples upon the humaner virtues."

LEWIS MUMFORD, *Men Must Act*

4. Avenge, O Lord, thy slaughtered saints, whose bones
Lie scattered on the Alpine mountains cold;
Even them who kept thy truth so pure of old,
When all our fathers worshiped stocks and stones,
Forget not: in thy book record their groans
Who were thy sheep, and in their ancient fold
Slain by the bloody Piemontese, that rolled
Mother with infant down the rocks. Their moans
The vales redoubled to the hills, and they
To heaven. Their martyred blood and ashes sow
O'er all the Italian fields, where still doth sway
The triple Tyrant; that from these may grow
A hundredfold, who, having learnt thy way,
Early may fly the Babylonian woe.

JOHN MILTON, "On the Late Massacre
in Piedmont"

12. AFFECTIVE COMMUNICATION

What I call the "auditory imagination" is the feeling for syllable and rhythm, penetrating far below the conscious levels of thought and feeling, invigorating every word; sinking to the most primitive and forgotten, returning to the origin and bringing something back, seeking the beginning and the end. It works through meanings, certainly, or not without meanings in the ordinary sense, and fuses the old and obliterated and the trite, the current, and the new and surprising, the most ancient and the most civilised mentality.

T. S. ELIOT

The devices of poetry are more than the devices of decoration, they are the devices of pressure.

JOSEPHINE MILES

THE LANGUAGE of science, as we have seen, is instrumental in getting done the work necessary for life, but it does not tell us anything about what life feels like in the living. We can communicate scientific facts to each other without knowing or caring about each other's feelings; but before love, friendship, and community can be established among men so that we *want* to co-operate and become a society, there must be a flow of sympathy between one man and another. This flow of sympathy is established, of course, by means of the affective uses of language. Most of the time, after all, we are not interested in keeping our feelings out of our discourse, but rather we are eager to express them as fully as we can. Let us examine, then, some more of the ways in which language can be made to work affectively.

Verbal Hypnotism

First, it should be pointed out again that fine-sounding speeches, long words, and the general *air* of saying something important are affective in result, regardless of what is being said. Often when we are hearing or reading impressively worded sermons, speeches, political addresses, essays, or "fine writing," we stop being critical altogether, and simply allow ourselves to feel as excited, sad, joyous, or angry as the author wishes us to feel. Like snakes under the influence of a snake charmer's flute, we are swayed by the musical phrases of the verbal hypnotist. If the author is a man to be trusted, there is no reason why we should not enjoy ourselves in this way now and then. But to listen or read in this way habitually is a debilitating habit. There is a kind of churchgoer who habitually listens in this way, however. He enjoys any sermon, no matter what the moral principles recommended, no matter how poorly organized or developed, no matter how shabby its rhetoric, so long as it is delivered in an impressive tone of voice with proper, i.e., customary, musical and physical settings. Such listeners are by no means to be found only in churches. The writer has frequently gnashed his teeth in rage when, after he has spoken before women's clubs on problems about which he wished to arouse thoughtful discussion, certain ladies have remarked, "That was such a lovely address, professor. You have such a nice voice." Some people, that is, never listen to *what* is being said, since they are interested only in what might be called the gentle inward massage that the *sound* of words gives them. Just as cats and dogs like to be stroked, so do some human beings like to be verbally stroked at fairly regular intervals; it is a form of rudimentary sensual gratification. Because listeners of this kind are numerous, intellectual shortcomings are rarely a barrier to a successful career in public life, on the stage or radio, on the lecture platform, or in the ministry.

More Affective Elements

The affective power of repetition of similar sounds, as in "catchy" titles and slogans (*The Mind in the Making, Live Alone and Like It,* Roosevelt or Ruin), has already been mentioned. Somewhat higher on the scale are repetitions not only of sounds but of grammatical structures, as in:

First in war,
first in peace,
first in the hearts of his countrymen . . .

Government of the people,
 by the people,
 for the people . . .

Elements of discourse such as these are, from the point of view of scientific reporting, extraneous; but without them, these phrases would not have impressed people. Lincoln could have signified just as much for scientific purposes had he said "government of, by, and for the people," or, even more simply, "a people's government." But he was not writing a scientific monograph. He hammers the word "people" at us three times, and with each apparently unnecessary repetition he arouses deeper and more affecting connotations of the word. It is impossible in a rapid survey to discuss in detail the complexities of the affective qualities of language that reside in sound alone, but it is important to remember that many of the attractions of literature and oratory have a simple phonetic basis—rhyme, alliteration, assonance, crossed alliteration, and all the subtleties of rhythm. All these sound effects are used to reinforce wherever possible the other affective devices.

Another affective device is the *direct address* to the listener or reader, as: "Keep off the grass. This means you!" The most painful example of this is Jimmie Fidler's "And I *do* mean you." It seeks to engage the listener's attention and interest by making him feel that he personally is being addressed. But the use of this device is by no means limited to the advertising poster and radio announcer. It softens the impersonality of formal speeches and adds what is called the "personal touch." When a speaker or writer feels a special urgency about his message, he can hardly help using it. It occurs, therefore, in the finest rhetoric as well as in the simplest. Almost as common as the "you" device is the "we" device. The writer in this case allies the reader with himself, in order to carry the reader along with him in seeing things as he does: "*We* shall now consider next . . ." "Let *us* take, for example . . ." "*Our* duty is to go forward . . ." This device is particularly common in the politer forms of exhortation used by preachers and teachers and is found throughout this book.

In such rhetorical devices as the *periodic sentence,* there is distortion of grammatical order for affective purposes. A periodic sentence is one in which the completion of the thought is, for the sake of the slight dramatic effect that can be produced by keeping the reader in suspense for a while, delayed. Then there are such devices as *antithesis,* a mild form of two-valued orientation—which is, as will be remembered, profoundly affective. In the antithesis, strongly opposed notions are placed close together or even laid side by side in parallel phonetic or grammatical constructions, so that the reader feels the contrast and is stirred by it: "Born a serf, he died a king." "The sweetest songs are those that tell of saddest thought." "The hungry judges soon the sentence sign, And wretches hang that jurymen may dine."

Metaphor and Simile

As we have seen, words have affective connotations in addition to their informative value, and this accounts for the fact that statements of this kind: "I've been waiting *ages* for you—you're an hour overdue!" "He's got *tons* of money!" "I'm so tired I'm simply *dead!*"—which are nonsensical if interpreted literally—nevertheless "make sense." The inaccuracy or inappropriateness of the informative connotations of our words are irrelevant from the point of view of affective communication. Therefore we may refer to the moon as "a piece of cheese," "a lady," "a silver ship," "a fragment of angry candy," or anything else, so long as the words arouse the desired feelings toward the moon or toward the whole situation in which the moon appears. This, incidentally, is the reason literature is so difficult to translate from one language to another—a translation that follows informative connotations will often falsify the affective connotations, and vice versa, so that readers who know both the language of the original and the language of the translation are almost sure to be dissatisfied, feeling either that "the spirit of the original has been sacrificed" or else that the translation is "full of inaccuracies."

During the long time in which *metaphor* and *simile* were regarded as "ornaments" of speech—that is, as if they were like embroidery, which improves the appearance of our linen but adds nothing to its utility—the psychology of such communicative devices was neglected. We have seen that as the result of what we have termed "confusion of levels of abstraction," we tend to assume that things that create in us the same responses are identical with each other. Let us say then, for example, that we are revolted by the conduct of an acquaintance at dinner and that we have had such a sense of revulsion before only when watching pigs at a trough. Our first, unreflecting reaction under such circumstances is naturally to say, "He is a pig." So far as our feelings are concerned, the man and the pig are identical with each other. Again, the soft winds of spring may produce in us agreeable sensations; the soft hands of lovely young girls also produce agreeable sensations; therefore, from the point of view of one expressing his feelings, "Spring has soft hands." This is the basic process by which we arrive at metaphor. Metaphors are not "ornaments of discourse"; they are direct expressions of feeling and are bound to occur whenever we have strong feelings to express. They are to be found in special abundance, therefore, in all primitive speech, in folk speech, in the speech of the unlearned, in the speech of children, and in the professional argot of the theater, of gangsters, and other lively occupations.

Simile

However, even at early stages of civilization it must have been apparent that calling a person a pig did not take sufficiently into consideration the differences between the person and the pig. Further reflection compels one to say, in modification of the original statement, "He is *like* a pig." Such an expression is called a *simile*—the pointing out of the similarities in our feelings towards the person and the pig. But it is important to notice the fact that the very notion of similarity implies the consciousness of differences, while at the earlier metaphor stage the pig and the person are identified. The simile, then, is something of a compromise stage between the direct, unreflective expression of feeling and the report, but of course closer to the former than to the latter.

Adequate recognition has never been given to the fact that what we call "slang" and "vulgarism" works on exactly the same principles as "great poetry" does. Slang makes constant use of metaphor and simile: "sticking his neck out," "to rubberneck," "out like a light," "baloney," "licorice stick" (clarinet), "punch-drunk," "weasel puss," "keep your shirt on." The imaginative process by which phrases such as these are coined is the same as that by which poets arrive at poetry. In poetry, there is the same love of seeing things in scientifically outrageous but emotionally expressive language:

> The hunchèd camels of the night
> Trouble the bright
> And silver waters of the moon.
>
> FRANCIS THOMPSON

> The snow doesn't give a soft white
> damn Whom it touches.
>
> E. E. CUMMINGS

> . . . the leaves dead
> Are driven, like ghosts from an enchanter fleeing,
> Yellow, and black, and pale, and hectic red,
> Pestilence-stricken multitudes.
>
> SHELLEY

> Sweet are the uses of adversity,
> Which like the toad, ugly and venomous,
> Wears yet a precious jewel in his head;
> And this our life exempt from public haunt,
> Finds tongues in trees, books in the running brook,
> Sermons in stones, and good in everything.
>
> SHAKESPEARE

> I saw Eternity the other night
> Like a great ring of pure and endless light.
>
> VAUGHAN

What is called "slang," therefore, might well be regarded as the poetry of everyday life, since it performs much the same function as poetry; that is, it vividly expresses people's feelings about life and about the things they encounter in life.

Personification

The reader is asked to recall the man in Chapter 9 who punched his car in the "eye." It will also be recalled that, to a limited extent, we all do something similar to this. So far as our feelings are concerned, there is no distinction between animate and inanimate objects. Our fright *feels* the same whether it is a creature or object that we fear. Therefore, in the expression of our feelings, a car may "lie down and die," the wind "kisses" our cheeks, the waves are "angry" and "roar" against the cliffs, the roads are icy and "treacherous," the mountains "look down" on the sea, machine guns "spit," revolvers "bark," volcanoes "vomit" fire, and the engine "gobbles" coal. This special kind of metaphor is called *personification* and is ordinarily described in textbooks of rhetoric as "making animate things out of inanimate." It is better understood, however, if we describe it as *not distinguishing between the animate and the inanimate.*

Dead Metaphor

No implication is intended, however, that because metaphor, simile, and personification are based ultimately upon primitive habits of thought they are to be avoided. On the contrary, they are among the most useful communicative devices we have, because by their quick affective power they often make unnecessary the inventing of new words for new things or new feelings. They are so commonly used for this purpose, indeed, that we resort to them constantly without realizing that we are doing so. For example, when we talk about the "head" of a cane, the "face" of a cliff, the "bowels" of a volcano, the "arm" of the sea, the "hands" of a watch, the "branches" of a river or an insurance company, we are using metaphor. A salesman "covers" an area; an engine "knocks"; a theory is "built up" and then "knocked down"; a government "drains" the taxpayers, and corporations "milk" the consumers. Even in so un-poetical a source as the financial page of a newspaper, metaphors are to be found: stock is "watered," shares are "liquidated," prices are "slashed" or "stepped up," markets are "flooded," the market is "bullish"; in spite of government efforts to "hamstring" business and "strangle" enterprise, there are sometimes "melons" to be "sliced"; although this is—but here we leave the financial page—"pure gravy" for some, others are left "holding the bag." Metaphors, that is to say, are so use-ful that they often pass into the language as part of its regular vocabulary. Metaphor is probably the most im-portant of all the means by which language develops, changes, grows, and adapts itself to our changing needs. When metaphors are successful, they "die"—that is, they become so much a part of our regular language that we cease thinking of them as metaphors at all.

To object to arguments, as is often done, on the ground that they are based on metaphors or on "metaphorical thinking" is rarely just. The question is not whether metaphors are used, but whether the metaphors represent valid similarities.

Allusion

Still another affective device is *allusion*. If we say, for example, standing on a bridge in St. Paul, Minnesota, in the early morning:

> Earth has not anything to show more fair;
> Dull would he be of soul who could pass by
> A sight so touching in its majesty . . .

we are evoking, in the mind of anyone familiar with the poem, such feelings as Wordsworth expressed at the sight of London in the early morning light in September, 1802, and applying them to St. Paul. Thus, by a kind of implied simile, we can give expression to our feelings. Allusion, then, is an extremely quick way of expressing and also of creating in our hearers shades of feeling. With a biblical allusion we can often arouse reverent or pious attitudes; with a historical allusion, such as saying that New York is "the modern Babylon," we can say quickly and effectively that we feel New York to be an extremely wicked and luxurious city, doomed to destruction because of its sinfulness; by a literary allusion, we can evoke the exact feelings found in a given story or poem as a way of feeling toward the event before us.

But allusions work as an affective device only when the hearer is familiar with the history, literature, people, or events alluded to. Family jokes (which are almost always allusions to events or memories in the family's experience) have to be explained to outsiders; classical allusions in literature have to be explained to people not familiar with the classics. Nevertheless, whenever a group of people—the members of a single family or the members of a whole civilization—have memories and traditions in common, extremely subtle and efficient affective communications become possible through the use of allusion.

One of the reasons, therefore, that the young in every culture are made to study the literature and history of their own linguistic or national groups is that they may be able to understand and share in the communications of the group. Whoever, for example, fails to understand such statements as "He is a regular Benedict Arnold," or "The president of the corporation is only a Charlie McCarthy; the Bergen of the outfit is the general manager," is in a sense an outsider to the popular cultural traditions of contemporary America. Similarly, one who fails to understand passing allusions to well-known figures in European or American history, to well-known lines in Chaucer, Shakespeare, Milton, Wordsworth, or the King James version of the Bible, or to well-known characters in Dickens, Thackeray, or Mark Twain may be said in the same sense to be an outsider to an important part of the traditions of English-speaking people. The study of history and of literature, therefore, is not merely the idle acquisition of polite accomplishments in order to be able to impress people, as "practical" men are fond of believing, but a necessary means both of increasing the efficiency of our communications and of increasing our understanding of what others are trying to communicate to us.

Irony, Pathos, and Humor

A somewhat more complex device, upon which much of humor, pathos, and irony depends, is the use of a metaphor, simile, or allusion that is so obviously inappropriate that a feeling of conflict is aroused: a conflict between our more obvious feelings towards that which we are talking about and the feelings aroused by the expression. In such a case, the conflicting feelings resolve themselves into a *third, new feeling*. Let us suppose, returning to our example above, that we are looking at an extremely ugly part of St. Paul, so that our obvious feelings are those of distaste. Then we arouse, with the

Wordsworth quotation, the feeling of beauty and majesty. The result is a feeling suggested neither by the sight of the city alone nor by the allusion alone, but one that is a product of the *conflict* of the two—a sharp sense of incongruity that compels us either to laugh or to weep, depending on the rest of the context. There are many complex shades of feeling that can hardly be aroused in any other way. If a village poet is referred to as the "Mudville Milton," for example, the conflict between the inglorious connotations of "Mudville" and the glorious connotations of "Milton" produces an effect of the ludicrous, so that the poet is exposed to contempt, although, if Craigenputtock can produce a Carlyle, there is no reason that Mudville should not produce a Milton. This somewhat more complex device may be represented graphically by a diagram borrowed from mathematics:

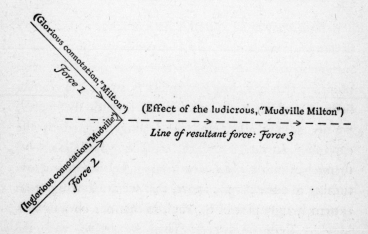

(Glorious connotation, "Milton")

Force 1

(Effect of the ludicrous, "Mudville Milton")

Line of resultant force: Force 3

(Inglorious connotation, "Mudville")

Force 2

The Affectiveness of Facts

We have already seen in the discussion of "slanting" that reports themselves, even if they are not intended to move the reader, may affect his feelings in one way or another. Even if we report as coldly and calmly as we can, "Although no anesthetics or surgical instruments were available, he said that the leg would have to be amputated. He performed the operation, therefore, with a butcher knife and a hatchet, while four men held the patient down," most readers will find such a report profoundly affective. Facts themselves, that is, are affective. There is, however, one important difference between the affectiveness of facts and the other affective elements in language. In the latter, the writer or speaker is expressing his own feelings; in the former, he is "suppressing his feelings"—that is to say, stating things in a way that would be verifiable, regardless of one's feelings.

Usually, as in the example given, a report with carefully selected facts is more affective in result than outright and explicit judgments. Instead of telling the reader, "It was a ghastly operation!" *we can make the reader say it for himself.* The reader is, so to speak, made to participate by being forced to draw his own conclusions. A skillful writer is often, therefore, one who is particularly expert at selecting the facts that are sure to move his readers in the desired ways. The following is a passage from a recent "Profile" in *The New Yorker:*

Several endocrinologists have tried vainly to argue Miss D—— into submitting to an examination. She is afraid of physicians. When sick, she depends on patent medicines. "When they get their hands on a monsterosity the medical profession is too snoopy," she says.

The facts reported about Miss D——, her fear of physicians, her addiction to patent medicines, the inelegance of her diction, and her reported mispronunciation of "monstrosity" lead almost inevitably to the conclusion that she is an ignorant and unintelligent person; but the writer *does not say so*. And we are therefore more likely to be convinced of this conclusion by such a passage than by explicit judgments to that effect because the writer does not ask us to take his word for it. The conclusion becomes, in a sense, our own discovery rather than his.

Levels of Writing

Reliance upon the affectiveness of facts—that is, reliance upon the reader's ability to arrive at the judgment we want him to arrive at—varies considerably, of course, according to the subject we are dealing with and the audience. When we say, for example, "His temperature was 105 degrees," practically any reader can be relied upon to feel, "What a bad fever!" but when we say,

"Mr. Jones's favorite poets were Edgar Guest and Shake-speare," there are among the possibilities such judgments as these: "How funny! Imagine not being able to distin-guish between Guest's tripe and Shakespeare's poetry!" and "Mr. Jones must be a nice fellow. They're my fa-vorites too." Now, if the remark is intended to be a sar-castic comment on Mr. Jones's undiscriminating taste, the sarcasm will altogether escape those who would give the latter response. This is what is meant by a remark being "over people's heads."

In this light, it is interesting to compare magazines and stories at different levels: the "pulp" and "confes-sion" magazines, the "slicks" (*Good Housekeeping, Mc-Call's, Esquire, Saturday Evening Post,* and so on), and the "quality" magazines (*Harper's, The New Yorker, The Nation,* for example). In all but the "quality" magazines, the writers rarely rely on the reader's ability to arrive at his own conclusions. In order to save any possible strain on the reader's intelligence, the writers *make the judgments for us.* In this respect there is little for us to choose between "pulps" and "slicks": they may give us statements in the form of reports, but they almost invariably accompany them with judgments, to make doubly and triply sure that the reader gets the point.

In the "quality" group, however, the tendency is to rely a great deal on the reader: to give no judgments at all when the facts "speak for themselves," or to give enough facts with every judgment so that the reader is free to make a different judgment if he so wishes. Passages of this kind, for example, are not uncommon in "pulps" and "slicks":

Elaine was—well, let's put it frankly—a trifle vulgar. She was pretty, of course, although in an obvious sort of way.

In the "quality" group, the treatment leaves a good deal more up to the reader:

Elaine dropped her cigarette into the remains of her coffee. As she stood up, she gave a couple of tugs at her skirt, and patted the ends of her curls.

The Evaluation of Literature

From what has been said, our first and most obvious conclusion is that since literature is principally the expression of feeling, affective elements are of the utmost importance in all literary writing. In the evaluation of a novel, poem, play, or short story, as well as in the evaluation of sermons, moral exhortations, political speeches, and directive utterances generally, the usefulness of the given piece of writing as a "map" of actual "territories" is always secondary—sometimes quite irrelevant. If this were not the case, *Gulliver's Travels, Alice in Wonderland, The Scarlet Letter,* or Emerson's *Essays* would have no excuse for existence.

Secondly, when we say that a given piece of affective writing is true, we do not mean "scientifically true." It may mean merely that we agree with the sentiment; it may also mean that we believe that a feeling has been accurately expressed; again, it may mean that the feelings it evokes are believed to be such as will lead us to better social or personal conduct. There is no end to the meanings "true" may have. People who feel that science and literature or science and religion are in necessary conflict have often in addition a two-valued orientation, so that everything is to them either "true" or "untrue." To such people, if science is "true," then literature or religion is nonsense; if literature or religion is "true," science is merely "pretentious ignorance." What should be understood when people tell us that certain statements are "scientifically true" is that they are useful and verifiable formulations, suitable for the purposes of organized co-operative workmanship. What should be understood when people tell us that the plays of Shakespeare or the Constitution of the United States are "eternally true" is that they produce in us attitudes toward our fellow men, an understanding of ourselves, or feelings of deep moral obligation that are valuable to humanity under any conceivable circumstances.

Thirdly, let us consider an important shortcoming of the language of reports and of scientific writing. John Smith in love with Mary is not William Brown in love

with Jane; William Brown in love with Jane is not
Henry Jones in love with Anne; Henry Jones in love
with Anne is not Robert Browning in love with Eliza-
beth Barrett. Each of these situations is unique; no two
loves are exactly alike—in fact, no love even between the
same two people is *exactly* the same from day to day.
Science, seeking as always laws of the widest possible
applicability and the greatest possible generality, would
abstract from these situations *only what they have in
common*. But each of these lovers is conscious only of
the *uniqueness* of his own feelings; each feels, as we all
know, that he is the first one in the world ever to have
so loved.

How is that sense of difference conveyed? It is here
that affective uses of language play their most important
part. The infinity of differences in our feelings towards
all the many experiences that we undergo are too subtle
to be reported; they must be expressed. And we express
them by the complicated manipulation of tones of voice,
of rhythms, of connotations, of affective facts, of metaphors, of allusions, of every affective device of language
at our command.

Frequently the feelings to be expressed are so subtle or
complex that a few lines of prose or verse are not enough
to convey them. It is sometimes necessary, therefore, for
authors to write entire books, carrying their readers
through numbers of scenes, situations, and adventures,

pushing their sympathies now this way and now that, arousing in turn their fighting spirit, their tenderness, their sense of tragedy, their laughter, their superstitiousness, their cupidity, their sensuousness, their piety. Only in such ways, sometimes, can the *exact* feelings an author wants to express be re-created in his readers. This, then, is the reason that novels, poems, dramas, stories, allegories, and parables exist: to convey such propositions as "Life is tragic" or "Susanna is beautiful," not by telling us so, but by putting us through a whole series of experiences that make us feel toward life or toward Susanna as the author did. *Literature is the most exact expression of feelings, while science is the most exact kind of reporting.* Poetry, which condenses all the affective resources of language into patterns of infinite rhythmical subtlety, may be said to be the language of expression at its highest degree of efficiency.

Scientific vs. Affective Communication

In a very real sense, then, people who have read good literature have lived more than people who cannot or will not read. To have read *Gulliver's Travels* is to have had the experience, with Jonathan Swift, of turning sick at the stomach at the conduct of the human race; to read *Huckleberry Finn* is to feel what it is like to drift down the Mississippi River on a raft; to have read Byron is to have suffered with him his rebellions and neuroses and to have enjoyed with him his nose-thumbing at society; to have read *Native Son* is to know how it feels to be frustrated in the particular way in which Negroes in Chicago are frustrated. This is the great task that affective communication performs: it enables us to feel how others felt about life, even if they lived thousands of miles away and centuries ago. It is not true that "we have only one life to live"; if we can read, we can live as many more lives and as many kinds of lives as we wish.

By means of scientific communication, then, with its international systems of weights and measures, international systems of botanical and zoological nomenclature, international mathematical symbols, we are enabled to exchange information with each other, pool our observations, and acquire collective control over our environment. By means of affective communication—by conversation and gesture when we can see each other, but by literature and other arts when we cannot—we come to understand each other, to cease being brutishly suspicious of each other, and gradually to realize the profound community that exists between us and our fellow men. Science, in short, makes us able to co-operate; the arts enlarge our sympathies so that we become willing to co-operate.

We are today equipped technologically to be able to get

practically anything we want. But our wants are crude. There seems to be only one ambition that is strong enough to impel us to employ our technological capacities to the full, and that ambition is the desire for tribal (national) aggrandizement—the desire to bomb our neighbors faster and more murderously than they can bomb us. The immediate task of the future, then, is not only to expand technology into fields where superstition now reigns—for example, economics and politics—and makes such calamities inevitable; it is also to bring, through the affective power of the arts and of literature, civilizing influences to bear upon our savage wills. We must not only be able to work together; we must actively want to work together.

Applications

All literary criticism that tries to find out what exactly an author is saying presupposes, of course, knowledge of principles such as those discussed in this chapter. Their real application can only be in abundant and careful reading and in the development of taste through *consciousness of what is going on* in every piece of literature one reads, whether it be a magazine serial, a Katherine Mansfield short story, or an Elizabethan play.

The subject of metaphor, however, offers an interesting side excursion. The following are additional examples of "dead metaphors." If their origin is not clear to you, look them up.

caterpillar tractor	incentive	auspicious
clew	poll tax	fourflusher
echelon	siren	crown gear
scale (in music)	High Sierras (mountains)	poached egg
pommel (of a saddle)		

The following expressions would look strange if one were conscious of the dead metaphors they contain. Look these up too, if you don't see why:

domestic economy
head of cabbage
afternoon matinee
They were good *companions*, but they never ate together.
He took the stars into *consideration*.
The *southpaw* was a *dextrous* pitcher and was exceedingly *adroit* in placing his fast curve ball. Nevertheless in most ways his manners were *gauche*, and there was something *sinister* about his appearance.

The reader may also find it instructive to make a list of the metaphorical expressions current in some one trade, profession, hobby, or sport with which he is familiar; for example, railroading, baseball, banking and finance, side show barking, aviation, jazz orchestra work, or the running of quick-lunch counters.

To get back, however, to the main business of this chapter, literary criticism: a useful practice, even for an experienced reader, is to take short passages of prose and verse—especially passages he has long been familiar with —and to find out by careful analysis not only what the author is saying, how he feels about his subject, and how he feels towards the reader, but also how the author conveys or reveals those feelings. The following passages may serve as additional material for this kind of analysis:

1. "It was a crisp and spicy morning in early October. The lilacs and laburnums, lit with the glory fires of autumn, hung burning and flashing in the upper air, a fairy bridge provided by kind Nature for the wingless wild things that have their home in the tree tops and would visit together; the larch and the pomegranate flung their purple and yellow flames in brilliant broad splashes along the slanting sweep of the woodland; the sensuous fragrance of innumerable deciduous flowers rose upon the swooning atmosphere; far in the empty sky a solitary oesophagus slept upon motionless wing; everywhere brooded stillness, serenity, and the peace of God."—MARK TWAIN

2. "They called a special meeting of the Board of Aldermen. A deputation waited upon her, knocked at the door through which no visitor had passed since she ceased giving china-painting lessons eight or ten years earlier. They were admitted by the old Negro into a dim hall from which a stairway mounted into still more shadow. It smelled of dust and disuse—a close, dank smell. The Negro led them into the parlor. It was furnished in heavy, leather-covered furniture. When the Negro opened the blinds of one window, they could see that the leather was cracked; and when they sat down, a faint dust rose sluggishly about their thighs, spinning with slow motes in the single sun-ray. On a tarnished gilt easel before the fireplace stood a crayon portrait of Miss Emily's father.

"They rose when she entered—a small, fat woman in black, with a thin gold chain descending to her waist and vanishing into her belt, leaning on an ebony cane with a tarnished gold head. Her skeleton was small and spare; perhaps that was why what would have been merely plumpness in another was obesity in her. She looked bloated, like a body long submerged in motionless water, and of that pallid hue. Her eyes, lost in the fatty ridges of her face, looked like two small pieces of coal pressed into a lump of dough as they moved from one face to another while the visitors stated their errand.

"She did not ask them to sit. She just stood in the door and listened quietly until the spokesman came to a stumbling halt. Then they could hear the invisible watch ticking at the end of the gold chain."—WILLIAM FAULKNER, "A Rose for Emily" [1]

3. "In this posture they travelled many hours, till they came into a wide and well-beaten road, which, as they turned to the right, soon brought them to a very fair promising inn, where they all alighted; but so fatigued was Sophia, that as she had sat her horse during the last five or six miles with great difficulty, so was she now incapable of dismounting from him without assistance. This the landlord, who had hold of her horse, presently perceiving, offered to lift her in his arms from her saddle; and she too readily accepted the tender of his service. Indeed fortune seems to have resolved to put Sophia to the blush that day, and the second malicious attempt succeeded better than the first; for my landlord had no sooner received the young lady in his arms, than his feet, which the gout had lately very severely handled, gave way, and down he tumbled; but, at the same time, with no less dexterity than gallantry, contrived to throw himself under his charming burden, so that he alone received any bruise from the fall; for the great injury which happened to Sophia was a violent

[1] Reprinted by permission of Random House, Inc.

shock given to her modesty by an immoderate grin, which, at her rising from the ground, she observed in the countenances of most of the bystanders. This made her suspect what had really happened, and what we shall not here relate for the indulgence of those readers who are capable of laughing at the offence given to a young lady's delicacy. Accidents of this kind we have never regarded in a comical light; nor will we scruple to say that he must have a very inadequate idea of the modesty of a beautiful young woman, who would wish to sacrifice it to so paltry a satisfaction as can arise from laughter."

HENRY FIELDING, *Tom Jones*

4.   To one who has been long in city pent,
        'Tis very sweet to look into the fair
        And open face of heaven—to breathe a prayer
    Full in the smile of the blue firmament.
    Who is more happy, when, with heart's content,
        Fatigued he sinks into some pleasant lair
        Of wavy grass, and reads a debonair
    And gentle tale of love and languishment?
    Returning home at evening, with an ear
        Catching the notes of Philomel—an eye
    Watching the sailing cloudlet's bright career,
        He mourns that day so soon has glided by:
    E'en like the passage of an angel's tear
        That falls through the clear ether silently.

JOHN KEATS

13. INTENSIONAL ORIENTATION

The man of understanding can no more sit quiet and resigned while his country lets its literature decay, and lets good writing meet with contempt, than a good doctor could sit quiet and contented while some ignorant child was infecting itself with tuberculosis under the impression that it was merely eating jam tarts.

EZRA POUND

Freedom of Communication

WE IN the United States, who enjoy about as much freedom of press and freedom of speech as can be found anywhere in the world, frequently forget that information in the form of books, news, and education was long considered too valuable a commodity to be distributed freely among the common people. This is still the case, of course, in many countries. All tyrannies, ancient and modern, go on the assumption on the part of the rulers that they know best what is good for the people, who should only have what information they think is advisable. Until comparatively recent times, education was withheld from all but the privileged classes. In some states of the union, for example, it used to be a criminal offense to teach Negroes to read and write. The idea of universal education was formerly regarded with as much horror by the "best people" as socialism is today. Newspapers, during the early days of journalism, had to be bootlegged, because governments were unwilling to permit them to exist. Books formerly could be published only after official permission had been obtained. It is no accident that freedom of speech and freedom of press go hand in hand with democracy and that censorship and suppression always accompany tyranny and dictatorship.

But the general suppression of information has rarely been completely successful, and since the invention of printing, telegraph, radio, and other means of communication, it has become even more difficult. Human beings, for the purposes of their own survival, insist upon getting knowledge from as many people as possible and also insist upon disseminating as widely as possible whatever knowledge they themselves may have found valuable. Authority and aristocratic privilege gain temporary victories, but for the past three or four hundred years at least, universal access to information has been, in spite of periodic war censorship, steadily increasing. In such a nation as the United States, where this tendency has had its fullest development, the principles of universal education and freedom of the press are rarely openly questioned. We can deliver speeches without showing our manuscripts in advance to the chief of police. Power presses, cheaper methods of printing, public circulating libraries, elaborate systems of indexing and reference which make possible the quick finding of practically any information anyone might want—these and many other devices are now in operation in order that we need not depend solely on our own experience, but may utilize the experience of the rest of humanity.

Nevertheless, the struggle for universal freedom of communication and the widest possible pooling of knowledge, even within the confines of the United States, is far from over. Standing in the way, first, are external difficulties. There are still millions of illiterates; good books are not everywhere available; there are many sections in our country without adequate schools; some communities have no libraries; our newspapers, although free of governmental interference, are too often in the control of those who tell us only what they want us to know.

Words as a Barrier

We are concerned here, however, with the conditions within ourselves that stand in the way of universal communication. The idealistic proponents of universal education believed that people able to read and write would automatically be wiser and more capable of intelligent self-government than illiterates. But we are beginning to learn that mere literacy is not enough. People who think like savages can continue to do so even after learning to read. As the result of the necessary abstractness of our vocabulary, general literacy has often had the effect of merely making our savagery more complicated and difficult to deal with than it was under conditions of illiteracy. And, as we have also seen, rapidity and ease of communication often make savagery infectious. Universal literacy has brought new problems of its own.

Because words are such a powerful instrument, we have in many ways a superstitious awe rather than an understanding of them—and even if we have no awe, we tend at least to have an undue respect for them. For example, when someone in the audience at a meeting asks the speaker a question, and when the speaker makes a long and plausible series of noises *without answering it, sometimes both the questioner and the speaker fail to notice that the question has not been answered; they both sit down apparently perfectly satisfied.* That is to say, the mere fact that an appropriate-sounding set of noises has been made satisfies some people that a statement has been made; thereupon they accept and sometimes memorize that set of noises, serenely confident that it answers a question or solves a problem.

Again, there are such incidents as the following. At a time when the action of a governor of Wisconsin in dealing with an official in the state university was being much discussed in the newspapers, the writer had occasion to travel through the state. Everywhere strangers and casual acquaintances who knew that the writer was connected with the university asked, "Say, what's the inside dope on that affair at the university? It's *all politics,* isn't it?" The writer never found out what anybody meant by "It's all politics," but in order to save trouble, he usually answered, "Yes, I suppose it is." Thereupon the questioner would look quite pleased with his own sagacity and say, "That's what I thought! Thanks for telling me." In short, the assurance that "politics" was the appropriate noise to make satisfied the questioner completely, in spite of the fact that the question which led to all the public discussion, namely, whether the governor had abused his political office or had carried out his political duty, had been left both unasked and unanswered. *This undue regard for words makes us tend to permit words to act as barriers between us and reality, instead of as guides to reality.*

Intensional Orientation

In previous chapters, we have analyzed particular kinds of misevaluation. All of these can now be summed up under one term: *intensional orientation*—the habit of guiding ourselves by *words alone,* rather than by the facts to which words should guide us. We all tend to assume, when professors, writers, politicians, or other apparently responsible individuals open their mouths, that they are saying something meaningful, simply because words have informative and affective connotations that arouse our feelings. When we open our own mouths, we are even more likely to make that assumption. The result of such indiscriminate lumping together of sense and nonsense is that "maps" pile up independently of "territory." And, in the course of a lifetime, we may pile up entire systems of meaningless noises, placidly unaware that they bear no relationship to reality whatever.

Intensional orientation may be regarded as the general cause leading to the multitude of errors already pointed out: the unawareness of contexts; the tendency towards signal reactions; the confusion of levels of abstraction— of what is inside one's head with what is outside; the consciousness of similarities, but not of differences; the habit of being content to explain words by means of definitions, that is, more words. By intensional orientation, "capitalists," "Bolsheviks," "farmers," and "working-men" "are" what we *say* they are; America "is" a democracy, because everybody *says* so; relief "destroys character" because it "logically follows" that if people are "given something for nothing," it's "bound to destroy their character."

Oververbalization

Let us take a term, such as "churchgoer," which *denotes* Smith$_1$, Smith$_2$, Smith$_3$ . . . , who attend divine services with moderate regularity. Note that the denotation says nothing about the "churchgoer's" character: his kindness to children or lack of it, the happiness or unhappiness of his married life, the honesty or dishonesty of his business practices. The term is applicable to a large number of people, some good, some bad, some poor, some rich, and so on. The intensional meanings or connotations of the term, however, are quite a different matter. "Churchgoer" suggests "good Christian"; "good Christian" *suggests* fidelity to wife and home, kindness to children, honesty in business, sobriety of living habits, and a whole range of admirable qualities. These suggestions further *suggest,* by two-valued orientation, that nonchurchgoers are likely not to have these qualities.

If our intensional orientations are serious, therefore, we can manufacture verbally a whole system of values—a whole system for the classification of mankind into sheep and goats—out of the connotations, informative and affective, of the term "churchgoer." That is to say, once the term is given, we can, by proceeding from connotation to connotation, keep going indefinitely. A map is independent of territory, so that we can keep on adding mountains and rivers after we have drawn in all the mountains and rivers that actually exist in the territory. Once we get started, we can spin out whole essays, sermons, books, and even philosophical systems on the basis of the word "churchgoer" without paying a particle of further attention to Smith$_1$, Smith$_2$, Smith$_3$ . . .

Likewise, give a good Fourth of July orator the word "Americanism" to play with, and he can worry it for hours, exalting "Americanism," making dreadful thundering noises at "foreign -isms," and evoking great applause from his hearers. There is no way of stopping this process by which free associations, one word "implying" another, can be made to go on and on. That is why, of course, there are so many people in the world whom one calls "windbags." That is why many orators, newspaper columnists, commencement day speakers, politicians, and high school elocutionists can speak at a moment's notice on any subject whatever. Indeed, a great many of the "English" and "speech" courses in our schools are merely training in this very thing—how to keep on talking importantly even when one hasn't a thing to say—or, to put it another way, how to conceal one's intellectual bankruptcy, not only from others, but also from oneself.

This kind of "thinking," which is the product of intensional orientation, is called *circular,* because, since all the possible conclusions are contained in the connotations of the word to start with, we are bound, no matter how hard or how long we "think," to come back to our starting point. Indeed, we can hardly be said ever to leave our starting point. How much energy is wasted per annum in the United States alone on this "circular thinking" is impossible to compute, but it must be enough to keep all the merry-go-rounds in the world going for a century. Of course, as soon as we are face to face with a fact, we are compelled to shut up or start over again somewhere else. That is why it is so "rude" in certain kinds of meetings and conversations to bring up any facts. They spoil everybody's good time.

Now let us go back to our "churchgoer." A certain Mr. William McDinsmore—the name is fictitious, of course—has had the term applied to him because of his habit of going to church. On examination, Mr. McDinsmore turns out to be, let us say, indifferent to his social obligations, unkind to his children, unfaithful to his wife, and dishonest in his trusteeship of other people's funds. If we have been habitually orientated towards Mr. McDinsmore by the intensional meanings of the word "churchgoer," this proves to be a shocking case. "How can a man be a churchgoer and so dishonest at the same time?" The problem is *completely incapable of solution for some people*. Unable to separate the intensional from the extensional "churchgoer," they are forced to one of three conclusions, all absurd:

1. "This is an exceptional case"—meaning, "I'm not changing my mind about churchgoers, who are always nice people *no matter how many exceptions you can find.*"
2. "He isn't *really* that bad! He *can't* be!"—that is, *denying* the fact in order to escape the necessity of accounting for it.
3. "All my ideals are shattered! A man can't believe any-

thing any more! My belief in human nature is destroyed!"—
that is, complete disillusionment, leading to cynicism.[1]

An unfounded complacency, which can so easily be followed by "disillusionment," is perhaps the most serious
consequence of intensional orientation. And, as we have
seen, we all have intensional orientation regarding some
subjects. Some of us go daily past gangs of WPA workers
sweating over the construction of roads and bridges and
still declare quite honestly, "I never saw a WPA worker
doing anything useful in all my life!" By the *definition*
some of us have, WPA is "made work"; "made work" is
not "real work"; therefore, even if WPA workers have
built schools, parks, and municipal auditoriums, they
weren't really working. Furthermore, many of us encounter daily hundreds of cars driven by women who
handle them expertly; yet we declare, again quite honestly, "I never saw a woman yet who could *really* drive
a car." By *definition,* women are "timid," "nervous," and
"easily frightened"; therefore, they "can't drive." If we
know women who have driven successfully for years, we
maintain that "they've just been lucky."

The important fact to be noticed about such attitudes

---

[1] Those who remember the storm of discussion that attended the publication of Sinclair Lewis's *Elmer Gantry* (1927) will recall how the
disputants divided into two main factions. First, there were those who
maintained that such a minister as Elmer Gantry—by intensional definition of "minister"—"couldn't possibly have existed," and that therefore Lewis had libeled the profession; secondly, there were the cynics
who hailed the book as "an exposé of religion." Neither conclusion
was, of course, justified by the novel.

towards "churchgoers," "WPA workers," and "woman drivers" is that we should never have made such mistakes nor so blinded ourselves if we had never heard anything about them beforehand. Such attitudes are not the product of ignorance; genuine ignorance doesn't have attitudes. They are the result of false knowledge—false knowledge that robs us of whatever good sense we were born with. As we have already seen, part of this false knowledge we make up for ourselves with our primitive habits of mind. However, a great deal of it is *manufactured* through our careless habits of *talking too much*.

Many people, indeed, are in a perpetual vicious circle. Because of intensional orientation, they are oververbalized; by oververbalization, they strengthen their intensional orientation. Such people burst into speech as automatically as juke boxes; a nickel in the slot, and they're off. With habits of this kind, it is possible for us to *talk ourselves into un-sane attitudes,* not only towards "woman drivers," "Jews," "capitalists," "bankers," and "labor unions," but also towards our personal problems: "mother," "relatives," "money," "popularity," "success," "failure"—and, most of all, towards "love" and "sex."

Outside Sources of Intensional Orientation: (1) Education

In addition to our own habits, there are verbal influences from without that tend to increase our intensional orientations. Of these, only three will be dealt with here: education, magazine fiction, and advertising.

Education really has two tasks. First, it is supposed to tell us facts about the world we live in: language is used *informatively*. Perhaps an even more important task, however, is that of inculcating ideals and "molding character"; that is, language is used *directively,* in order that students should conform to the usages and traditions of the society in which they live. In their directive function, therefore, schools tell us the "principles" of democracy— how democracy *ought* to work. But often they fail to perform their informative function. That is, they may fail to tell us how democracy *does* work: how the patronage system operates; what precinct captains and ward heelers do; how mayors, governors, and presidents are sometimes controlled by powers behind the throne; how legislative logrolling—"You vote for my bill and I'll vote for yours" —determines the fate of many bills.[1]

Again, schools tell how "good English" *ought* to be spoken and not how it *is* spoken. For example, we are all told that a double negative makes a positive, although nowhere is there any record of an officer of law holding a man on a charge of murder on the grounds that since the prisoner had said, "I ain't killed nobody," his words were actually a confession that he *had* killed *somebody.*

[1] There is today, however, a vigorous movement, especially on the part of social science teachers, to make secondary school education in such subjects as civics and government more informative than has been customary in the past.

Also, English teachers say that "there is no such word" as "ain't." They ignore the fact that the language of hill-billies, rustics, gangsters, and mugs is often more expressive, especially for purposes of affective communication, than what they call "good English."

Perhaps the greater part of education in some subjects is directive rather than informative. Law schools say much more about how law ought to work than about how it does work; the effects of the stomach ulcers, domestic troubles, and private economic views of judges upon their decisions are not regarded as fit topics for discussion in most law schools. History teachers of every nation often suppress or gloss over the disgraceful episodes in the histories of their nations. The reason for these silences and suppressions is that, although such statements may be informatively true, it is feared that they may, as directives, have bad effects on "impressionable minds."

Unfortunately, neither students nor teachers are in the habit of distinguishing between informative and directive utterances. Teachers issue such statements as "The United States is the greatest country in the world" and "Water is composed of oxygen and hydrogen" and ask their students to regard them as "true," *without telling them to distinguish between the two senses of the word "true."* Students thereupon find that some things their teachers say check with experience, while others are either questionable or false when examined as if they were informative statements. This creates among students, especially at around high school age, an uneasiness—a sense that their teachers are "stringing them along"—that leads many of them to leave school prematurely. Getting out of school, they feel that their suspicions about their teachers were correct, because, having mistaken the directive utterances they learned for informative, scientific utterances, they naturally find that they were "badly misinformed." Such experiences are probably the basis for that contempt for the "academic mind" which is so common in some circles. The fault is both the teacher's and the student's.

But those who continue in school are often no better off. Having indiscriminately lumped together directive and informative statements, they suffer shock and disillusionment when they get to a college where education is more realistic than that to which they have been accustomed. Other people continue all the way through college to confuse the directive and the informative; they may be aided in doing so by the unrealistic educational programs offered by the college. In such cases, the longer they go to school, the more badly adjusted they become to actualities. We have seen that directive language consists essentially of "maps" of "territories-to-be." We cannot attempt to cross a river on a bridge that is yet-to-be without falling into the water. Similarly students cannot be expected to guide their conduct exclusively by such statements as "Good always triumphs over evil" and "Our system of government ensures equality of opportunity to all men" without getting some terrible shocks. This may account in part for the fact that "bitterness," "disillusionment," and "cynicism" are particularly common among people during the first ten years after their graduation from college. Some people, indeed, never get over their shocks.

Education has to be, of course, both informative and directive. We cannot simply give information to students without giving them some "aspirations," "ideals," and "aims" so that they will know what to do with their information when they get it. But it is just as important to remember that we must not give them ideals alone without some factual information upon which to act; without such information they cannot even begin to bring their ideals to fruition. Information alone, students rightly insist, is "dry as dust." Directives alone, impressed upon the memory by frequent repetition, produce only intensional orientations that unfit students for the realities of life and render them liable to shock and cynicism in later years.

Outside Sources of Intensional Orientation: (2) Magazine Fiction

The next time the reader gets a printed slip giving "instructions for installation" with a car radio, a fog light, or similar piece of apparatus, he should notice how much close *attention* the reading of such a slip requires—how much constant checking with extensional facts: "The wires are distinguished from each other by colored threads in the insulation." We check and see if this is so. "Connect the positive wire, indicated by a red thread"—we find the wire—"with the terminal marked with the letter A . . ."

He should then contrast such a task of reading with that of reading a magazine story in one of the "pulp" or "slick" magazines. This latter task can be performed with hardly any attention whatever; we can keep the radio going full blast, we can be munching chocolates, we can be teasing the cat with our feet, we can even carry on desultory conversations without being unduly distracted from the story. The reading of the average magazine story, that is, requires no extensional checking whatsoever, neither by looking at the extensional world around us nor by furrowing our foreheads in attempts to recall apposite facts. The story follows nice, easy paths of *already established intensional orientations*. As we have already seen, the expected judgments are accompanied by the expected facts. The straying hubby returns to his mate, and the little wife who is "true blue" triumphs over the beautiful but unscrupulous glamour girl; the little son is a "tousled, mischievous, but thoroughly irresistible little darling"; the big industrialist is "stern, but has a kindly twinkle in his eye." Such stories are sometimes cleverly contrived, but they never, if they can help it, disturb anyone's intensional orientations. Although in real life communists are sometimes charming people, they are never presented as such, because in the light of intensional orientations, anyone called "communist" cannot at the same time be "charming." Although in real life Negroes often occupy positions of dignity and professional responsibility, in magazine stories they are never permitted to appear except as comic characters or as servants, because, by intensional orientation, Negroes should never be anything else.

There are two important reasons for the maintenance of intensional orientation in mass-production fiction, political articles, books, and radio dramas. The first is that it is easy on the reader. The reader is, after all, seeking relaxation. The housewife has just got the kids to bed; the businessman has had "a hard day at the office." They do not want to try to account for unfamiliar or disturbing facts. They *want* to daydream.

The other reason is, of course, that such writing is easy on the writer. In order to keep the market supplied, he has to produce so many thousands of words a week. Proceeding by intension, as we have seen, the orator can go on talking for hours. Likewise proceeding by intension, the "pulp" or "slick" story writer can, unencumbered by new facts to be explained or differences to be noted, keep on writing page after page. The resulting product is, to be sure, like paper towels, fit only to be used once and thrown away. Nobody ever reads a magazine story twice.

But, the reader may ask, since very few people take such stuff seriously anyway, why bother about it? The reason is that although we may not "take it seriously," our intensional orientations, which result from the word-deluge we live in, are deepened by such reading matter, although we may be quite unaware of the fact at the time. We must not forget that our excessive intensional orientations blind us to the realities around us.

Outside Sources of Intensional Orientation: (3) Advertising

Perhaps the worst offender of all in the creation of intensional orientations is advertising as it is now practiced. The fundamental purpose of advertising, the announcing of products, prices, new inventions, and special sales, is not to be quarreled with; such announcements deliver needed information, which we are glad to get. But advertising long ago ceased to restrict itself to the giving of needed information, and its principal purpose, especially in so-called "national advertising," has become the creating, in as many of us as possible, of *signal reactions*. That is to say, there is nothing that would profit the na-

tional advertiser more than to have us *automatically* ask
for Coca-Cola whenever we walked to a soda fountain,
automatically take Alka-Seltzer whenever we felt ill,
automatically ask for Chesterfields whenever we wanted
to smoke. Such automatic reactions are produced, of
course, by investing "brand names" with all sorts of desirable affective connotations, suggestive of health, wealth,
social prominence, domestic bliss, romance, personal popularity, fashion, and elegance. The process is one of creating in us *intensional orientations toward brand names:*

If you want love interest to thrive, then try this dainty way.
. . . For this way is glamorous! It's feminine! It's alluring!
. . . Instinctively, you prefer this costly perfume of Kashmir
Soap . . . It's a fragrance men love. Massage each tiny ripple
of your body daily with this delicate, cleansing lather . . .
Thrill as your senses are kissed by Kashmir's exquisite per-
fume. Be radiant.

Advertisers further promote intensional habits of mind
by playing on words: the "extras" of skill and strength
that enable champions to win games are equated with the
"extras" of quality that certain products are claimed to
have; the "protective blending" that harmonizes wild
animals with their environment and makes them invisible
to their enemies is equated with the "protective blending" of whiskies; a business association has for some time
been publicizing this masterpiece of obfuscation: "If you
work for a living you're in Business; what helps Business

helps you!" Even the few facts that advertising gives us are charged with affective connotations: "It's got vitamins! It's chock-full of body-building, bone-building, energy-building VITAMINS!!" Meaningless facts are also charged with significance: "See the New Hy-Speed Electric Iron. It's STREAMLINED!"

Advertising has become, in short, the art of overcoming us with words. When the consumer demands that, as a step towards enabling him to orientate himself by facts rather than by the affective connotations of brand names, all products be required by law to have informative labels and verifiable government grading, the entire advertising industry, backed by newspapers and magazines, raises a hue and cry about "government interference with business." The advertiser *prefers,* that is, that we be governed by signal reactions in favor of brand names rather than by consideration of the facts about products. This, of course, works considerable injustice on those advertisers—there are many—who have actual facts to talk about; they are likely to meet with a skepticism that they have done nothing to deserve.

When this advertising by verbal "glamorizing" succeeds in producing these intensional orientations, the act of washing with Kashmir Soap becomes, in our minds, a thrilling experience; brushing our teeth with Briten-Whyte Tooth Paste becomes, in our minds, a dramatic and timely warding off of terrible personal calamities, such as getting fired or losing one's girl friend; the smoking of cigarettes becomes, in our minds, the sharing of the luxuries of New York's Four Hundred; the taking of dangerous laxatives becomes, in our minds, "following the advice of a world-renowned Viennese specialist."[1] That is to say, we are sold daydreams with every bottle of mouth-wash, and delusions of grandeur with every package of breakfast-food.

The reader may say, again: If people want to pay for daydreams in their bath salts and want to battle imaginary diseases with imaginary cures, isn't that their business? It isn't entirely. The willingness to rely on words instead of examining facts is a disorder in the communicative process. Anything so important as the degeneration of human intercommunication is the concern of all of us. Intensional orientations—and they are increasing on every hand throughout the world as the result of the spread of literacy and the wide use of the radio— are, one might almost say, a kind of disease of the human evaluational process. It is our concern if our neighbors

---

[1] "But," some people are in the habit of saying, "surely nationally advertised products *must* be good! It stands to reason that a big advertiser couldn't afford to risk his reputation by selling inferior products!" A more perfect illustration of intensional orientation could hardly be found. Such people fail to realize, of course, that this is precisely the attitude that advertisers bank on. Yet these same people would hesitate to say, "Our public officials *must* be honest! It stands to reason that men in their position couldn't afford to risk their reputations by betraying the public interest."

have smallpox. It is also our concern if our fellow men are un-sane in their reactions to words; this disease too is, as we have seen, infectious. The uncritical response to the incantations of advertising is a serious symptom of widespread evaluational disorder. And it does not seem beyond the bounds of possibility that today's suckers for national advertising will be tomorrow's suckers for the master political propagandist who will, by playing up the "Jewish menace" in the same way as national advertisers play up the "pink tooth-brush menace," and by promising us national glory and prosperity in the same way as national advertisers promise us personal glory and prosperity, sell fascism in America.

14. RATS AND MEN

We have unprecedented conditions to deal with and novel adjustments to make—there can be no doubt of that. We also have a great stock of scientific knowledge unknown to our grandfathers with which to operate. So novel are the conditions, so copious the knowledge, that we must undertake the arduous task of reconsidering a great part of the opinions about man and his relations to his fellow-men which have been handed down to us by previous generations who lived in far other conditions and possessed far less information about the world and themselves. We have, however, first to create an unprecedented attitude of mind to cope with unprecedented conditions, and to utilize unprecedented knowledge.

JAMES HARVEY ROBINSON

SOME readers may have seen the article and pictures in the magazine *Life* of March 6, 1939, reporting an experiment with a rat, performed by Dr. N. R. F. Maier of the University of Michigan. The rat is first trained to jump off the edge of a platform at one of two doors. If it jumps to the right, the door holds fast, and the rat falls to the floor; if it jumps to the left, the door opens, and the rat finds a dish of food. When the rat is well trained to these reactions, the situation is reversed; the food is put behind the right door, and the left door is made fast. The rat, however, *continues to jump at the left door,* each time bumping its nose and falling to the floor. Finally, it refuses to jump at all and has to be pushed. When pushed, it again jumps to the *left*. Thereupon the right door is opened so that *the food is visible,* and again the rat is forced to jump. The rat, says the report, "persistently jumps at the same door as before, bumps its nose, grows more and more nervous as it finds it is up against an insoluble problem. In desperation, it leaps off the platform and races around the floor, bounces about like a kangaroo. When it stops, exhausted, it goes into trembling convulsions, then falls into a coma." In this passive state, it refuses to eat, refuses to take any interest in anything: it can be rolled up into a ball or suspended in the air by its legs—the rat has ceased to care what happens to it. It has had a "nervous breakdown." [1]

It is the "insolubility" of the rat's problem that leads to its nervous breakdown, and, as Dr. Maier cautiously intimates, it is the "insolubility" of human problems that leads many human beings to have nervous breakdowns. Rats and men seem to go through pretty much the same stages. First, they are trained to make habitually a given choice when confronted by a given problem; secondly, they get a terrible shock when they find that the conditions have changed and that the choice doesn't produce

[1] This account of Dr. Maier's experiment is, I am told, inaccurate. But since the inaccuracies are matters of detail which do not alter the principles involved, I have permitted it to stand as originally written on the basis of the article in *Life*.

the expected results; third, they continue making that choice anyway; fourth, they sullenly refuse to act at all; fifth, when by external compulsion they are forced to make a choice, they again make the one they were originally trained to make—and again get a bump on the nose; finally, even *with the goal visible in front of them,* to be attained simply by making a different choice, they go crazy out of frustration. They tear around wildly; they sulk in corners and refuse to eat; they cease to care what happens to them; bitter, cynical, disillusioned, they may even commit suicide.

Is this an exaggerated picture? It hardly seems so. The pattern recurs throughout human life, from the small tragedies of the home to the world-shaking tragedies among nations. In order to cure her husband's faults, a wife may nag him. His faults get worse, so she nags him some more. Naturally his faults get worse still—and she nags him even more. Governed, like the rat, by signal reactions to the problem of her husband's faults, she can meet it only in one way. The longer she continues, the worse it gets, until they are both nervous wrecks; their marriage is destroyed, and their lives are shattered.

Again, an industrialist may want to prevent strikes in his plant and may believe that the only way to do this is to prevent the formation of unions. He therefore fires union men. This may provoke his men into wanting to form a union strong enough to fight arbitrary dismissals, so that there is an increase of union activity. The increase in union activity makes the employer increase his anti-union activities; he hires labor spies and pays "loyal employees" to beat up union men and run them out of town. The more the union men are beaten up, the more determined they become; they want to "get back at him." The more aware the employer becomes of the hostility of his workers, the more angry and violent become his tactics. He stocks up on tear gas and munitions and organizes an army of company police. In the end, his plant is completely tied up in the bitter and bloody strike he was trying to avoid. When the National Labor Relations Board orders him to recognize the union, he nearly has an apoplectic fit. His physician recommends "complete quiet and rest"; reason, "nervous breakdown."

Again, a nation may believe that the only way to secure peace and dignity is through strong armaments. This makes neighboring nations anxious, so that they increase their armaments too. There is a war. The lesson of the war, the first nation declares when it is all over, is that we were not strongly enough armed to preserve peace; we must *double* our armaments. This naturally makes the neighboring nations twice as anxious, so that they double their armaments too. There is another war, bigger and bloodier. When this is over, the first nation declares: "We have learned our lesson. Never again shall we make the mistake of underestimating our defense needs. This time we must be *sure* to be sufficiently armed to preserve peace. This time we must *triple* our armaments. . . ."

Of course these instances are purposely oversimplified, but are not vicious circles of this kind responsible for the fact that we often are unable to get at or do anything about the conditions that lead to such tragedies? The pattern is frequently recognizable; the goal may be in sight, attainable only by a change in methods. Nevertheless, governed by signal reactions, the rat "cannot" get food, the wife "cannot" cure her husband's faults, strikes "cannot" be prevented, and wars "cannot" be stopped.

"Insoluble" Problems

How about our other apparently insoluble problems? Why do people maintain, in spite of all the fruit that is permitted to rot, all the grain that has to be stored away, all the coffee that has to be burned and dumped into the ocean in order to "stabilize prices," that we "cannot afford" to feed the unemployed and the undernourished? Why does every nation want to manufacture and sell to the people within its borders at higher prices the things it could import more cheaply from elsewhere? Why, if it continues to send away more of its natural resources, more of the products of its soil's fertility, more of the products of its labor than it receives in exchange from other nations, does it consider that it has a "favorable" balance of trade? Why do people speak bitterly about the illiteracy and ignorance of Negroes and then use their illiteracy and ignorance as grounds for opposing any measures for ameliorating their condition? The world is full of such absurd paradoxes, the most tragic feature of which is not simply that they exist and have existed for a long time, but that they are steadily becoming worse even as we struggle over their solution.

These are problems which "conservatives" and "liberals" agree are serious and fundamental. Almost all of us recognize that dislocations like these are likely to wreck us. Yet we are incapable of doing anything to save ourselves. Why? Is there not enough intelligence and understanding in the minds of human beings to find a way out? Are we incapable of finding grounds for agreement sufficient to act upon?

The fault does not lie in any lack of "brains." Nor does it lie in our inability to control our physical environment, for human beings have amply demonstrated that they can perform near miracles in science, medicine, and the construction of machinery. The point at which we fail is in organizing human co-operation—in using the machinery of human communication.

These problems which were touched upon above are admittedly complex. It is not a question of their being "all in the mind," and it is not denied that one reason they are so difficult is that many conflicting interests are involved.

They are not, however, insoluble. Perhaps the most dramatic thing about human behavior is how many "insoluble" problems are promptly solved when the necessity is pressing enough. It would have been "impossible" to send the slum children of London to the country for the sake of their health. But when the war began, the evacuation took place over a week end. It was demonstrated time and again that it was "impossible" for German economy to continue without a gold supply. That was seven or eight years ago. Of course the things done in wartime are not always good things. But they do show the almost unlimited capacity of human beings for performing the "impossible" when driven to it. What is tragic is that they have to be driven. The things that should be done to prevent disasters are thought of as "impossible" for too long.

That is another of the "insoluble" problems of our democracy, the inability to act before it is too late. This is a reference not only to war preparations. We had to wait until a third of our irreplaceable topsoil had been eroded away before taking proper conservation measures; we waited until the Indian population was almost wiped out by disease and their ancient culture had almost been destroyed by miseducation and economic stress before beginning to mend our ways in the treatment of Indians and trying to revive their almost vanished arts. What prevents us from acting? First of all, of course, there is the inertia which makes us prefer the evils that we have over others that we know not of. But our national resistance to any and all changes involves more than that; it has elements of pathology in it.

Why We Are Stalled

It is natural, though often shortsighted, for people whose pocketbooks or personal comfort will be immediately affected to oppose specific suggestions. A farmer whose land will be flooded by a proposed dam quite naturally would rather have the dam flood someone else's land. Nevertheless, if the dam is for the benefit of hundreds of thousands of people whose interests outweigh those of the farmer, he is compensated for the land and required to move. Here the question is quite simple and capable of extensional examination. "What," we ask, "will be the results? How many members of society will be benefited, and in what ways? How many will be harmed, and in what ways?" The decision follows the results of the examination.

There are cases, however, in which no such examination of extensional facts takes place, at least on the part of the general public. In at least one instance, the enforced removal of farm families was made the basis for opposition to a dam, and all sorts of appeals were made to the public to resist "government oppression" and to defend "justice" and "human rights." The instigators of the appeals were not the farmers who were being removed, but other people who had other reasons for opposing the dam. Doubtless, however, because they thought their own case was not very strong, they conducted the fight *at a higher level of abstraction*—on the basis of the "oppression" of the "underdog."

Now "rights" and "justice" being very fine things and "oppression" being a very bad thing, an intensionally orientated public responded like automatons to this appeal to their two-valued orientation. The fact was overlooked that whenever a highway, a railroad, or an army camp is to be located in a particular place, many people suffer from the enforced condemnation of land. If the power to condemn did not exist, many things society needs could never be built. Nevertheless, a great deal of hysterical sympathy was aroused for the farmers, so that even those who benefited from the dam when it was finally built were in many cases unhappy about the benefits; they felt that a "wrong principle" had triumphed, and their intensional definition of "government" as an "oppressive power" was deepened and perpetuated. All this could have been debated sanely with reference to the extensional facts if it had not been for the profound intensional orientations which existed in people's minds, ready to be exploited by those who wished to exploit them.

In any one case of proposed change, what portion of society will be benefited and what portion will be adversely affected can be demonstrated within a reasonable margin of error. The issues debated, however, are never put in the form: "Will the (extensional) results outweigh the (extensional) hardships involved?" Instead the proposal is denounced as "visionary," "reactionary," "leading towards state socialism," or "paving the way for dictatorship." There are few facts which the defenders of the scheme can bring forward that will stand up against powerful words such as these with an intensionally orientated public.

The affective connotations of a word are more powerful than the informative. "Planning" has become such a loaded word that to accuse a politician of advocating "planning" may ruin his political career. This in spite of the fact that "planning" under other names is essential not only to any well-run business, but to the conduct of the life of an individual. This, also, when these same people who denounce "planning" suffer from many of the economic hardships which come as a result of *not* "planning." The word, however, suggests to the intensionally orientated "the Five Year Plan" and, going up the abstraction ladder, "communism," "oppression," "regimentation," and "godlessness." If we were all extensionally orientated, however, our worry would not be whether or not the suggestion can be classified as "planning," but *what is planned* and what good or harm it is going to do.

These mental blockages which so many of us have prevent us from meeting our "insoluble" problems with the only approach which can ever help us solve them: the extensional approach—for we cannot distribute goods or carry on trade by intensional definitions or high level abstractions. That which is done in the extensional world must be done by extensional means, no matter who does them. If we as citizens of a democracy are going to carry our share in the important decisions about the things that concern us so greatly, we must prepare ourselves to do so by coming down out of the clouds of abstractions and learning to consider the extensional problems of our society as we now consider the extensional problems of feeding ourselves and getting clothes and shelter. If, however, we continue to cling to our intensional orientations, with the signal reactions they produce, we shall have to continue behaving like Dr. Maier's rat. We shall be victims of whoever wishes to call forth our signal reactions for whatever purposes. We shall remain pathologically incapable of changing our ways of behavior, and there will be nothing for us to do but, like the rat, to try the same wrong solutions over and over again. After prolonged repetition of such futile conduct, would it be remarkable if we found ourselves finally in a condition of political "nervous breakdown"—sick of trying, and willing to permit a dictator to dangle us upside down by our tails?

Science is daily putting new and wonderful instruments into our hands for the controlling of our environment and therefore for the potential enrichment of our lives. But they require adult *human* nervous systems for their safe handling. A chimpanzee, as we have seen, cannot drive a car in a stream of modern traffic without bringing disaster upon both himself and others. Similarly, if the majority of human beings are governed in their personal, social, and political thinking by signal reactions, they can hardly be expected to handle the resources of modern civilization without bringing disaster upon themselves. Yet not only are persons of great influence, including rulers of nations, willing to exploit the signal reactions of others; many of them have as many and as serious signal reactions as any of the people whom they govern. And such rulers, using the press and radio to spread their own verbal confusions as well as to arouse the tribal, religious, and economic superstitions of their people, make madness epidemic. No wonder, then, that the skies of Europe and Asia are filled with bombing planes.

The Scientific Attitude

Can we do no better than rats? Of course we can, and in some things we do. The scientist, when he finds a problem "insoluble," frequently solves it. It was "impossible" to devise means of traveling over twenty miles an hour, but now we can travel four hundred miles an hour. It was "impossible" for man to fly—people "proved" it again and again—but now we can fly across oceans. The scientist may almost be called the professional accomplisher of the "impossible." He does this because, as scientist, he is extensionally orientated. He may be, and often is, intensionally orientated towards what he calls "nonscientific subjects"; therefore, the scientist talking about politics or ethics is often no more sensible than the rest of us.

As we have seen, scientists have special ways of talking about the phenomena they deal with, special "maps" describing their "territories." On the basis of these "maps," they make predictions; when things turn out as predicted, they regard their "maps" as "true." If things do not turn out as predicted, however, they *discard* their "maps" and make new ones; that is, they act on new sets of hypotheses that suggest *new courses* of action. Again, they check their "map" with the "territory." If the new one does not check, they cheerfully discard it and make still more hypotheses, until they find some that *work*. These they regard as "true," but "true" *for the time being only.* When, later on, they find new situations in which they do not work, they are again ready to discard them, to re-examine the extensional world, and to make new "maps" that again suggest *new courses of action.*

When scientists work with a minimum of interference from pecuniary or political influences—when, that is, they are free to pool their knowledge with their co-workers all over the world and to check the accuracy of each other's "maps" by observations independently made and freely exchanged—they make rapid progress. Highly multi-valued and extensional in their orientations, they are troubled less than any other men by fixed dogmas and nonsense questions. The last thing a scientist would do would be to cling to a "map" because he inherited it from his grandfather or because it was used by George Washington or Abraham Lincoln. By intensional orientation, "If it was good enough for Washington and Lincoln, it's good enough for us." By extensional orientation, *we don't know until we have checked.*

The Left-Hand Door Again

Notice the differences between the technological, scientific attitudes that we have towards some things and the intensional attitudes that we have towards others. When we are having a car repaired, we do not ask: "Is the remedy you suggest consistent with the principles of thermodynamics? What would Faraday or Newton have done under similar circumstances? Are you sure this does not

represent a degenerative, defeatist tendency in the technological traditions of our nation? What would happen
if we did this to *every* car? What has Aristotle to say on
this?" These are nonsense questions. We only ask, "What
will be the *results?*"

But a different thing happens when we are trying to
have society repaired. Few people ask what will be the
practical results of a proposed social change. Remedies
suggested are almost always discussed in the light of questions to which verifiable answers cannot be given: "Are
your proposals consistent with sound economic policy?
Do they accord with the principles of justice and reason?
What would Alexander Hamilton, Thomas Jefferson, or
Andrew Jackson have said? Would it be a step in the
direction of communism or fascism? What would happen in the long run if everybody followed your scheme?
Why don't you read Aristotle on politics?" And we spend
so much time discussing nonsense questions that often we
never get around to finding out exactly what the results
of proposed actions would be.

During the course of our weary struggles with such
nonsense questions, someone or other is sure to come
along with a campaign to tell us, "Let's get *back* to nor-
malcy. . . . Let's stick to the good *old-fashioned, tried-
and-true* principles. . . . Let's *return* to *sound* economics
and *sound* finance. . . . America must get *back* to this.
. . . America must get *back* to that. . . ." Most of such

appeals are, of course, merely invitations to take another jump at the left-hand door—in other words, INVITATIONS TO CONTINUE DRIVING OURSELVES CRAZY. In our confusion we accept those invitations—with the same old results.

15. EXTENSIONAL ORIENTATION

> *It is evident that all the sciences have a relation, greater or less, to human nature; and that, however wide any of them may seem to run from it, they still return back by one passage or another. . . . Here, then, is the only expedient, from which we can hope for success in our philosophical researches: to leave the tedious lingering method which we have hitherto followed, and, instead of taking now and then a castle or village on the frontier, to march directly to the capital or center of these sciences—to human nature itself—which, being once masters of, we may elsewhere hope for an easy victory.*
>
> DAVID HUME

Rules for Extensional Orientation

JUST as a mechanic carries around a pair of pliers and a screw driver for use in an emergency—just as we all carry around in our heads tables of multiplication for daily use—so can we all carry with us in our heads convenient rules for extensional orientation. These rules need not be complicated; a short, rough-and-ready set of formulas will do. Their principal function will be to prevent us from going around in circles of intensional thinking, to prevent signal reactions, to prevent us from trying to answer unanswerable questions, to prevent us from repeating old mistakes endlessly. They will *not* magically show us what better solutions are possible, but they will *start us looking* for better courses of action than the old ones. The following rules, then, are a brief summary of the more important parts of this book. These rules should be *memorized*.

1. A map is NOT the territory it stands for; words are NOT things.

A map does not represent ALL of a territory; words never say ALL about anything.

Maps of maps, maps of maps of maps, and so on, can be made indefinitely, with or without relationship to a territory.

2. Contexts determine meaning.

> I like fish. (Cooked, edible fish.)
> He caught a fish. (Live fish.)
> You poor fish! (Not fish at all.)
> To fish for compliments. (To seek.)

3. The meanings of words are NOT in the words; they are in US.

4. Beware of the word *"is,"* which can cause more trouble than any other word in the language:

The grass *is* green. (But what about the part our nervous system plays?)
Mr. Miller *is* a Jew. (Beware of confusing levels of abstraction.)

Business *is* business. (A directive.)
A thing *is* what it *is*. (Is it? And for how long?)

5. DON'T try to cross bridges that aren't built yet. Distinguish between directive and informative statements.

6. DON'T sock a car in the eye when it stalls.

7. The two-valued orientation is the *starter, not the steering apparatus*.

8. BEWARE OF DEFINITIONS: In one way, they say *too much*—a "chair" is *not always* "something to sit in"; in another way, they *never say enough,* because characteristics are left out in any verbalization.

9. Use INDEX NUMBERS and DATES as reminders that NO WORD EVER HAS EXACTLY THE SAME MEANING TWICE.

Cow_1 is *not* cow_2, cow_2 is *not* cow_3, . . .
Jew_1 is *not* Jew_2, Jew_2 is *not* Jew_3, . . .
$Smith_{1939}$ is *not* $Smith_{1940}$, $Smith_{1940}$ is *not* $Smith_{1941}$, . . .

10. When you are "disillusioned," "cynical," and "beset with doubts," DOUBT YOUR DOUBT.

If these rules are too much to remember, the reader is asked to memorize *at least* this much:

COW_1 IS NOT COW_2, COW_2 IS NOT COW_3, . . .

This is the simplest and most general of the rules for extensional orientation. The word "cow" gives us the intensional meanings, informative and affective; it calls up in our minds the features that this "cow" has *in common* with other "cows." The index number, however, reminds us that this one is *different;* it reminds us that "cow" does *not* tell us "all about" the event; it reminds us of the *characteristics left out* in the process of abstracting; it prevents us from equating the word with the thing, that is, from confusing the abstraction "cow" with the extensional cow and having a signal reaction.

Symptoms of Disorder

Not to observe, consciously or unconsciously, such principles of interpretation is to think and react like savages or children. There are a number of ways in which we can detect signal reactions in ourselves. One of the most obvious symptoms is sudden displays of temper. When blood pressure rises, quarrels become excited and feverish, and arguments end up in snarling and name calling, there is usually a signal reaction somewhere in the background.

Another obvious symptom is worry—when we keep going round and round in circles. "I love her. . . . I love her. . . . Oh, if I could only forget that she is a *waitress!* . . . What will my friends think if I marry a *waitress?* . . . But I love her. . . . If only she weren't a *waitress.*" But waitress$_1$ is not waitress$_2$. "Gosh, what a terrible governor we've got! . . . We thought he was a businessman, but he proves to be only a *politician.* . . . Now that I think of it, the last governor wasn't too bad. . . . Oh,

but he was a *politician,* too, and how he *played politics!*
. . . Can't we ever get a governor who isn't a *politician?"*
But politician₁ is not politician₂. As soon as we break these
circles and think about *facts* instead of *words,* new light
is thrown on our problems.

Still another symptom of our signal reactions is a tendency to be "oversensitive," "easily hurt," and "quick to
resent insults." The infantile mind, equating words with
things, regards unkind words as unkind acts. Attributing to harmless sets of noises a power of injuring, such a
person is "insulted" when those noises are uttered at him.
So-called "gentlemen" in semi-savage and infantile societies used to dignify signal reactions of this kind into
"codes of honor." By "honor," they meant extreme readi-
ness to pull out swords or pistols whenever they imagined
that they had been "insulted." Naturally, they killed each
other off much faster than was necessary, illustrating
again a principle often implied in this book: the lower
the boiling point, the higher the mortality rate.

It has already been pointed out that the tendency to
talk too much and too readily is an unhealthy sign. We
should also be wary of "thinking too much." It is a mistake to believe that productive thinkers necessarily "think
harder" than people who never get anywhere. They only
think more efficiently. "Thinking too much" often means
that somewhere in the back of our minds there is a "certainty"—an "incontrovertible fact," an "unalterable law,"

an "eternal principle"—some statement which we believe "says all" about something. Life, however, is constantly throwing into the face of our "incontrovertible certainties" facts that do not fit our preconceptions: "communists" who *don't* need a shave, "politicians" who *aren't* corrupt, "friends" who *aren't* faithful, "benevolent societies" that *aren't* benevolent, "insurance companies" that *don't* insure. Refusing to give up our sense of "certainty" and yet unable to deny the facts that do not fit, we are forced to "think and think and think." And, as we have seen before, there are only two ways out of such dilemmas: first, to deny the facts altogether, and secondly, to reverse the principle altogether, so that we go from *"All* insurance companies are safe" to *"No* insurance companies are safe." Hence such infantile reactions as, "I'll *never* trust another woman!" "Don't *ever* say politics to me again!" "I'm through with newspapers for good!" "Men are all alike, the heels!"

The mature mind, on the other hand, knows that words never say all about anything, and it is therefore *adjusted to uncertainty*. In driving a car, for example, we never know what is going to happen next; no matter how often we have gone over the same road, we never find *exactly* the same traffic conditions. Nevertheless, a competent driver travels over all kinds of roads and even at high speeds without either fear or nervousness. As driver, he is adjusted to uncertainty—the unexpected blowout or the sudden hazard—and he is not insecure.

Similarly the intellectually mature person does not "know all about" anything. And he is not insecure, because he knows that the only kind of security life offers is the *dynamic security that comes from within: the security derived from infinite flexibility of mind—from an infinite-valued orientation.*

"Knowing all" about this, "knowing all" about that, we have only ourselves to blame when we find certain problems "insoluble." With some working knowledge of how language acts, both in ourselves and others, we save both time and effort; we prevent ourselves from being driven mad in verbal squirrel cages. With an extensional orientation, we are adjusted to the inevitable uncertainties of all our science and wisdom. And whatever other problems the world thrusts upon us, we at least escape those of our own making.

Reading Towards Sanity

A few words, finally, need to be said on the subject of reading as an aid to extensional orientation. Studying books too often has the effect of producing excessive intensional orientation; this is especially true in literary study, for example, when the study of words—novels, plays, poems, essays—becomes an end in itself. When the study of literature is undertaken, however, not as an end in itself, but as a guide to life, its effect is extensional in the best sense.

Literature works by intensional means; that is, by the manipulation of the informative and affective connotations of words. By these means, it not only calls our attention to facts not previously noticed, but it also is capable of arousing feelings not previously experienced. These new feelings in turn call our attention to still more facts not previously noticed. Both the new feelings and the new facts, therefore, upset our intensional orientations, so that our blindness is little by little removed.

The extensionally orientated person, as has been repeatedly said, is governed not by words only, but by the facts to which the words have guided him. But supposing there were no words to guide us? Should we be able to guide ourselves to those facts? The answer is, in the vast majority of cases, no. To begin with, our nervous systems are extremely imperfect, and we see things only in terms of our training and interests. If our interests are limited, we see extremely little; a man looking for cigarette butts in the street sees little else of the world passing by. Furthermore, as everyone knows, when we travel, meet interesting people, or have adventures before we are old enough to appreciate such experiences, we often feel that we might just as well not have had them. Experience itself is an extremely imperfect teacher. Experience does not tell us what it is we are experiencing. Things simply happen. And if we do not know *what to look for* in our experience, they often have no significance to us whatever.

Many people put a great deal of stock in experience as such; they tend automatically to respect the person who has "done things." "I don't want to sit around reading books," they say; "I want to get out and *do things!* I want to travel! I want to have experiences!" But often the experiences they go out and get do them no good whatever. They go to London, and all they remember is their hotel and the American Express Company office; they go to China, and their total impression is that "there were a lot of Chinamen there"; they may be caught in a South American revolution in the course of their travels and remember only their personal discomforts. The result often is that people who have never had these experiences, people who have never been to those places, know more about them than people who have. We all tend to go around the world with our eyes shut unless someone opens them for us.

This, then, is the tremendous function that language, in both its scientific and its affective uses, performs. In the light of abstract scientific generalizations, "trivial" facts lose their triviality. When we have studied, for example, surface tension, the alighting of a dragonfly on a pool of water is a subject for thought and explanation. In the light of reading *The Grapes of Wrath,* a trip through California is a doubly meaningful experience. And we turn and look at migrant families in all other parts of the country as well, because Steinbeck has created in us new ways of feeling about a subject that we may formerly have ignored. In the light of the subtleties of feeling aroused in us by the great literature and poetry of the past, every human experience is filled with rich significances and relationships.

The communications we receive from others, insofar as they do not simply retrace our old patterns of feeling and tell us things we already know, increase the efficiency of our nervous systems. Poets, as well as scientists, have truly been called "the window washers of the mind"; without their communications to widen our interests and increase the sensitivity of our perceptions, we could very well remain as blind as puppies.

Much of this book may have sounded like warnings against words. Such has not been its purpose. Words are, as has been said from the beginning, the essential instruments of man's humanity. This book only asks the reader to treat them as such.

READINGS

I. From Chapter XIV of

THE ADVENTURES OF HUCKLEBERRY FINN [1]

by MARK TWAIN

The feeling that one's own way of talking is the only sensible way to talk has rarely been expressed so eloquently or with such devastating logic as by Jim, the runaway slave.

WHY, HUCK, doan' de French people talk de same way we does?"

"*No,* Jim; you couldn't understand a word they said—not a single word."

"Well, now, I be ding-busted! How do dat come?"

"*I* don't know; but it's so. I got some of their jabber out of a book. S'pose a man was to come to you and say Polly-voo-franzy—what would you think?"

"I wouldn' think nuffin; I'd take en bust him over de head—dat is, if he warn't white. I wouldn't 'low no nigger to call me dat."

"Shucks, it ain't calling you anything. It's only saying, do you know how to talk French?"

"Well, den, why couldn't he say it?"

"Why, he *is* a-saying it. That's a Frenchman's *way* of saying it."

---

[1] Reprinted by permission of Harper and Brothers, Inc.

"Well, it's a blame ridicklous way, en I doan' want to hear no mo' 'bout it. Dey ain' no sense in it."

"Looky here, Jim; does a cat talk like we do?"

"No, a cat don't."

"Well, does a cow?"

"No, a cow don't, nuther."

"Does a cat talk like a cow, or a cow talk like a cat?"

"No, dey don't."

"It's natural and right for 'em to talk different from each other, ain't it?"

"Course."

"And ain't it natural and right for a cat and a cow to talk different from us?"

"Why, mos' sholy it is."

"Well, then, why ain't it natural and right for a *Frenchman* to talk different from us? You answer me that."

"Is a cat a man, Huck?"

"No."

"Well, den, dey ain't no sense in a cat talkin' like a man. Is a cow a man?—er is a cow a cat?"

"No, she ain't either of them."

"Well, den, she ain't got no business to talk like either one er the yuther of 'em. Is a Frenchman a man?"

"Yes."

"*Well,* den! Dad blame it, why doan he *talk* like a man? You answer me *dat!*"

II. From "Sixth-Century Political Economy,"
    Chapter XXXIII, of

A CONNECTICUT YANKEE
IN KING ARTHUR'S COURT [1]

by MARK TWAIN

There are still millions of Brother Dowleys among us, to whom ten dollars "is" ten dollars regardless of context—here, the price system. Energetically demanding higher wages, but doing nothing to protect themselves against higher prices, they are often deprived of their wage increases as fast as they get them. Accordingly, even when living costs have risen fifty per cent, they may still derive a sense of progress from the fact that they now get "three dollars" where they used to get "two dollars."

"In your country, brother, what is the wage of a . . . swineherd?"

"Twenty-five milrays a day . . ."

The smith's face beamed with joy. He said:

"With us they are allowed the double of it! And what may a mechanic get . . . ?"

"On the average, fifty milrays . . ."

"Ho-ho! With us they are allowed a hundred! . . ."

And his face shone upon the company like a sunburst. But I didn't scare at all. I rigged up my pile-driver, and

---

[1] Reprinted by permission of Harper and Brothers, Inc.

allowed myself fifteen minutes to drive him into the earth—drive him *all* in—drive him in till not even the curve of his skull should show above-ground. Here is the way I started in on him. I asked:

"What do you pay a pound for salt?"

"A hundred milrays."

"We pay forty. What do you pay for beef and mutton—when you buy it?" That was a neat hit; it made the color come.

"It varieth somewhat, but not much; one may say seventy-five milrays the pound."

"*We* pay thirty-three. What do you pay for eggs?"

"Fifty milrays the dozen."

"We pay twenty. . . . What do you pay for a stuff gown for the wife of the laborer or the mechanic?"

"We pay eight cents, four mills."

"Well, observe the difference: you pay eight cents and four mills, we pay only four cents." I prepared now to sock it to him. I said: "Look here, dear friend, *what's become of your high wages you were bragging so about a few minutes ago?*"—and I looked around on the company with placid satisfaction, for I had slipped up on him gradually and tied him hand and foot, you see, without his ever noticing that he was being tied at all. "What's become of those noble high wages of yours—I seem to have knocked the stuffing all out of them, it appears to me."

But if you will believe me, he merely looked surprised, that is all! He didn't grasp the situation at all, didn't know he had walked into a trap, didn't discover that he was *in* a trap. I could have shot him, from sheer vexation. With cloudy eye and a struggling intellect he fetched this out:

"Marry, I seem not to understand. It is *proved* that our wages be double thine; how then may it be that thou'st knocked therefrom the stuffing? . . ."

Well, I was stunned; partly with this unlooked-for stupidity on his part, and partly because his fellows so manifestly sided with him and were of his mind—if you might call it mind. My position was simple enough, plain enough; how could it be simplified more? However, I must try:

"Why, look here, brother Dowley, don't you see? Your wages are merely higher than ours in *name,* not in *fact.*"

"Hear him! They are the *double*—ye have confessed it yourself."

"Yes-yes, I don't deny that at all. But that's got nothing to do with it; the *amount* of the wages in mere coins, with meaningless names attached to them to know them by, has got nothing to do with it. The thing is, how much can you *buy* with your wages?—that's the idea. While it is true that with you a good mechanic is allowed about three dollars and a half a year, and with us only about a dollar and seventy-five—"

"There—ye're confessing it again, ye're confessing it again!"

"Confound it, I've never denied it, I tell you! What I say is this. With us *half* a dollar buys more than a *dollar* buys with you—and *therefore* it stands to reason and the commonest kind of common sense, that our wages are *higher* than yours."

He looked dazed, and said, despairingly:

"Verily, I cannot make it out. Ye've just *said* ours are the higher, and with the same breath ye take it back."

III.

THE DEACON'S MASTERPIECE:
OR THE WONDERFUL "ONE-HOSS SHAY"
A Logical Story

by OLIVER WENDELL HOLMES

Here is the account of a vehicle manufactured by purely intensional methods. Holmes often showed his impatience with logicians, whose facility in the manipulation of "maps" never seemed to him commensurate with their acquaintance with the "territories" their maps were supposed to stand for. "I value a man," he says in *The Autocrat of the Breakfast-Table,* "mainly for his primary relations with truth . . . not for any secondary artifice in handling his ideas."

Have you heard of the wonderful one-hoss shay,
That was built in such a logical way
It ran a hundred years to a day,

And then, of a sudden, it—ah, but stay,
I'll tell you what happened without delay,
Scaring the parson into fits,
Frightening people out of their wits—
Have you ever heard of that, I say?

Seventeen hundred and fifty-five
Georgius Secundus was then alive—
Snuffy old drone from the German hive;
That was the year when Lisbon-town
Saw the earth open and gulp her down,
And Braddock's army was done so brown,
Left without a scalp to its crown.
It was on the terrible Earthquake-day
That the Deacon finished the one-hoss shay.

Now in the building of chaises, I tell you what,
There is always *somewhere* a weakest spot—
In hub, tire, felloe, in spring or thill,
In panel, or crossbar, or floor, or sill,
In screw, bolt, thoroughbrace—lurking still,
Find it somewhere you must and will—
Above or below, or within or without—
And that's the reason, beyond a doubt,
A chaise *breaks down,* but doesn't *wear out.*

But the Deacon swore (as Deacons do,
With an "I dew vum," or an "I tell *yeou*"),

He would build one shay to beat the taown
'N' the keounty 'n' all the kentry raoun';
It should be so built that it *couldn'* break daown—
"Fur," said the Deacon, " 't's mighty plain
Thut the weakes' place mus' stan' the strain;
'N' the way t' fix it, uz I maintain,
 Is only jest
T' make that place uz strong uz the rest."

So the Deacon inquired of the village folk
Where he could find the strongest oak,
That couldn't be split nor bent nor broke—
That was for spokes and floor and sills;
He sent for lancewood to make the thills;
The crossbars were ash, from the straightest trees,
The panels of whitewood, that cuts like cheese,
But lasts like iron for things like these;
The hubs of logs from the "Settler's ellum"—
Last of its timber—they couldn't sell 'em,
Never an ax had seen their chips,
And the wedges flew from between their lips,
Their blunt ends frizzled like celery tips;
Step and prop iron, bolt and screw,
Spring, tire, axle, and linchpin too,
Steel of the finest, bright and blue;
Thoroughbrace bison skin, thick and wide;
Boot, top, dasher, from tough old hide

Found in the pit when the tanner died.
That was the way he "put her through."
"There!" said the Deacon, "naow she'll dew."

Do! I tell you, I rather guess
She was a wonder, and nothing less!
Colts grew horses, beards turned gray,
Deacon and deaconess dropped away,
Children and grandchildren—where were they?
But there stood the stout old one-hoss shay
As fresh as on Lisbon earthquake day!

EIGHTEEN HUNDRED—it came and found
The Deacon's masterpiece strong and sound.
Eighteen hundred increased by ten—
"Hahnsum kerridge" they called it then.
Eighteen hundred and twenty came—
Running as usual; much the same.
Thirty and forty at last arrive,
And then come fifty, and FIFTY-FIVE.

Little of all we value here
Wakes on the morn of its hundredth year
Without both feeling and looking queer.
In fact, there's nothing that keeps its youth,
So far as I know, but a tree and truth.
(This is a moral that runs at large;
Take it.—You're welcome.—No extra charge.)

FIRST OF NOVEMBER—the Earthquake-day.
There are traces of age in the one-hoss shay,
A general flavor of mild decay,
But nothing local, as one may say.
There couldn't be—for the Deacon's art
Had made it so like in every part
That there wasn't a chance for one to start.
For the wheels were just as strong as the thills,
And the floor was just as strong as the sills,
And the panels just as strong as the floor,
And the whippletree neither less nor more,
And the back crossbar as strong as the fore,
And spring and axle and hub *encore.*
And yet, *as a whole,* it is past a doubt
In another hour it will be *worn out!*

First of November, 'Fifty-five.'
This morning the parson takes a drive.
Now, small boys, get out of the way!
Here comes the wonderful one-hoss shay,
Drawn by a rat-tailed, ewe-necked bay.
"Huddup!" said the parson.—Off went they.

The parson was working his Sunday's text—
Had got to *fifthly,* and stopped perplexed
At what the—Moses—was coming next.
All at once the horse stood still,
Close by the meet'n'-house on the hill.

—First a shiver, and then a thrill,
Then something decidedly like a spill—
And the parson was sitting upon a rock,
At half-past nine by the meet'n'-house clock—
Just the hour of the Earthquake shock!
What do you think the parson found,
When he got up and stared around?
The poor old chaise in a heap or mound,
As if it had been to the mill and ground.
You see, of course, if you're not a dunce,
How it went to pieces all at once—
All at once, and nothing first—
Just as bubbles do when they burst.

End of the wonderful one-hoss shay.
Logic is logic. That's all I say.

IV. From

THE GRAPES OF WRATH [1]

by JOHN STEINBECK

Tom Joad makes an acute analysis of the presymbolic character of the filling-station operator's words.

". . . But what's the country comin' to? That's what I wanta know. What's it comin' to? Folks can't make a

---

[1] Copyright, 1939, by John Steinbeck. Reprinted by permission of The Viking Press.

livin' farmin'. I ask you, what's it comin' to? I can't figure her out. Ever'body I ask, they can't figure her out.
Fella wants to trade his shoes so he can get a hunderd
miles on. I can't figure her out." He took off his silver
hat and wiped his forehead with his palm. . . .

Al started the motor and backed the truck to the gas
pump. "Fill her up. She'll take about seven," said Al.
"We'll give her six so she don't spill none. . . ."

Casy said, "I been walkin' aroun' in the country. Ever'-
body's askin' that. What we comin' to? Seems to me we
don't never come to nothin'. Always on the way. Always
goin' and goin'. Why don't folks think about that?
They's movement now. People moving. We know why,
an' we know how. Movin' 'cause they got to. That's why
folks always move. Movin' 'cause they want somepin better'n what they got. An' that's the on'y way they'll ever
git it. Wantin' it an' needin' it, they'll go out an' git it.
It's bein' hurt that makes folks mad to fightin'. I been
walkin' aroun' the country, an' hearin' folks talk like
you."

The fat man pumped the gasoline and the needle
turned on the pump dial, recording the amount. "Yeah,
but what's it comin' to? That's what I want ta know."

Tom broke in irritably. "Well, you ain't never gonna
know. Casy tries to tell ya an' you jest ast the same thing
over. I seen fellas like you before. You ain't askin'
nothin'. You're jus' singin' a kinda song. 'What we comin'

to?' You don' wanta know. Country's movin' aroun', goin' places. They's folks dyin' all aroun'. Maybe you'll die pretty soon, but you won't know nothin'. I seen too many fellas like you. You don't want to know nothin'. Just sing yourself to sleep with a song—'What we comin' to?'"

V. From Chapter VII of *The Folklore of Capitalism*
THE TRAPS WHICH LIE IN DEFINITIONS AND POLAR WORDS [1]

by THURMAN W. ARNOLD

Mr. Arnold is, as his record as Assistant Attorney General in charge of the Antitrust Division shows, one of the most extensionally orientated people in public life today. The following passages from his *The Folklore of Capitalism* are cited, first, in support of the principle that "the two-valued orientation is the starter, but not a steering wheel," and second, in support of the contention that "orientation by definition" should be avoided.

One who would escape from the culture of his own time long enough to view it from the outside, as the historian views the French Revolution or the anthropologist views a primitive people, must beware of the hidden traps which lie in the terminology of that culture which he must necessarily use. He is confronted with the same dif-

[1] Reprinted by permission of the author and the Yale University Press.

ficulty the anthropologist would face if he had to write his observations in the language of the tribe he was observing. He would find all the words used in connection with their sacred institutions so heavily freighted with little mental pictures of the ideals and phobias of the tribe that they would imperfectly describe the actual moving effect of those ideals on the tribe. This is such a dangerous handicap to one who describes modern society that it is necessary to digress from our main theme for a chapter in order to explain it.

We may take an example from the development of physics. In the last century the terminology of physics was tied up with little mental pictures of a world composed of matter and energy. Matter was little lumps, of which the atom was the smallest. Time was a sequence. Space was a frame. These word-images were taken from the general images of the day. They could not be used to describe a world in which time was a dimension and matter a form of energy.

Today we realize that word-images of ordinary discourse cannot be used to describe the phenomena of physics. They are too hopelessly confused with the view of the universe as made up of little lumps of matter. Einstein's great contribution to science is the fact that he made men realize that mental pictures had their distinct limitations as scientific tools. He escaped from these little pictures through symbols of mathematics which had the advantage of carrying no concrete mental images along with them. The fourth dimension and the Riemann metric, both of which Einstein used, either mean absolutely nothing when translated into language or they become completely absurd. However, when one gets used to them, they appear to have meaning enough to use, just as the symbol for zero is treated as a number in mathematics. . . .

Therefore, it becomes necessary for anyone thinking objectively about human institutions to realize the traps which lie beneath words. This is a familiar enough idea. What is not so familiar, however, is the kind of trap which lies behind peculiar types of words often called "polar" words. These have no meaning by themselves. They require an opposite term in order to be used at all. Let us illustrate.

The term "up" has no meaning apart from the term "down." The term "fast" has no meaning apart from the term "slow." And in addition such pairs of terms have no meaning even when used together, except when confined to a very particular situation. The realization of this fact in physics is called the principle of relativity. "Up" and "down" are very useful terms to describe the movement with reference to an elevator. They are utterly useless and, indeed, lead us into all sorts of errors when we talk about interstellar spaces. The reason is that these words require a frame of reference which does not work in astronomy. The idea that the sun went "down" and that the sky was "up" was among the great stumbling blocks to astronomical science for centuries.

The observer of social institutions must face a similar difficulty because most of our language about the organization and objectives of government is made up of such polar terms. "Justice" and "injustice" are typical. A reformer who wants to abolish injustice and create a world in which nothing but justice prevails is like a man who wants to make everything "up." Such a man might feel that if he took the lowest in the world and carried it up to the highest point and kept on doing this, everything would eventually become "up." This would certainly move a great many objects and create an enormous amount of activity. It might or might not be useful, according to the standards which we apply. However, it would never result in the abolishment of "down."

The battle between justice and injustice is a similar struggle. It leads to change. It also leads to civil wars. What we call "progress" is a consequence of this activity, as well as what we call "reaction." Our enthusiasms are aroused by these words and therefore they are excellent tools with which to push people around. Both the Rebels and the Loyalists in Spain are fighting for justice. That is what enables them to kill so many people in such a consecrated way.

Since justice is a nice word, we refuse to apply it to

people who are struggling for things we do not like. The pacifist will refuse to admit that any war can be a war for justice. The born fighter will say that men who refuse to fight for justice do not really care for justice at all. Each side gets morale from the use of such terms and obtains the confidence necessary to make faces at the other side, knowing that God is with him. However, these polar terms are purely inspirational. They are not guides. Each side always claims to have "justice" on its side. Even organized criminals fight each other in the interest of justice.

All this does not, of course, mean that such words are foolish. They are, on the contrary, among the most important realities in the world. Take the term "efficiency," for example, which is an ideal of the business world. It has no meaning whatever unless there exists something which is called "inefficiency." One does not speak of a mountain as either efficient or inefficient. I recently engaged in a discussion with a newspaper editor, whose paper had a policy of taking care of all its old employees. This editor was very much in favor of an "efficient" society. He therefore wondered whether the policy of taking care of old employees was really "efficient." What was happening in his mind was simply this. Being a man of kindly impulses, he wanted the people whom he knew to be well fed. Being engaged in a struggle for economic power, he liked to see his paper make money. If he had

desired to fire some of the older employees, he would
have obtained the moral courage to do so by saying that
newspaper "efficiency" demanded it. He desired to keep
his old employees. Therefore, the word "efficient," with
its little mental pictures of making profits, created a conflict. In order to resolve that conflict he had to invent a
new term. He was for humanitarianism and against
cruelty. Here was another pair of polar words which
gave him support because it put him on the side of the
nice word. His competitor, who was firing his employees
when they got old, would of course have been troubled
by this new set of polar words. He would not want to
be called cruel. He would like to be considered humanitarian. Therefore, in order to resolve this conflict, he
would proceed to prove that in the long run temporary
cruelty led to humanitarianism. This is a complicated
idea and therefore it takes a great many economic books
to prove it. The idea that humanitarianism is better than
efficiency is an inspirational idea and can be proved by
a sermon. However, it requires a number of learned
books to prove that present cruelty results in long-run
humanitarianism. Economic theory is always equal to
such a task. The humanitarian is shown to be an advocate of "paternalism" and against "rugged individualism."

These arguments never get anywhere in persuading the
other side. However, they perform a real function in bol-

stering up the morale of the side on which they are used. The trick is to find a pair of polar words, in which the nice word justifies your own position and the bad word is applied to the other fellow.

Thus keeping on old employees is not "efficiency." Answer: But it is humanitarian, which is the only proper objective of efficiency. Apparent efficiency which leads to inhumanitarian results is really "inefficiency." Reply: But humanitarianism which destroys rugged individualism is in reality paternalism, which in the long run leads to more suffering than it cures and hence is inhumanitarian. Rebutter: But rugged individualism which destroys the morale of the individual by depriving him of security in the interests of selfish profits in the long run is in its essence Fascism. Surrebutter: Now the cat is out of the bag. You are attacking the profit motive and that leads to Communism.

This sort of thing can be kept up all night. It doesn't get anywhere and it doesn't mean anything. However, it makes both sides feel that God is with them. It is a form of prayer. . . .

Definition is ordinarily supposed to produce clarity in thinking. It is not generally recognized that the more we define our terms the less descriptive they become and the more difficulty we have in using them. The reason for this paradox is that we never attempt to define words which obtain a proper emotional response from our listeners. Logical definition enters when we are using words which we are sure "ought" to mean something, but none of us can put our finger on just what that meaning is. In such situations priestly-minded men believe that definition will make the meaning clearer. Most of this kind of definition occurs in the use of the polar words which we have just been describing.

We may illustrate with a homely example. There is no conflict in a farmer's mind about the meaning of the words "horse" and "duck." The one is not used as a polar term to the other. If you tell a farmer to bring you a horse, he never comes out of the barn leading a duck.

Suppose that the farmer attempted to define the difference. If he took the task at all seriously, he would find millions of differences. His definition would become so involved that he could no longer talk about the animals intelligibly. He would probably end up by thinking that horses were really ducks and vice versa, because this is an ordinary effect of the close concentration on particular pairs of terms; they tend to merge, and the distinctions between the two grow less and less sharp.

Of course, you say, the farmer would never attempt such a thing. This is true in the ordinary situation. But suppose that a conflict arose between an abstraction and a need which required the use of the words in pairs. We can easily imagine such a hypothetical situation.

Suppose, for example, we had a statute that taxed horses at ten dollars a head and ducks at ten cents. This does not create any conflict, because it seems to be a fair enough classification according to the prevailing folklore of taxation. However, suppose, in addition, that due to the automobile, or some other cause, horses became completely worthless and ducks became very valuable. Suppose that the original statute had been passed by ancestors of such great respectability that it would be tearing down the Constitution to repeal it and use new words. Obviously, if we want to collect revenue in such a situation, we must begin to define the real essence of the difference between a horse and a duck. We set our legal scholars to work. They discover that there are all sorts of immaterial differences apparent to the superficial eye. The mind of the scholar, however, is able to penetrate to the real essence of the distinction, which is value. The horse is the more valuable animal. It is clear that the fathers thought that this was the difference, because Thomas Jefferson once remarked to his wife that his horses were worth much more than his ducks. Differences between feathers and hair were never mentioned by any of the founders. Therefore, it is apparent that the webfooted animals are really horses, and the creatures with hoofs are really ducks. (Such observations are called "research.")

This works all right so far as the taxing situation is

concerned. Revenue begins to flow in again. However, scholarly definitions are supposed to go through the surface and to the core of things. Ordinary men feel a conflict, because deep down in their hearts they feel that there is something wrong somewhere. This conflict makes them celebrate the truth of the definition by ceremony. If the conflict is a minor one, a procession once a year in which ducks are led around with halters and equipped with little saddles will be sufficient. A supreme court is also helpful in such situations. However, if the conflict is sufficiently keen, we shall find farmers all over the country forced to feed ducks on baled hay. Ducks will not die because of this, however. They will actually be kept alive by low-class politicians sneaking into the barn at night and giving them the proper food. (Thus a great organization of bootleggers gave us our liquor only a few years ago.) If this situation is finally accepted as inevitable, scholars will be called in to prove that the particular food which is being fed to the ducks is actually baled hay, even though to a superficial observer it looks like something else. This definition will mix men up along some other lines and the literature will continue to pile up so long as the conflict exists. When the conflict disappears, the need of definition will go with it.

The illustration sounds absurd, but the writer has tried many cases involving exactly that type of situation. A plaster company was scraping gypsum from the surface of the ground. If it was a mine, it paid one tax; if a manufacturing company, it paid another. Expert witnesses were called who almost came to blows, such was their disgust at the stupidity of those who could not see that the process was essentially mining, or manufacturing. A great record was built up to be reviewed by the State Supreme Court on this important question of "fact."

A typical piece of theology of this type is the transformation of the due process clause in the fifth amendment from a direction regarding criminal trials to a prohibition against the regulation of great corporations. The word "property" in a like manner has changed from something which was tangible to the right of a great organization to be free from governmental interference. Such changes appear to have something wrong about them, because the older response to the sound of the word "property" is still instinctively felt. A spiritual conflict is created which requires a great deal of literature or ceremony to resolve.

How may the observer of social institutions avoid such traps? The answer is that in writing *about* social institutions he should never define anything. He should try to choose words and illustrations which will arouse the proper mental associations with his readers. If he doesn't succeed with these, he should try others. If he ever is led into an attempt at definition, he is lost.

VI.

"GOVERNMENT" VS. "BUSINESS" [1]

A Short Study in Applied Semantics

by STUART CHASE

Mr. Chase has spoken of his work in semantics as by and for the layman. His *The Tyranny of Words* contains a wealth of illuminating and amusing applications and illustrations drawn from his experiences in business, public controversy, economics, and government service. In the following, he shows the reader how to orientate himself extensionally regarding "government" and "business."

Government is destroying the confidence of Business. . . .

If Government would leave Business alone, the depression would soon be over. . . .

Business is sabotaging recovery. . . .

If Business were not so blind, it would realize that Government is chiefly engaged in bolstering up Capitalism. . . .

Government and Business must co-operate if this nation is to march forward. . . .

To show that these paraphrases are not unfair, here are two run-of-the-mine samples clipped from the New York *Times* of April 28, 1938: Alfred P. Sloan: "The ex-

[1] " 'Government' vs. 'Business,' " *Common Sense,* June, 1938. Reprinted by permission of *Common Sense.*

ploitation of industry by regimentation means the death knell of individual enterprise." Henry Ford: "If finance would get out of government, and government would get out of business, everything would go again."

Mr. Sloan identifies "industry" with "business," and "regimentation" with "government." Mr. Ford complicates the situation by introducing something called "finance" which is in government's hair and should get out. Most commentators do not make this nice distinction; they lump "finance" with "business"; i.e., bankers are assumed to be businessmen.

Similar statements can be found by the square yard in any newspaper, in almost any magazine, radio address, column by General (Iron Pants) Johnson, speech at the annual banquet of the American Widget Manufacturers, baccalaureate sermon. . . . Government and Business glowering at each other over the barbed wire and shell holes of no man's land. Such pronouncements are gravely received by millions of Americans who are certified by life insurance examiners as sane. It is widely held that something of moment is being said and that the cause of human understanding and knowledge is advanced.

Wherever you drive in the country, you are likely to see a billboard advertising a business magazine. The sign shows a gigantic baby about to burst into tears, with the caption: "What hurts Business hurts me." You are not to conclude that Business is a crying baby, but that Business provides milk and shoes for children, especially for your child. But what is Business and what are the things that hurt it? The sign does not say, nor do the columnists and orators. They could not tell you. It would be a tough job of analysis for anyone to tell you. This article will indicate some ways of going about that job.

Initially we must recognize that there are two prevalent motives in the minds of those who use the terms "government" and "business." Some of the talkers wish to create a prejudice for or against a definite measure (say a tax bill), for or against a definite person or group of persons (say Mr. Roosevelt or Mr. Willkie and his friends). They are using loose talk consciously and deliberately to confuse the issue, and will of course continue to do so. They are not interested in saying what they mean, and would be greatly alarmed if attempts were made to clarify their verbiage.

Other talkers, and I think they are in the majority, really want more knowledge about political and industrial affairs. They want to know clearly what is going on so that suitable inferences may be drawn and suitable action taken. They are like persons in a theater when a fire breaks out—where are the exits, what shall we do? —except that political and industrial fires, while just as dangerous, do not burn so fast. To them, semantics offers certain fire-fighting tools—to continue the analogy. Semantics does not merely encourage the habit of rejecting windy abstractions; it also provides a series of tests by which you can be sure that you are thinking straight when you tackle a mental problem with the serious intention of solving it. . . .

People talk as though they saw an iron-booted entity "government" jumping on a frail, defenseless "business," or, per contra, a gross, recalcitrant "business" hurling a shower of monkey wrenches at a hard-working, conscientious "government." In the world that we actually see with our eyes or touch with our hands, there is no entity "government" and no "business." A man with a camera could not take a picture of either. He can take a picture of Dr. Bennett of the Soil Conservation Service, or a picture of Mr. Alfred P. Sloan. He can take a picture of Grand Coulee Dam—indeed I have a copy—where thousands of men working for a "business" contractor are building the biggest "government" structure in history, bossed by "government" engineers. He can take a picture of a fleet of "business" trucks running on U.S. 1, a "government" road, or a picture of a little "business" man made happy by an RFC "government" loan.

A brief grounding in semantics makes it clear that most of the talk, emotion, fury, this pounding of tables, these apoplexies in club armchairs, these editorials, upheavals of columnists, banquet orators, soapbox fireworks, are without meaning. The uproar is not about events in space and time, but about events in Cloud-Cuckoo-Land. No fiery combatant knows what "government" or "business" means to his equally fiery opponent. He could not make an intelligent appraisal of what these terms mean to himself—not, if you please, because he does not stop to think, but because the words themselves are so abstract that they defy comprehensive appraisal by even the most careful appraiser. That is the kind of loose, general words they happen to be.

It follows that specific action taken by any combatant must be loose, random, and confused. It will be on a par with action taken by Congo villagers when they beat drums to exorcise demons in the forest. The demons seem real to the villagers. "Government" and "business" seem real to most Americans.

Before Citizen A and Citizen B can intelligently communicate to one another about "government," it is necessary that they both go down the verbal ladder to events in the real world which both can see and agree upon. At this lower level, Citizen A can point to his income tax blank and say to Citizen B: "By 'government' I mean this. Take it, look at it, add it up. Isn't it the damnedest thing?" But Citizen B may say: "I pay no income tax. I'm on the Federal Arts Project. It saved my life. Look at these sketches for my new high school mural. By 'government,' I mean *this!*" Income tax blanks and high school murals and millions of other tangible objects, acts, events, constitute the reality behind the term "government." Ditto for "business." How are you going to get A and B to agree in this situation? You cannot get them to agree. So they shout. But observe: if they stop shouting about "government," it may be possible for B to agree with A that his income tax is a complicated accounting monstrosity and for A to agree with B that his high school mural sketch is admirable.

If two or more persons are going to understand one another and make sense in an abstract discussion, they must find a common object or event to which their words refer. Otherwise their discussions will be meaningless because (1) they have different referents for their words, and so are talking about different events, or (2) they have no referents at all. For such a term as "the sublime" there are no referents at all. Without a common referent, A and B can make noises at one another, but they cannot communicate. It is as though one talked in Chinese and the other in Eskimo. Each can let the other know that he is very much stirred up, but not what he is stirred up about.

The student of semantics cannot get excited about all the acts of "government" because he does not know, and never can know, what all the acts are. Ditto for "business." He can get excited about Mr. Roosevelt, or Mr. Hopkins, about the acts of certain government officials, or about the behavior of Jim Hill or of Richard Whitney. But is the behavior of Richard Whitney to be taken as the mode for the behavior of "business"? I ask any corporation official if this is justifiable. Yet that same official may be growling to Mrs. Official over the *Times* and coffee cups tomorrow morning: "Look at that fellow Earle in Pennsylvania. That's government for you. That's why we can't make any progress in this country."

Words are not things. You cannot sleep on the word "bed" or eat the word "roast beef." The thing comes before the word and is recognized by the senses on the nonverbal level. A dog knows what "roast beef" is, right enough, but he makes no conversation about it. Man alone of the animals invents labels for things in his environment and makes conversations about them. If A and B discuss a side of beef on the table in front of them, they both see the referent; they can touch it, taste it, smell it. Here communication difficulty is at a minimum. Similarly, scientists talk clearly to one another—sometimes aided by a special language called mathematics—because they constantly check their talk with physical experiments. They perform operations and find common referents. They must, if they are to continue to be scientists. When they turn their backs on the laboratory and begin to argue, they resemble philosophers. Most philosophers, incidentally, do not like semantics. It is beneath their attention. It certainly is—far down the verbal ladder.

"Well," cries one enthusiastic convert to semantics, "let's get rid of abstract terms and stick to Rover—the actual dog out on the lawn there." We cannot get rid of abstractions; we require them constantly. This article I am writing is full of them. No. Relief is available not by striking abstractions from the language, *but by using them accurately;* by realizing which level of the verbal ladder we are on; by going down the ladder at frequent intervals to find the real events at the bottom. We should use abstractions cautiously, and the last thing we should do is to get excited about them. To become emotional about a high order abstraction is pretty good evidence that we have mistaken a word for a thing, personified the label, and so delivered ourselves over, bag and baggage, to word-magic.

Rover is never as goofy as this. He does not get excited about "private property" as a sacred principle. He gets excited when somebody steals his bone. It is sane to get excited about stolen bones or stolen bonds. It is not sane to get excited about verbal machinery. The structure of language as it has developed down the ages, whether English, French, or Hottentot, makes us tend to believe in things which are not there. Adjustment to the environment is a difficult business, as any dog or robin or bee knows. Men have made that adjustment far

more difficult by peopling the environment with ghosts
and demons derived from bad language.

Consider savages in New Guinea. In addition to floods,
storms, insects, wild beasts, pestilences, the distraught
native must contend with evil spirits in trees, caves,
clouds, and soul boxes. This doubles the job. We are just
beginning to realize from the semantic studies of Ogden,
Richards, Korzybski, and others that similar conditions
obtain among civilized peoples today. They must deal
not only with droughts, dust storms, floods, erosion,
mortgages, men out of work, syphilis, slums, busted
banks, wars, but with demons lurking behind such terms
as "red," "Wall Street," "fascism," "democracy," "plutocracy," "collective security," "isolation," "the profit system," "dictatorship," "government," "business," "regimentation," "the bosses," and hundreds more. Foggy language about "dictatorship" killed the reorganization bill
in Congress recently. (Part of it was, of course, intended
deliberately to be foggy.) Foggy language about "spending" and "balanced budgets" may cut the national income to fifty billions or less and give us more years like
1932. We work so much harder than we would need to
work if we could understand what we are talking about.

Opium is a beneficial drug in certain limited fields of
medical practice. Indiscriminately used, it is a curse. Similarly, the abstract terms "government" and "business"
are useful in limited contexts, and breeders of confusion

in others. If one says "governments all over the world in 1938 are spending more for armaments," the statement is clear, and can be checked by inspection of government budgets, nation by nation. But if one says, "the sole purpose of government is tyranny and oppression," clear use gives way to a ghost hunt.

Where are the referents behind the word "government"? Great God, where are they not? Posssibly five million individuals in America today are acting as representatives of the community in one capacity or another. There are thousands of laws on statute books, three hundred million acres of land, hundreds of great ships, schoolhouses, courthouses, dams, highways, mines. These individuals, buildings, printed laws, pieces of land, are referents for "government," in one context or another. Here is a typical abstraction ladder:

1. My neighbor, Roger Holmes, dogcatcher for the town.
2. Dogcatchers as a class.
3. Local police officers.
4. Town governments.
5. County governments.
6. State governments.
7. Federal governments.
8. The concept of government.

That is a long way from Roger Holmes. Furthermore, I have heard Roger, a good Republican, violently attack the encroachment of "government" on "personal liberty." Is he attacking himself? Does he know what he is attacking? Or is he just making a loud noise about a pair of spooks?

It is highly probable that Mr. Holmes is not objecting so much to "government" as he is to Mr. Roosevelt. Why doesn't he say so? To identify Mr. Roosevelt with "government" is to leave out some five million other individuals as referents for the term. No one of them is so important as Mr. Roosevelt today, but they do a tremendous number of important jobs, whoever happens to be President. Persons on government pay rolls furnish us with pure water supplies, fire protection, schools for our children, concrete highways. They protect us from contagious diseases. Does this undermine our personal liberty? Do these acts make "government" an interloper and a menace? If we fired every government official who is performing some economic activity today, we should soon be in a fine jam. Consider the state of the roads alone, without traffic controls of any kind. Our hospitals would be filled to the roof—except that many of them, being government institutions, would have shut up shop. Quarrel with Mr. Roosevelt if you wish, for that is your traditional privilege as a sovereign voter, but do not talk nonsense about throwing out "government" because you would like to throw out Mr. Roosevelt.

Congress, says Mr. A, is all right, for it licked the President in the reorganization bill. Part of Congress would

be more accurate, for the bill was defeated by eight votes.
But Congressmen are important referents for that "government" which so tyrannizes over Mr. A's liberties.
Does he mean that government is bad but that a bare
majority of Congress is good? Does Mr. A recall, however, the shouts of approval with which he welcomed the
news that Congress had adjourned, thus "allowing business to go back to work"?

Mr. A's opinion of the Supreme Court is high. At least,
he bitterly resented a proposal to change its membership.
Yet the justices of that court are also important referents
for "government." Are these gentlemen interfering with
his business, tearing up his liberties, prostrating him with
taxes, taking orders from Moscow?

One could go on like this for pages. Once the semantic
analysis is grasped, any high order abstraction can be
chased down the ladder, where tangible referents often
make a mockery of passionate opinions as to the abstraction itself. It is plain goofy to become passionate about
things which are not there or about things which represent only a very small fraction of the total situation under
discussion.

Turning now to "business," we find a similar situation,
except that "business" is of a higher order and even vaguer
than "government." You can at least line up and count
government employees. How do you line up business-

men? The unconscious stereotype back of the label is probably the independent merchant of the early nineteenth century. There are some still left in America, but large corporations are liquidating them rapidly. Most Americans in "business" work for corporations and have not much independent action left. Important decisions are made higher up. Are professional men in business? Are farmers businessmen? Is an investor a businessman? Is a filling station owner a businessman or a laboring man? When I shut my ears to labels and project my imagination over the America I have seen with my eyes, I find it impossible to visualize a definite army of private businessmen. I can pick out some real entrepreneurs, but in the picture are millions of corporation employees, engineers, chain store managers, architects, college presidents, all sorts of people. Furthermore, these various groups are frequently in violent conflict. One group wants free trade and another protection. One group wants to control retail stores by corporate devices while the neighborhood store man runs to "government" for laws prohibiting chains. Railroads fight shippers. Coal men fight oil men. Managers of large corporations oust legal owners from all but a semblance of control over their "private property." Some groups want a free market; more powerful groups want prices fixed by executive fiat, and fix them. Mr. Ford thinks the trouble with "business" is "finance."

Here are two abstraction ladders, reading down:

Business	Business
The oil business	The oil business
Oil production	Oil production
Hot oil production	Standard oil producing com-panies
Hot oil wells in Texas	
Mr. X, a hot oil runner in Texas, violently opposed to proration	Mr. Y, of a Standard company in Texas, violently in favor of proration

In these cases, referents for "business" at the bottom of the ladder are found in two gentlemen with policies belligerently and diametrically opposed.

Certain astute politicians in the United States Chamber of Commerce and the National Manufacturers' Association wangle resolutions through their respective organizations. I suppose these men are as close to the "voice of business" as one can get. But obviously they represent only a limited group.

Where does "business" end and "government" begin? At the margin, we find a hopeless confusion of referents. Ford builds cars, and government builds roads. No roads, no Fords. Is transportation a government or a business activity or a mixture of both? How about enterprises "affected with a public interest" like the utilities, where rates and investment policies are controlled in name at least by regulatory commissions? How about the 600 million dollars the government has lent to the railroads to bail out the widows and orphans holding railroad bonds? Suppose these loans had not been made. What would have been the effect on the investment market and on "confidence"? How about government loans for housing projects? You cannot tear these operating realities apart —except in your head.

Meanwhile, one can say categorically that most persons buying and selling goods and services have benefited to some degree by government spending programs . . . Such persons may hold the program morally wrong and economically odious, but they have not neglected to take the dollars as they rolled along from reliefer to retailer to wholesaler to manufacturer to banker.

Some stockbrokers, manufacturers, merchants, investors, have lost money because of some laws passed and enforced since 1933. Undoubtedly true. Some have made money and avoided loss because of laws passed. Also true. For example, had it not been for certain fiscal laws passed in March and April of 1933, most bankers would have lost their banks. Nobody knows what the net effects of laws and the acts of government officials have been on the balance sheets and operating accounts of all corporations, partnerships, and proprietorships. Nobody can know. The matter is too complex for appraisal. Many business activities in 1938 are not as profitable as they were in 1928. Ha! The New Deal is guilty! But they are

considerably more profitable than they were in 1932. Ha!
Mr. Hoover is guilty—and a government dominated by
Republicans is worse for business than a government
dominated by Democrats.

So the conclusions spin round and round until the
mind reels. This kind of thing gets nowhere because it
is about nothing. Generalizations about "government"
destroying the confidence of "business," kicking the stuffing out of "business," are just windy salutes in the
spring air. People on private pay rolls are worried. But
people on public pay rolls are worried too. The whole
damned population is worried, and has been since 1929.
Rather than dig into the causes of that universal worry,
people call each other names.

I happen to be an employee on part time of a small
corporation in New York City. The undistributed profits
tax hit this concern pretty hard in 1937. I feel that this
tax is sometimes unfair to small companies. I am prepared to ask Congress to exempt certain classes of small
corporations. But I do not propose to accompany the pro-
test with loud yells about the "government" destroying
confidence. You have to take these things as they come.
In 1934, when the Treasury began to borrow and spend,
my business began to pick up. I happen to be a shrewd
enough businessman to grasp the connection. When the
Treasury halted spending last year, my business took a
nose dive. (Name of my company on request.)

Here, you see, I am dealing with real referents—a business I know thoroughly and a certain act of Congress whose effects on that business I know. I made out the tax form. I can talk intelligently, I hope, about this business and this law. But as a student of semantics the last thing I propose to do is to identify my business with all "business" or to identify this law with all "government." Such a technique may be good enough for naked savages; it is not good enough for civilized men.

What business enterprise has been hurt? What is the connection between a given law and a given hurt? How was it hurt? When was it hurt? What laws have helped this business? What is the net loss or gain? Such questions and answers make sense. Referents are found. Communication is aided. Laws can be intelligently discussed and perhaps rendered more just.

In this semantic exercise, I have tried to set forth a method. I have not examined the policies of Mr. Roosevelt or the policies of those who oppose him. This is an analytical essay directed against the whirlwind of bad language which fills the press and the air waves today. It is not supposed that this attack will have much tangible effect. But I venture the opinion that until enough of us, in this or some future generation, begin to separate mental machinery from things under our noses, we shall continue to tilt at verbal windmills, while the ob-

jective of making the environment a tolerable and peaceful place in which to live remains only a pious hope.

VII.

SCIENCE AND LINGUISTICS [1]

by BENJAMIN LEE WHORF

Every normal person in the world, past infancy in
years, can and does talk. By virtue of that fact, every person—civilized or uncivilized—carries through life certain
naive but deeply rooted ideas about talking and its relation to thinking. Because of their firm connection with
speech habits that have become unconscious and automatic, these notions tend to be rather intolerant of opposition. They are by no means entirely personal and hap-
hazard; their basis is definitely systematic, so that we
are justified in calling them a system of natural logic—
a term that seems to me preferable to the term common
sense, often used for the same thing.

According to natural logic, the fact that every person
has talked fluently since infancy makes every man his
own authority on the process by which he formulates
and communicates. He has merely to consult a common
substratum of logic or reason which he and everyone
else are supposed to possess. Natural logic says that talk-

[1] "Science and Linguistics," *The Technology Review,* April, 1940.
Reprinted by permission of the author and *The Technology Review.*

ing is merely an incidental process concerned strictly with communication, not with formulation of ideas. Talking, or the use of language, is supposed only to "express" what is essentially already formulated nonlinguistically. Formulation is an independent process, called thought or thinking, and is supposed to be largely indifferent to the nature of particular languages. Languages have grammars, which are assumed to be merely norms of conventional and social correctness, but the use of language is supposed to be guided not so much by them as by correct, rational, or intelligent *thinking*.

Thought, in this view, does not depend on grammar but on laws of logic or reason which are supposed to be the same for all observers of the universe—to represent a rationale in the universe that can be "found" independently by all intelligent observers, whether they speak Chinese or Choctaw. In our own culture, the formulations of mathematics and of formal logic have acquired the reputation of dealing with this order of things, i.e., with the realm and laws of pure thought. Natural logic holds that different languages are essentially parallel methods for expressing this one-and-the-same rationale of thought and, hence, differ really in but minor ways which may seem important only because they are seen at close range. It holds that mathematics, symbolic logic, philosophy, and so on, are systems contrasted with language which deal directly with this realm of thought, not that they are themselves specialized extensions of language. The attitude of natural logic is well shown in an old quip about a German grammarian who devoted his whole life to the study of the dative case. From the

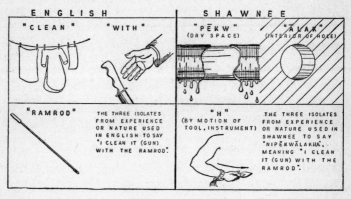

Fig. 1. Languages dissect nature differently. The different isolates of meaning (thoughts) used by English and Shawnee in reporting the same experience, that of cleaning a gun by running the ramrod through it. The pronouns "I" and "it" are not shown by symbols, as they have the same meaning in each case. In Shawnee "ni-" equals "I"; "-a" equals "it."

point of view of natural logic, the dative case and grammar in general are an extremely minor issue. A different attitude is said to have been held by the ancient Arabians: Two princes, so the story goes, quarreled over the honor of putting on the shoes of the most learned grammarian of the realm; whereupon their father, the caliph, is said to have remarked that it was the glory of his kingdom that great grammarians were honored even above kings.

The familiar saying that the exception proves the rule contains a good deal of wisdom, though from the standpoint of formal logic it became an absurdity as soon as "prove" no longer meant "put on trial." The old saw began to be profound psychology from the time it ceased to have standing in logic. What it might well suggest to us today is that if a rule has absolutely no exceptions, it is not recognized as a rule or as anything else; it is then part of the background of experience of which we tend to remain unconscious. Never having experienced anything in contrast to it, we cannot isolate it and formulate it as a rule until we so enlarge our experience and expand our base of reference that we encounter an interruption of its regularity. The situation is somewhat analogous to that of not missing the water till the well runs dry, or not realizing that we need air till we are choking.

For instance, if a race of people had the physiological defect of being able to see only the color blue, they would hardly be able to formulate the rule that they saw only blue. The term blue would convey no meaning to them, their language would lack color terms, and their words denoting their various sensations of blue would answer to, and translate, our words light, dark, white, black, and so on, not our word blue. In order to formulate the rule or norm of seeing only blue, they would need exceptional moments in which they saw other colors. The phenomenon of gravitation forms a rule without exceptions; needless to say, the untutored person is utterly unaware of any law of gravitation, for it would never enter his head to conceive of a universe in which bodies behaved otherwise than they do at the earth's surface. Like the color blue with our hypothetical race, the law of gravitation is a part of the untutored individual's background, not something he isolates from that background. The law could not be formulated until bodies that always fell were seen in terms of a wider astronomical world in which bodies moved in orbits or went this way and that.

Similarly, whenever we turn our heads, the image of the scene passes across our retinas exactly as it would if the scene turned around us. But this effect is background, and we do not recognize it; we do not see a room turn around us but are conscious only of having turned our heads in a stationary room. If we observe critically while turning the head or eyes quickly, we shall see no motion, it is true, yet a blurring of the scene between two clear views. Normally we are quite unconscious of this continual blurring but seem to be looking about in an unblurred world. Whenever we walk past a tree or house, its image on the retina changes just as if the tree or house were turning on an axis; yet we do not see trees or houses turn as we travel about at ordinary speeds. Sometimes ill-fitting glasses will reveal queer movements in the

scene as we look about, but normally we do not see the
relative motion of the environment when we move; our

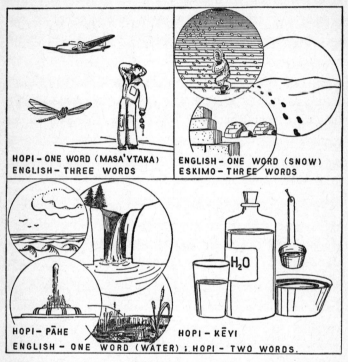

HOPI – ONE WORD (MASA'YTAKA)   ENGLISH – ONE WORD (SNOW)
ENGLISH – THREE WORDS   ESKIMO – THREE WORDS

HOPI – PĀHE   HOPI – KĒYI
ENGLISH – ONE WORD (WATER) ; HOPI – TWO WORDS.

*Fig. 2. Languages classify items of experience differently. The
class corresponding to one word and one thought in language A
may be regarded by language B as two or more classes corresponding to two or more words and thoughts.*

psychic make-up is somehow adjusted to disregard whole
realms of phenomena that are so all-pervasive as to be
irrelevant to our daily lives and needs.

Natural logic contains two fallacies: First, it does not see that the phenomena of a language are to its own speakers largely of a background character and so are outside the critical consciousness and control of the speaker who is expounding natural logic. Hence, when anyone, as a natural logician, is talking about reason, logic, and the laws of correct thinking, he is apt to be simply marching in step with purely grammatical facts that have somewhat of a background character in his own language or family of languages but are by no means universal in all languages and in no sense a common substratum of reason. Second, natural logic confuses agreement about subject matter, attained through use of language, with knowledge of the linguistic process by which agreement is attained; i.e., with the province of the despised (and to its notion superfluous) grammarian. Two fluent speakers, of English let us say, quickly reach a point of assent about the subject matter of their speech; they agree about what their language refers to. One of them, A, can give directions that will be carried out by the other, B, to A's complete satisfaction. Because they thus understand each other so perfectly, A and B, as natural logicians, suppose they must of course know how it is all done. They think, e.g., that it is simply a matter of choosing words to express thoughts. If you ask A to explain how he got B's agreement so readily, he will simply repeat to you, with more or less elaboration or abbreviation, what he said to B. He has no notion of the process involved. The amazingly complex system of linguistic patterns and classifications which A and B must have in common before they can adjust to each other at all, is all background to A and B.

These background phenomena are the province of the grammarian—or of the linguist, to give him his more modern name as a scientist. The word linguist in common, and especially newspaper, parlance means something entirely different, namely, a person who can quickly attain agreement about subject matter with different people speaking a number of different languages. Such a person is better termed a polyglot or a multilingual. Scientific linguists have long understood that ability to speak a language fluently does not necessarily confer a linguistic knowledge of it—i.e., understanding of its background phenomena and its systematic processes and structure—any more than ability to play a good game of billiards confers or requires any knowledge of the laws of mechanics that operate upon the billiard table.

The situation here is not unlike that in any other field of science. All real scientists have their eyes primarily on background phenomena that cut very little ice, as such, in our daily lives; and yet their studies have a way of bringing out a close relation between these unsuspected realms of fact and such decidedly foreground activities as transporting goods, preparing food, treating the sick, or growing potatoes, which in time may become very much modified simply because of pure scientific investigation in no way concerned with these brute matters themselves. Linguistics is in quite similar case; the background phenomena with which it deals are involved in all our foreground activities of talking and of reaching agreement, in all reasoning and arguing of cases, in all law, arbitration, conciliation, contracts, treaties, public opinion, weighing of scientific theories, formulation of scientific results. Whenever agreement or assent is arrived at in human affairs, and whether or not mathematics or other specialized symbolisms are made part of the procedure, *this agreement is reached by linguistic processes, or else it is not reached.*

As we have seen, an overt knowledge of the linguistic processes by which agreement is attained is not necessary to reaching some sort of agreement, but it is certainly no bar thereto; the more complicated and difficult the matter, the more such knowledge is a distinct aid, till the point may be reached—I suspect the modern world has about arrived at it—when the knowledge becomes not only an aid but a necessity. The situation may be likened to that of navigation. Every boat that sails is in the lap of planetary forces; yet a boy can pilot his small craft around a harbor without benefit of geography, astronomy, mathematics, or international politics. To the captain of an ocean liner, however, some knowledge of all these subjects is essential.

When linguists became able to examine critically and scientifically a large number of languages of widely different patterns, their base of reference was expanded; they experienced an interruption of phenomena hitherto held universal, and a whole new order of significances came into their ken. It was found that the background linguistic system (in other words, the grammar) of each language is not merely a reproducing instrument for voicing ideas but rather is itself the shaper of ideas, the program and guide for the individual's mental activity, for his analysis of impressions, for his synthesis of his mental stock in trade. Formulation of ideas is not an independent process, strictly rational in the old sense, but is part of a particular grammar and differs, from slightly to greatly, as between different grammars. We dissect nature along lines laid down by our native languages. The categories and types that we isolate from the world of phenomena we do not find there because they stare every observer in the face; on the contrary, the world is presented in a kaleidoscopic flux of impressions which has to be organized by our minds—and this means largely by the linguistic systems in our minds. We cut nature up, organize it into concepts, and ascribe significances as we do, largely because we are parties to an agreement to organize it in this way—an agreement that holds throughout our speech community and is codified

OBJECTIVE FIELD	SPEAKER (SENDER)	HEARER (RECEIVER)	HANDLING OF TOPIC RUNNING OF THIRD PERSON
SITUATION 1 a.			ENGLISH..."HE IS RUNNING".
			HOPI ... "WARI". (RUNNING, STATEMENT OF FACT.)
SITUATION 1 b.			ENGLISH..."HE RAN".
OBJECTIVE FIELD BLANK DEVOID OF RUNNING			HOPI ... "WARI". (RUNNING, STATEMENT OF FACT.)
SITUATION 2.			ENGLISH HE IS RUNNING
			HOPI ..."WARI". (RUNNING, STATEMENT OF FACT)
SITUATION 3.			ENGLISH..."HE RAN".
OBJECTIVE FIELD BLANK			HOPI ... "ERA WARI".(RUNNING, STATEMENT OF FACT FROM MEMORY)
SITUATION 4.			ENGLISH..."HE WILL RUN".
OBJECTIVE FIELD BLANK			HOPI ... "WARIKNI", (RUNNING, STATEMENT OF EXPECTATION)
SITUATION 5.			ENGLISH..."HE RUNS", (E.G. ON THE TRACK TEAM.)
OBJECTIVE FIELD BLANK			HOPI ..."WARIKNGWE", (RUNNING, STATEMENT OF LAW.)

Fig. 3. Contrast between a "temporal" language (English) and a "timeless" language (Hopi). What are to English differences of time are to Hopi differences in the kind of validity.

in the patterns of our language. The agreement is, of course, an implicit and unstated one, *but its terms are absolutely obligatory;* we cannot talk at all except by subscribing to the organization and classification of data which the agreement decrees.

The fact is very significant for modern science, for it means that no individual is free to describe nature with absolute impartiality but is constrained to certain modes of interpretation even while he thinks himself most free. The person most nearly free in such respects would be a linguist familiar with very many widely different linguistic systems. As yet no linguist is in even any such position. We are thus introduced to a new principle of relativity, which holds that all observers are not led by the same physical evidence to the same picture of the universe, unless their linguistic backgrounds are similar, or can in some way be calibrated.

This rather startling conclusion is not so apparent if we compare only our modern European languages, with perhaps Latin and Greek thrown in for good measure. Among these tongues there is a unanimity of major pattern which at first seems to bear out natural logic. But this unanimity exists only because these tongues are all Indo-European dialects cut to the same basic plan, being historically transmitted from what was long ago one speech community; because the modern dialects have long shared in building up a common culture; and because much of this culture, on the more intellectual side, is derived from the linguistic backgrounds of Latin and Greek. Thus this group of languages satisfies the special case of the clause beginning "unless" in the statement of the linguistic relativity principle at the end of the preceding paragraph. From this condition follows the unanimity of description of the world in the community of modern scientists. But it must be emphasized that "all modern Indo-European-speaking observers" is not the same thing as "all observers." That modern Chinese or Turkish scientists describe the world in the same terms as Western scientists means, of course, only that they have taken over bodily the entire Western system of rationalizations, not that they have corroborated that system from their native posts of observation.

When Semitic, Chinese, Tibetan, or African languages are contrasted with our own, the divergence in analysis of the world becomes more apparent; and when we bring in the native languages of the Americas, where speech communities for many millenniums have gone their ways independently of each other and of the Old World, the fact that languages dissect nature in many different ways becomes patent. The relativity of all conceptual systems, ours included, and their dependence upon language stand revealed. That American Indians speaking only their native tongues are never called upon to act as scientific observers is in no wise to the point. To exclude the evidence which their languages offer as to what the human mind can do is like expecting botanists to study nothing but food plants and hothouse roses and then tell us what the plant world is like!

Let us consider a few examples. In English we divide most of our words into two classes, which have different grammatical and logical properties. Class 1 we call nouns, e.g., "house," "man"; Class 2, verbs, e.g., "hit," "run." Many words of one class can act secondarily as of the other class, e.g., "a hit," "a run," or "to man" the boat, but on the primary level the division between the classes is absolute. Our language thus gives us a bipolar division of nature. But nature herself is not thus polarized. If it be said that strike, turn, run, are verbs because they denote temporary or short-lasting events, i.e., actions, why then is fist a noun? It also is a temporary event. Why are lightning, spark, wave, eddy, pulsation, flame, storm, phase, cycle, spasm, noise, emotion, nouns? They are temporary events. If man and house are nouns because they are long-lasting and stable events, i.e., things, what then are keep, adhere, extend, project, continue, persist, grow, dwell, and so on, doing among the verbs? If it be objected that possess, adhere, are verbs because they are stable relationships rather than stable percepts, why then should equilibrium, pressure, current, peace, group, nation, society, tribe, sister, or any kinship term, be among the nouns? It will be found that an "event" to *us* means "what our language classes as a verb" or something analogized therefrom. And it will be found

that it is not possible to define event, thing, object, relationship, and so on, from nature, but that to define them
always involves a circuitous return to the grammatical
categories of the definer's language.

In the Hopi language, lightning, wave, flame, meteor,
puff of smoke, pulsation, are verbs—events of necessarily
brief duration cannot be anything but verbs. Cloud and
storm are at about the lower limit of duration for nouns.
Hopi, you see, actually has a classification of events (or
linguistic isolates) by duration type, something strange
to our modes of thought. On the other hand, in Nootka,
a language of Vancouver Island, all words seem to us to
be verbs, but really there are no Classes 1 and 2; we have,
as it were, a monistic view of nature that gives us only
one class of word for all kinds of events. "A house occurs"
or "it houses" is the way of saying "house," exactly like
"a flame occurs" or "it burns." These terms seem to us
like verbs because they are inflected for durational and
temporal nuances, so that the suffixes of the word for
house event make it mean long-lasting house, temporary
house, future house, house that used to be, what started
out to be a house, and so on.

Hopi has a noun that covers every thing or being that
flies, with the exception of birds, which class is denoted
by another noun. The former noun may be said to denote
the class FC—B—flying class minus bird. The Hopi actually call insect, airplane, and aviator all by the same

word, and feel no difficulty about it. The situation, of course, decides any possible confusion among very disparate members of a broad linguistic class, such as this class FC—B. This class seems to us too large and inclusive, but so would our class "snow" to an Eskimo. We have the same word for falling snow, snow on the ground, snow packed hard like ice, slushy snow, wind-driven flying snow—whatever the situation may be. To an Eskimo, this all-inclusive word would be almost unthinkable; he would say that falling snow, slushy snow, and so on, are sensuously and operationally different, different things to contend with; he uses different words for them and for other kinds of snow. The Aztecs go even farther than we in the opposite direction, with cold, ice, and snow all represented by the same basic word with different terminations; ice is the noun form; cold, the adjectival form; and for snow, "ice mist."

What surprises most is to find that various grand generalizations of the Western world, such as time, velocity, and matter, are not essential to the construction of a consistent picture of the universe. The psychic experiences that we class under these headings are, of course, not destroyed; rather, categories derived from other kinds of experiences take over the rulership of the cosmology and seem to function just as well. Hopi may be called a timeless language. It recognizes psychological time, which is much like Bergson's "duration," but this "time" is quite unlike the mathematical time, *T,* used by our physicists. Among the peculiar properties of Hopi time are that it varies with each observer, does not permit of simultaneity, and has zero dimensions; i.e., it cannot be given a number greater than one. The Hopi do not say, "I stayed five days," but "I left on the fifth day." A word referring to this kind of time, like the word day, can have no plural. The puzzle picture (Fig. 3), will give mental exercise to anyone who would like to figure out how the Hopi verb gets along without tenses. Actually, the only practical use of our tenses, in one-verb sentences, is to distinguish among five typical situations, which are symbolized in the picture. The timeless Hopi verb does not distinguish between the present, past, and future of the event itself but must always indicate what type of validity the *speaker* intends the statement to have: (a) report of an event (situations 1, 2, 3 in the picture); (b) expectation of an event (situation 4); (c) generalization or law about events (situation 5). Situation 1, where the speaker and listener are in contact with the same objective field, is divided by our language into the two conditions, 1*a* and 1*b,* which it calls present and past, respectively. This division is unnecessary for a language which assures one that the statement is a report.

Hopi grammar, by means of its forms called aspects and modes, also makes it easy to distinguish between momentary, continued, and repeated occurrences, and to

indicate the actual sequence of reported events. Thus
the universe can be described without recourse to a concept of dimensional time. How would a physics con-
structed along these lines work, with no T (time) in its
equations? Perfectly, as far as I can see, though of course
it would require different ideology and perhaps different
mathematics. Of course V (velocity) would have to go
too. The Hopi language has no word really equivalent
to our "speed" or "rapid." What translates these terms
is usually a word meaning intense or very, accompanying
any verb of motion. Here is a clew to the nature of our
new physics. We may have to introduce a new term I,
intensity. Every thing and event will have an I, whether
we regard the thing or event as moving or as just endur-
ing or being. Perhaps the I of an electric charge will turn
out to be its voltage, or potential. We shall use clocks to
measure some intensities, or, rather, some *relative* intensities, for the absolute intensity of anything will be meaningless. Our old friend acceleration will still be there but
doubtless under a new name. We shall perhaps call it V,
meaning not velocity but variation. Perhaps all growths
and accumulations will be regarded as V's. We should
not have the concept of rate in the temporal sense, since,
like velocity, rate introduces a mathematical and linguistic time. Of course we know that all measurements
are ratios, but the measurements of intensities made by
comparison with the standard intensity of a clock or a

planet we do not treat as ratios, any more than we so treat a distance made by comparison with a yardstick.

A scientist from another culture that used time and velocity would have great difficulty in getting us to understand these concepts. We should talk about the intensity of a chemical reaction; he would speak of its velocity or its rate, which words we should at first think were simply words for intensity in his language. Likewise, he at first would think that intensity was simply our own word for velocity. At first we should agree, later we should begin to disagree, and it might dawn upon both sides that different systems of rationalization were being used. He would find it very hard to make us understand what he really meant by velocity of a chemical reaction. We should have no words that would fit. He would try to explain it by likening it to a running horse, to the difference between a good horse and a lazy horse. We should try to show him, with a superior laugh, that his analogy also was a matter of different intensities, aside from which there was little similarity between a horse and a chemical reaction in a beaker. We should point out that a running horse is moving relative to the ground, whereas the material in the beaker is at rest.

One significant contribution to science from the linguistic point of view may be the greater development of our sense of perspective. We shall no longer be able to see a few recent dialects of the Indo-European family, and the rationalizing techniques elaborated from their patterns, as the apex of the evolution of the human mind; nor their present wide spread as due to any survival from fitness or to anything but a few events of history—events that could be called fortunate only from the parochial point of view of the favored parties. They, and our own thought processes with them, can no longer be envisioned as spanning the gamut of reason and knowledge but only as one constellation in a galactic expanse. A fair realization of the incredible degree of diversity of linguistic system that ranges over the globe leaves one with an inescapable feeling that the human spirit is inconceivably old; that the few thousand years of history covered by our written records are no more than the thickness of a pencil mark on the scale that measures our past experience on this planet; that the events of these recent millenniums spell nothing in any evolutionary wise, that the race has taken no sudden spurt, achieved no commanding synthesis during recent millenniums, but has only played a little with a few of the linguistic formulations and views of nature bequeathed from an inexpressibly longer past. Yet neither this feeling nor the sense of precarious dependence of all we know upon linguistic tools which themselves are largely unknown need be discouraging to science but should, rather, foster that humility which accompanies the true scientific spirit, and thus forbid that arrogance of the mind which hinders real scientific curiosity and detachment.

VIII.

A LAWYER LOOKS AT LANGUAGE

by JEROME FRANK

"Words are the daughters of earth and things are the sons of heaven," wrote Dr. Samuel Johnson, in 1755, in the preface to his dictionary (probably repeating a Hindustani proverb). Mr. Justice Miller, in 1878, told a friend that he favored the kind of education which sought "the knowledge of things instead of the knowledge of words." Mr. Justice Holmes, in 1899, said, "We must think things not words," and then added, "or at least we must constantly translate our words into the things for which they stand." That addition made the aphorism sensible. For no one can think things directly; we need words in order to think. They are pointers to things; they make it possible for us to devise ideas and theories, about the complicated world of things, which enable us to manipulate our environment and to communicate those ideas and theories to other men. Thomas Hobbes remarked, almost three centuries ago, that "the most noble and profitable invention of all others was that of speech . . . whereby men register their thoughts, recall them when they are past, and also declare them for mutual utility and conversation; without which, there had been amongst men neither Commonwealth, nor Society, nor Contract, nor

Peace, no more than amongst lions, bears and wolves."

But, alas, if words are indispensable to thought, they can also be its worst enemy. For words are not only signs, pointing to things, but also, being derived from animal grunts and squeals,[1] are noises used to stir up and communicate emotions. That is fair enough; many implements have at least two uses. We both eat and kiss with our mouths. However, we seldom confuse eating and kissing. But we do, too often, confuse the two functions of language, and believe that a word is an idea-carrier when it is merely an emotion-transmitter. Then, too, we all too frequently assume that, since some words are signs for things, all words are; that every word must, directly or indirectly, refer to something which exists in the external world. But many words do not. Many of them are guide posts to nothing; and some of them point not to what exists but merely to what might perhaps be made to exist. We tend to regard everything as real if it has a name, failing to recognize that names can be assigned to non-existent things. One of our worst verbal habits has to do with abstractions: We devise names for certain aspects

[1] "A metaphysician," wrote Anatole France, pessimistically, "possesses, to build up his system of the Universe, only the perfected cries of apes and dogs. What he styles profound speculation and transcendental method is only setting in a row, arbitrarily arranged, the onomatopoetic noises wherewith the brutes expressed hunger and fear and desire in the primeval forests, and to which have gradually become attached meanings that are assumed to be abstract, only because they are less definite."

of or relations between things; those abstractions—such as Beauty, Goodness, Art, Intelligence, Capitalism—since they refer to actualities, are, of course, part of the actual; they are immensely useful short-hand expressions. But we "thingify" those words and then waste precious time striving to adjust our lives to their assumed independent reality, worship them as if they were more real than the totality of events and experiences part of which they were invented to describe. The classic illustration is Ingraham's: "We do not often have occasion to speak, as of an indivisible whole, of the group of phenomena involved in or connected with the transit of a Negro over a rail fence with a watermelon under his arm while the moon is just passing under a cloud. But if this collocation of phenomena were of frequent occurrence and, if we did have occasion to speak of it often, and if its happening were likely to affect the money market, we should have some name such as 'Wousin' to denote it by. People would in time be disputing whether the existence of a Wousin involved necessarily a rail fence, and whether the term could be applied when a white man is similarly related to a stone wall."

And so, through such Word Magic, words can and do distract us from the actual—or potentially actual—world into a fictitious word-world or, rather, a fake word-heaven where dwell bogus verbal entities, all words and no substance. We become the dupes or slaves of words, get drugged with them. We quarrel bitterly over ghost-words. We even die for them: many of the bloodiest wars in history began as Word Wars. Beveridge and others have concluded that there is much reason to believe that our own Civil War might have been averted if the poisoned-word distillers had not sold their wares widely and thus arrested sane thinking; if monstrous, over-powering words—ABOLITION, SECESSION, STATES' RIGHTS—had not taken possession of men's minds. On the other hand, in our era, the word-mongers have used "appease-ment" to destroy the will of free men to fight against degradation. . . . Word Magic, word madness, are, then, among the deadliest foes of human welfare.

Ever and again, over the centuries, a few men have perceived the dangers of such verbomania; have sought to lead a revolt against the Dictatorship of the Vocabu-lary; have endeavored to help make mankind a little more the master of things by making it at least the master of words. They have tried to stir up a Word Revolution. That kind of revolutionary movement is not new. It had its beginnings in the ancient world; the nominalists of the Middle Ages, like William of Occam, were its fellow travelers; as were (to choose at random) such men as Hobbes [2] and Locke in the seventeenth cen-

---

[2] He warned that "words are wise men's counters, they do but reckon by them: but they are the money of fools . . ."; and that the wise man has "need to remember what every name he uses stands for, and to

tury, and Schopenhauer in the nineteenth. (One thinks of what Hitler has done to Germany when he finds Schopenhauer saying that "at the sound of certain words . . . the German's head begins to swim, and falling straight away into a kind of delirium, he launches into high flown phrases which have no meaning whatever. He takes the most remote and empty conceptions, and strings them together artificially, instead of fixing his eyes on the facts, and looking at things and relations as they really are.")

In this century, the revolt against Word Slavery broke out all over the place. In the English-speaking world, the leading twentieth century enemies of such slavery were C. K. Ogden, I. A. Richards, and Alfred Korzybski. Others rapidly joined them. Their most recent adherent is the author of the present volume. Hayakawa has done what none of his predecessors has tried to accomplish: he has addressed himself to the average man. As a result, this book will not, I hope, be a mere prod to the high-brows; indeed, I hope it will begin to make the Word Revolution a mass movement.

Such a movement has already profoundly affected the thinking of one group—the lawyers. What makes that development interesting is that lawyers have been, par

place it accordingly, or else he will find himself entangled in words, as a bird in lime-twigs; the more he struggles, the more belimed." And he said, "The Light of humane minds is Perspicuous Words, but . . . first snuffed and purged from ambiguity."

excellence, word-intoxicated men. Perhaps just because word worship was most excessive and pernicious in lawyerdom, some lawyers have been among the leading word-iconoclasts: Bacon, one of the ablest lawyers of the seventeenth century, was explicitly word-conscious. Among the chief indictments he brought against the medieval schoolmen was their preoccupation with words as against observation of things; that preoccupation, he charged, was one of the three "distempers of learning." True, Harvey said of Bacon that "he wrote on science like a Lord Chancellor." For all that, Bacon railed effectively against what he described as "delicate learning" whereby "words usurp the place of substance, and polished phrases are accepted for real weight of meaning": "Of this vanity," he said, "Pygmalion's frenzy is a good emblem; for words are but the images of matter, and except they have life of reason and invention, to fall in love with them is all one as to fall in love with a picture." Or again: "Men believe that their reason governs words, but it is also true that words, like arrows from a Tartar bow, are shot back upon and react upon the mind." (That is almost as good as twentieth century philosopher Whitehead's comment, "It is the task of reason to understand and purge the symbols on which humanity depends.") In the eighteenth century, Lord Mansfield, wisest English judge of his day, said, "Many of the disputes in the world arise over words."

It must be admitted that such insight was then rare in the profession. But in the nineteenth century, some seventy years ago, when most lawyers and other men were still being narcotized by words, Mr. Justice Holmes, our greatest American judge, began a vigorous attack on that sort of drug traffic. Perceiving the misleading ambiguity of the word "law," and that an unrealistic legal theology had grown out of that ambiguity, he rejected the notion that "law" is "a brooding omnipresence in the sky," and, shocking many of his colleagues, defined "lawyers' law" as merely "the prophecies of what the courts will do in fact, and nothing more pretentious." That led him to see and to say that judges "have other motives for decision, outside their own arbitrary will, besides the commands" of the law-makers, so that "the only question for the lawyer is, how will the judges act?" He spoke of the tendency of judges "to dodge difficulty and responsibility with a rhetorical phrase"; he had no confidence in "veiling words." He said from the bench, "A word is not a crystal, transparent and unchanged, it is the skin of a living thought and may vary greatly in color and content according to the circumstances and the time in which it is used." In the same vein, he wrote to a Chinese friend that "the only use of forms [words] is to present their contents, just as the only use of a pint pot is to present the beer . . . and infinite meditation upon the pot will never give the beer."

There was, at first, little response in the legal profession to this Holmesian wisdom. Verbal fundamentalism was then too deeply entrenched. Canonized, profound, Capital Letter Words, like Rights and Duties, were regnant.

However, in the last ten years or so, Leon Green, Walter Cook, Thurman Arnold, and others of us, inspired by Holmes, undertook the dissection of legal terminology. We skinned the peel off much legal jargon; many law-words (not all, of course) then proved to be like onions—you peeled and peeled and there was nothing left.[3] Some critics asserted that that was sheer vandalism; they maintained that such word dissectors were trying to show that all words were dangerous instrumentalities. Of course, that criticism was absurd: To urge men not to become drug-fiends is not to urge the abandonment by physicians of the use of morphine or cocaine; to advocate that surgical implements be antiseptic does not signify a disbelief in the worth of surgical implements. Words convey not only valuable ideas but also lies. (Page Hitler.) Like many another valuable instrument—such as dynamite, roach-powder, or formal logic, for instance—words can serve bad as well as good purposes.

The legal word skeptics were engaged in a worth-while job. For the meaning of words, as they affect citizens in-

[3] If you were sensitive, your eyes watered.

volved in law suits—and any citizen may be, any day—
is fearfully important. Every week, men are hanged or
jailed for life, women are divorced or lose the custody of
their children, sons and daughters lose all they have in
the world, labor unions are destroyed, employers become
bankrupt—all because of the meaning the courts give to
such words as "due process," "income," "willful," "reasonable," or "interstate commerce." Our constitutional history is little more than a series of contests about the vocabulary employed by the founding fathers in the Constitution. There are twenty-eight closely typed volumes of
a work entitled, *Words and Phrases Judicially Defined*.
What Congress meant when it passed a law is a subject
discussed and argued almost every day in some court.
Sometimes the courts stick to the literal or "plain" meaning; but for many years they have refused to do this when
such an interpretation would lead to absurd or futile results. More recently—and here the word-revolutionary
movement seems to have been a factor—the United
States Supreme Court has said that the plain meaning is
to be ignored when "at variance with the policy of the
legislation," no matter how clear the verbiage may appear
on superficial examination; the judges then turn to the de-
bates in the legislature or other sources to ascertain what
the lawmakers were trying to accomplish. Sometimes the
legislature inserts in the statute an "interpretation section," purporting to define the words used in that statute;

for instance, we are told that "words importing the plural member may include the singular." But, as an English judge once said, "these interpretation clauses are often the parts of the Act most difficult to be understood."

The difficulty, however, is not primarily with the law-makers; it lies in the impossibility of foreseeing all the situations which may arise in the future to which the words of the statute may be applied. What to do in such cases has been discussed as long ago as when Aristotle was writing. But today, with many lawyers, there is, more than ever, a highly conscious facing of the problem of verbal imprecision and an awareness of this consequence: that the courts play an unavoidably important role in law-making.[4] Lord MacMillan said recently that "at least half the contents of the law have their origin in the ambiguous use of language," that "great questions of principle turn upon a word, and valuable rights and interests depend on the meaning assigned to it." [5] It is for that reason that

[4] "I recognize without hesitation," said Mr. Justice Holmes in 1917, "that judges do and must legislate, but they can do so only inter-stitially. . . ." Mr. Justice Cardozo wrote: "I take judge-made law as one of the realities of life." Sir Frederick Pollock remarked, "No intelligent lawyer would in this day pretend that the decisions of the courts do not add to and alter the law." And Dicey wrote: "Judge-made law is real law, though made under the form of, and often described by judges no less than jurists as, the mere interpretation of law . . . Whole branches, not of ancient but of very modern law, have been built up, developed or created by action of the courts."

[5] He added that "it is consoling to reflect . . . that imperfectly framed statutes will, at any rate, save many lawyers from swelling the ranks of the unemployed. . . . The imperfections of the human vocabulary are as lucrative to the legal practitioner as our physical frailties are to the physician."

John Chipman Gray, a successful, conservative American lawyer and one of our keenest legal thinkers, was fond of quoting Bishop Hoadly's remark: "Nay, whoever hath an absolute authority to interpret any written or spoken laws, it is He who is truly the Law Giver to all intents and purposes, and not the Person who first wrote and spoke them." Gray said as to "interpretation" of statutes: "The fact is that the difficulties of so-called interpretation arise when the legislature had no meaning at all; when the question which is raised on the statute never occurred to it; when what the judges have to do is, not to determine what the legislature did mean on a point which was present to its mind, but to guess what it would have intended on a point not present to its mind . . ." Holmes, in an opinion in 1908, expressed himself in a somewhat similar vein in language which, in the past few years, the Supreme Court has twice quoted with approval: "A statute may indicate or require as its justification a change in the policy of the law, although it expresses that change only in the specific cases most likely to occur to the mind. The Legislature has the power to decide what the policy of the law shall be, and if it has intimated its will, however indirectly, that will should be recognized and obeyed. The major premise of the conclusion expressed in a statute, the change of policy that induces the enactment, may not be set out in terms, but it is not an adequate discharge of duty for the courts to say: 'We see what you are driving at, but you have not said it, and therefore we shall go on as before.'"

Far more important are the word habits the ordinary man adopts as he is faced with national and international crises. As Hayakawa says in this book, the very future of mankind may depend upon a rectification of word-habits. An attitude toward language such as Hayakawa recommends can and should be an *important agency of national defense.* It can and should aid us to think straight in this time of world war and in the peace that will be possible if we meet our world problems in his spirit. For it is a commonplace that this war is, in large part, a war of ideas—both as to weapons and as to aims; and the clear thinking we must have, if Hitlerism is to be defeated, can be had only if we know how to use and respond to words in the way Hayakawa describes. The abolition of what Hayakawa calls "linguistic naïveté," will help to make this a better world. For (as I've suggested elsewhere[6]) much of the thinking of the American people is in danger of being imprisoned by Big Words. We are often the captives of Nouns. Our capacity to face, realistically and intelligently, our gravest national problems, is frequently paralyzed by a few terrifying Combinations of the Alphabet—combinations in restraint of the intellect. A frontal attack on a certain kind of Capital-

[6] *Save America First* (1938), pp. 15-19.

ism—the kind that consists of vague Capital-letter Words and Phrases—is long overdue.

Take "Determinism," for instance. That has been the Marxists' verbal opiate for the masses; they derived it from Hegel; more recently it has been borrowed by the Nazis, who have used it to seduce many men into believing that their new "world order" is "inevitable" and is being washed forward irresistibly on the "wave of the future." A good dose of "extensional thinking" will prevent that sort of infection.

And then there are "Monopoly" and "Competition"; they are usually pictured as sharply divided entities, when, in truth, there are large areas of business activity in which there is—and should be—an intermixture of the two. This renders futile any attempt to solve the "problem of monopoly" through any over-simplified program; some intelligent economists have focused attention on the real nature of the problem by coining the phrase "monopolistic competition." There are those who say that the way out of the dilemma is to recognize that more and more industries are becoming "public utilities"; that, however, is nothing but a label for those industries in which monopoly, properly regulated, is regarded as desirable; the difficulty is to determine which industries should be thus treated. Indeed, the words "public utility" and "regulation" are so supersaturated with emotion, and evoke so many images of a not particularly successful way of coping with the railroads and power companies, that it might be well to abandon those words and substitute new, made-up, emotionless terms—like "ugg-wugg" for "public utility" and "agwag" for "regulate." All businesses do not require governmental "regulation"; and, even as to those that do, the kind of "regulation" should vary with the particular type of industry, being far more drastic as to some than as to others.

The great majority of Americans believe in "free Enterprise"—so far as it is attainable in the modern industrial world. But that label means different things to different men. The SEC, in a report published the other day, referred to that mouth-filling cluster of words, "Interference with Free Enterprise." The SEC said that some persons "define it as any act of government which prohibits any conduct—no matter how undesirable—especially if that conduct is anti-competitive and tends to interfere with free enterprise. Their surprising reasoning, on the few occasions when it is made explicit, runs thus: (1) If competition or free enterprise is unprotected by government, it sometimes produces, in some areas of business, practices which are anti-competitive or monopolistic; (2) such anti-competitive or monopolistic practices are, therefore a 'natural' outcome of free enterprise or competition; (3) when government prevents such anti-competitive or monopolistic practices, it is, therefore, intruding on the 'natural' course of events and thus 'interfering with free enterprise.' Back of such a sophistical argument is an unspoken anarchic philosophy, one which regards all laws, whether or not designed to afford protection to citizens, as 'interferences' with freedom and accordingly 'unnatural.' "

NOTE: As an enthusiastic semanticist for more than a decade, I feel entitled to register the following objections to the failure of some of my fellows to recognize that semantics is not a universal panacea: (1) While words dripping with emotion block clear thinking, yet the word-doctors, with their word-therapy, often promise too much. They are treating something which is, in part, but a symptom. Men often use opiate words because of an underlying emotional craving for anodynes. The elimination of drugged words, while immensely helpful, will not, alone, do the trick. To induce a dipsomaniac to stop drinking may not cure his neurosis, if it derives from deeper causes. The removal of symptoms is not to be decried. But a skin specialist is not very thorough, if his therapy is only skin-deep. Herbert Spencer wrote at length of the unfortunate effects of bias on thinking; but he remained one of the most prejudiced of men. There are diseases of thought not altogether due to diseases of language. *Drastic revision of bad word-habits is so important that we should not discredit it by claiming too much for it.* (2) The leaky character of words is not *always* an unmixed evil. Isn't it, perhaps, lucky that "democracy" was not frozen in its meaning in 1800? Where would we be if the words in our Constitution had been given inflexible definitions? Safety-valve terms ("weasel words") like "due care" or "good faith" are not without some value in a legal system. (3) What about "fictions"—that is, "as if's" or "let's-pretend" phrases—such as the "social contract," for instance? They are not maps either of the existent or the possible; but they are "useful lies"—deliberate distortions of "reality" which effectively overcome difficulties in coping with "reality." They are vicious only if mistaken for hypotheses or dogmas. (4) Some semanticists tend to discredit all phrases embodying generalizations and abstractions. We sorely need such phrases. They symbolize relations; and relations are part of the world as we know it.

As to the foregoing, see, e.g., Frank, *Law and The Modern Mind* (1930) 87-91, 312-322, 37-40; Frank, *Are Judges Human?,* 80 Un. of Pa. Law Review (1931) 233 at 264-265; Vaihinger, *Philosophy of "As If"* (transl. 1924); Tourtoulon, *Philosophy in the Development of Law* (transl. 1922).

ACKNOWLEDGMENTS AND
BIBLIOGRAPHY

THE SEMANTIC principles in this book have been drawn mainly from the "General Semantics" (or "non-Aristotelian system") of Alfred Korzybski. I have also drawn considerably from the work done in more specialized fields of semantics by other distinguished writers: especially I. A. Richards, C. K. Ogden, Bronislaw Malinowski, Leonard Bloomfield, Eric Temple Bell, Thurman Arnold, Jean Piaget, Lucien Lévy-Bruhl, Karl Britton, and Rudolf Carnap.

The necessity of synthesizing the often conflicting terminologies and sometimes conflicting views of these and other authorities has produced, I am afraid, a result that will completely satisfy none of them. I make here my apologies to them all for the liberties I have taken with their work: the omissions, the distortions, the changes of emphasis, which in some cases are so great that the originators of the theories may well have difficulty in recognizing them as their own. If mistaken impressions have been given of any of their views, or if, through the omission of quotation marks around words of misleading implications (such as "mind," "intellect," "emotion"), I have increased rather than reduced the difficulties of the subject, the fault is mine. Whenever such unscientific terms have been used, however, they have been the result of the exigencies of idiomatic expression rather than the result of willful negligence. I have usually attempted (although not always successfully, perhaps) to remove in the surrounding context the erroneous implications of popular terminology.

In an attempt at popular synthesis such as this, I have thought it wiser not to try to make individual acknowledgments of my borrowings, since this could hardly be done without making the pages unduly formidable in appearance. Therefore, a brief list of works to which I am especially indebted is provided here to serve in lieu of footnotes and a more detailed bibliography.

I am indebted to many friends and colleagues throughout the United States for their suggestions and criticism, both by letter and in conversation, during the preparation of this book. My greatest indebtedness, however, is to Alfred Korzybski. Without his system of General Semantics, it appears to me difficult if not impossible to systematize and make usable the array of linguistic information, much of it new, now available from all quarters, scientific, philosophical, and literary. His principles have in one way or another influenced almost every page of this book, and his friendly criticism and patient comments have facilitated at every turn the task of writing it.

SELECTED BIBLIOGRAPHY

Thurman W. Arnold, *The Symbols of Government,* Yale University Press, 1935.
—— *The Folklore of Capitalism,* Yale University Press, 1937.
A. J. Ayer, *Language, Truth and Logic,* Oxford University Press, 1936.
Eric Temple Bell, *The Search for Truth,* Reynal and Hitchcock, 1934.
—— *Men of Mathematics,* Simon and Schuster, 1937.
Leonard Bloomfield, *Language,* Henry Holt and Company, 1933.
Boris B. Bogoslovsky, *The Technique of Controversy,* Harcourt, Brace and Company, 1928.
P. W. Bridgman, *The Logic of Modern Physics,* The Macmillan Company, 1927.
Karl Britton, *Communication: A Philosophical Study of Language,* Harcourt, Brace and Company, 1939.
Rudolf Carnap, *Philosophy and Logical Syntax,* Psyche Miniatures (London), 1935.
Stuart Chase, *The Tyranny of Words,* Harcourt, Brace and Company, 1938.
Felix S. Cohen, "Transcendental Nonsense and the Functional Approach," *Columbia Law Review,* Vol. 35, pp. 809-849 (June, 1935).
Committee on the Function of English in General Education, *Language in General Education* (Report for the Commission on Secondary School Curriculum), D. Appleton-Century Company, 1940.
John Dewey, *How We Think,* D. C. Heath and Company, 1933.

William Empson, *Seven Types of Ambiguity,* Chatto and Windus (London), 1930.

Ernest Fenellosa, *The Chinese Written Character* (ed. Ezra Pound), Stanley Nott (London), 1936.

Jerome Frank, *Law and the Modern Mind,* Brentano's, 1930 (also Tudor Publishing Company, 1936).

Lancelot Hogben, *Mathematics for the Million,* W. W. Norton and Company, 1937.

T. E. Hulme, *Speculations,* Harcourt, Brace and Company, 1924.

H. R. Huse, *The Illiteracy of the Literate,* D. Appleton-Century Company, 1933.

Wendell Johnson, *Language and Speech Hygiene: An Application of General Semantics,* Institute of General Semantics (Chicago), 1939.

Alfred Korzybski, *The Manhood of Humanity,* E. P. Dutton and Company, 1921.

—— *Science and Sanity: An Introduction to Non-Aristotelian Systems and General Semantics,* Science Press Printing Company (Lancaster, Pa.), 1933. Second edition, 1941.

Q. D. Leavis, *Fiction and the Reading Public,* Chatto and Windus (London), 1932.

Irving J. Lee, "General Semantics and Public Speaking," *Quarterly Journal of Speech,* December, 1940.

Vernon Lee, *The Handling of Words,* Dodd, Mead and Company, 1923.

Lucien Lévy-Bruhl, *How Natives Think,* Alfred A. Knopf, 1926.

Kurt Lewin, *Principles of Topological Psychology,* McGraw-Hill Book Company, 1936.

B. Malinowski, "The Problem of Meaning in Primitive Languages," Supplement I in Ogden and Richards' *The Meaning of Meaning.*

C. K. Ogden, *Opposition:* A Linguistic and Psychological Analysis, Psyche Miniatures (London), 1932.

C. K. Ogden and I. A. Richards, *The Meaning of Meaning,* Harcourt, Brace and Company, third edition, revised, 1930.

Jean Piaget, *The Language and Thought of the Child,* Harcourt, Brace and Company, 1926.

—— *The Child's Conception of the World,* Harcourt, Brace and Company, 1929.

Oliver L. Reiser, *The Promise of Scientific Humanism,* Oskar Piest (New York), 1940.

I. A. Richards, *Science and Poetry,* W. W. Norton and Company, 1926.

—— *Practical Criticism,* Harcourt, Brace and Company, 1929.

—— *The Philosophy of Rhetoric,* Oxford University Press, 1936.

—— *Interpretation in Teaching,* Harcourt, Brace and Company, 1938.

James Harvey Robinson, *The Mind in the Making,* Harper and Brothers, 1921.

Edward Sapir, *Language,* Harcourt, Brace and Company, 1921.

Vilhjalmur Stefansson, *The Standardization of Error,* W. W. Norton and Company, 1927.

Allen Upward, *The New Word: An Open Letter Addressed to the Swedish Academy in Stockholm on the Meaning of the Word* IDEALIST, Mitchell Kennerley (New York), 1910.

Thorstein Veblen, *The Theory of the Leisure Class,* The Modern Library.

A. P. Weiss, *The Theoretical Basis of Human Behavior,* R. G. Adams and Company (Columbus, Ohio), 1925.

V. Welby, *What Is Meaning?* Macmillan and Company, 1903.

INDEX